Lifemaking

Lifemaking

Political Philosophy for
Human Flourishing in African Perspective

NIMI WARIBOKO

Published by State University of New York Press, Albany

For information, contact State University of New York Press, Albany, NY
www.sunypress.edu

Library of Congress Cataloging-in-Publication Data

Name: Wariboko, Nimi, 1962– author.
Title: Lifemaking : political philosophy for human flourishing in African
  perspective / Nimi Wariboko.
Other titles: Political philosophy for human flourishing in African perspective
Description: Albany : State University of New York Press, [2024] | Includes
  bibliographical references and index.
Identifiers: LCCN 2023048612 | ISBN 9781438498218 (hardcover : alk. paper) |
  ISBN 9781438498232 (ebook)
Subjects: LCSH: Kalabari (African people)—Nigeria—Niger River Delta—Social life
  and customs. | Kalabari (African people)—Nigeria—Niger River Delta—Politics
  and government. | Quality of life—Nigeria—Niger River Delta. | Political
  science—Philosophy. | Nigeria—Politics and government—1960–
Classification: LCC DT515.45.I35 W37 2024 | DDC 966.9004963—dc23/eng/20231018
LC record available at https://lccn.loc.gov/2023048612

To Mrs. Ibidun Spiff

Contents

Acknowledgments

Acknowledgment is the recognition of the power of "and" in scholarship. It is where the author pays homage to the eros of "and." The "and" is erotic as in the author and their helpers belonging together. The "and" conjoins the writer to their helpers in some dense connectivity of creativity. The "erotic" here is used in the old philosophical sense, meaning the power to connect, yearning for something new, driving to wholeness and thus to overcome estrangement, or driving to exceed the given. Thus, a book's acknowledgment page celebrates the erotic quality of "and" in our social existence and its glory as a community-building power.

The "and" and the acknowledgment pages that bear witness to it anytime you open a book proclaim that without the author's relationships with other human beings the existence of the book would have been impossible. They say though the author claims the title of the creator of the book, its ideas were actually inseminated, wombed, birthed, and nurtured together with others. A certain effable and ineffable "and" that conjures and conjuncts the author and their helpers is the true creator of the book. Acknowledgment pages say the work stands in and stands out of the dense relationality of human coexistence. The acknowledgment pages publicly recognize this being-with at the heart of the lonely world of scholarship or creativity.

These are the great men and women I want us to celebrate in this acknowledgment space. Thanks to Dr. Oluwabunmi Tope Bernard of Obafemi Awolowo University, Nigeria, for preparing the bibliography for me. Thanks to James Peltz, codirector and editor-in-chief at SUNY Press, who worked with me at various stages of this book. Other staff of SUNY, Diane Ganeles, John Britch, Julia Cosacchi, and Aimee Harrison did wonderful work in bringing this book to the public.

Finally, let me thank Rowman & Littlefield for permission to reuse a revised portion (35–62) of my book *Ethics and Time: Ethos of Temporal Orientation in Politics and Religion of Niger Delta* (2010), permission conveyed through Copyright Clearance Center, Inc. Thanks also to Africa World Press for permission to reuse portions (139–77) of my book *The Depth and Destiny of Work: An African Theological Interpretation* (2008).

Preface

Nobel Laureate Wole Soyinka writes: "The man dies in all who keep silent in the face of tyranny."

—The Man Died: Prison Notes of Wole Soyinka

Nigerian American novelist Okey Ndibe writes: "A story that must be told never forgives silence."

—Arrows of Rain

In this exciting new work, I seek to develop a viable philosophical account of what it takes to create and to keep lifemaking as the restrainer of necropolitics in Africa. If politics is to have lifemaking as its essential nature, we cannot enact it without making a choice between two existential paths of Africa: life and anti-life. See, I set before you today two visions of Africa: life and death; lifemaking and necropolitics; playing children and dead children. Choose wisely. As for me, I will choose life.

Vision I: The Child Lives

The child lives. She laughs. She is happy, always surrounded by smiling faces. She is never hungry. She has friends. She has toys, books, and electronic gadgets. Her room is clean, lively, and colorful. Her father adores her and plays catch with her almost every day on the well-manicured lawn of their suburban home.

Her mother asks her, "What would you like to be when you grow up?" She says: "I want to be the chief executive officer of the biggest oil company in Nigeria and from there become the minister of petroleum resources in the country." No one doubts her and she does not doubt herself. Everyone, including her four grandparents, tell her she is unique and would initiate something new in their community.

She has realized in her short years that she would gain access to the relevant communal-institutional forms to realize her dreams. The adults who listen to her dreams believe that every human being carries the possibility to act in totally unexpected ways that might constitute a fresh start for their social existence. It is a general viewpoint in the community that every child is a miracle to the world and a potential source of miracle. The community regards every child as a miracle, as something that has never happened in the world before, and thus remains open and willing to allow and support her to actualize her potentialities. They have prepared the way for her to become the best that she can be given her natural endowments and gifts.

She laughs, she plays, she dreams, and she lives.

Vision II: The Child Died

The child died. He was only five years old. He died alone. No one was there to close his eyes or to shed a tear for him. When he was found two days after he gave up the ghost, rigor mortis had set in. His hands were raised as if he were holding on to something. His sore-infested tender legs looked awkward. There was no beauty that we should desire him. His dead body was expelling intestinal worms from almost all its orifices. His still pretty face stared in cold surprise at the majestic presence of premature Death in the room—a face indicting the world, humanity, God, and, indeed, the government as perpetrators. He was wounded for our transgressions. His only possession, a tattered T-shirt, stuck to his skin in one last merciless paradoxical act of mocking and embracing his wretched life. His lifeless body was guarded by mud cakes created by tears, sweat, and urine that mixed with the bare, dusty earth floor on which he gave fight to Death. Ants, roaches, and mosquitoes were menacingly circling around his hapless, helpless body like a ferocious army of a superpower. Lizards and geckos were on the walls of the ugly room as drones and satellites of a superpower's space force.

His mother was not around when he died because she had gone to the nearby city to secure the ever-elusive employment that might resist ever-advancing Poverty's army of locusts, caterpillars, and cankerworms that devour the lifeforce of the masses.

His grandfather, his primary caregiver, had gone out to beg for food on the streets to feed him. The grandfather never came back because four policemen, the terrible horsemen of the apocalypse, falsely accused him of a crime and threw him into a dark guardroom at their stenchy station. He had no money to bribe them for his release. He pleaded with them that his grandson was dying at home for lack of food. On hearing this, they laughed at him and whipped him with *koboko* (horse whip).

The policemen that seized the old man were working in cahoots with leading local politicians. They were on orders to shake the masses down for money. These same politicians embezzled the money that the central government allotted to the town for a small factory that would have generated employment for citizens like the child's mother. The news of the coming factory had raised the hopes of the town's poor. Alas, the town is now only a giant factory of death. Every day children die in droves. And the child died!

At his birth, his parents, from different ethnic groups, filled with high hopes, named him Dumo Anikulapo. They had hoped that he was the one who was going to redeem them from poverty, stop the macabre rotations of *abiku* (*menji-ogbo*) children in their family, and launch them into a flourishing life. Dumo in Kalabari means "life"; Anikulapo in Yoruba means "the one who has captured death in his bag." Did he ever have life or subdue death? Don't count him as a failure. No, no! He held on to life as much as his feeble, malnourished hands could bear. He did not give up the ghost. His hands gave in. Death bagged him. Therefore, the grave is licking its lips in anticipation, opening its mouth wide.[1] Ouch, the child died!

There are three that bear witness in Nigerian politics: Enjoyment, Death, and Life. These three are one. Unethical politicians obscenely enjoy themselves. Leaders deliver death to the people. And life is marked more by its fleetingness than its endurance—it is, indeed, driven by death.

What do I mean by *enjoyment*? Ethics, arguably, is about making sacrifices for the sake of the public or community. It is about transcending our private self-interest, a person sacrificing her own enjoyment for the sake of the whole creation, community, group, or another person. It is about doing something for the common good. Enjoyment is about doing something for oneself from a limited perspective, resisting identification with the symbolic order. It is through enjoyment, with all its uncanniness, uniqueness, rejection (ignoring) of taking others into account, and even doing so at the expense of the other, that Nigerian politicians most vividly display their deviation from ethics, the public (social) good. In their enjoyment they slowly strangle the joy of life of their fellow citizens. They are necrophilous leaders. They are the *lotus-selves* masterminding the necropolitics of Nigeria.[2]

Theirs is politics as *death drive*—Nigeria is governed by leaders who do not desire the nation's good. Death is injected into the forward movement of life and throws it off its course. Nigerian politics harbors death within it as an excess that relentlessly disrupts the movement of life. Currently, politics is nothing but the ability of politicians and leaders to act against the good of life or reject what is in the self-interest of the nation. Nigerian leaders enjoy Nigeria insofar as its good is lost; the good socioeconomic development and excellence (virtue) remain lost. The practices of supporting life to flourish and contribute to the common good of the nation are basically absent.

Lifemaking (*dumo-nama*[3]) offers us a way to conceptualize what is structurally absent in the everyday world of Nigerian politics. By focusing on lifemaking this book exposes the fundamental absence that structures the political system in Nigeria. At this juncture, it is germane to mention that lifemaking is not a metaphysic but a method of sociohistorical analysis. It is a method of interpreting politics or political systems in which the critical importance of supporting life over and against necropolitics is strongly expressed and in which, at the same time, the creative actualization of potentialities of human-beings-in-sociality in the course of history is preferentially and concretely promoted.

Life (as potentiality-to-be) is the condition of possibility for a community and its members. The ways in which the community and its members posit themselves generate the life's structure, movements, and limits. It is in the act of positing that lifemaking occurs and community or person affirms itself as free, enslaved, or oriented to death. Lifemaking is a tracing or recording of these ways. Lifemaking exists relationally between life and the people (community of practice). This statement is important to make because the features or traces that make up lifemaking are neither in life itself nor in the community itself alone.

Lifemaking as a signifier is charged with ambiguity. It can be interpreted as life's making, life getting made, becoming life, making lifeful, or making life. Lifemaking (or *lifepoiesis*, an English-Greek neologism) as discursive strategy (a reflection on the nature of the making of life) for crafting an indigenous African political philosophy exploits these semantic excesses to illustrate that full (not perfect) human becoming in Kalabari-Ijo corresponds to life getting made, becoming life. *Lifepoetics* is the supreme capacity of human beings; politically it is identical with human flourishing. This poetics is guaranteed by each new birth in the community: the child as a new beginning, a new promise, the possibility of renewal.[4] Life exists, lifemaking insists. Lifemaking insists on life existing. In this insistence, it incessantly remakes the "substantial existence" of life. Life enfolds, refolds, unfolds, and folds in and out of the creativity of lifemaking; life possibility finds its actualization in the *poiesis* (materialization) of life. Life (human life) does not preexist humans. Life, human beings, and the endless process of their interactivity "become together, make each other even as [any one of them comes] unmade."[5] These matterings, existence and insistence, their entanglements, create, express, articulate, and distribute human flourishing, their *telos* (not in the sense of perfection or closure, but an end without end). For our limited purpose in this book, political philosophy is interpreted as a conceptual construction of this operant human flourishing, giving words to the deep structure of the plays of entanglements and their telic dialectic.

Lifemaking is an answer to existential needs; it figures (transfigures) and it is in turn figured (transfigured) by existence. It answers the questions of human existence (situation) by correlating the resources (history, dynamic foundational truths, notions of the sacred, culture, and tradition) of a community to the questions members of the community are asking. One of the tasks of this book is to show how the questions implicit in existence are met and answered by the Kalabari (Niger Delta, Nigeria) form of lifemaking. Life is their own making, and, as in any other society, the Kalabari make it according to their social, political, and economic circumstances existing already. In telling their story, this book also offers the *lifemaking method* of discovering a community's answers to human existential questions through interpretation of observable practices, ideas, data, and transcripts of the sacred.[6] This method mobilizes a tripartite system of analysis to unlock the answers.

This book attempts to bring together three vital elements (principles) in philosophical thinking for the interpretation of politics: the sacred (as in the universal set of possibilities, creativity),[7] form (the abyss of the universal set of possibilities manifesting or being given form), and human flourishing, which unites the first and second principles, the universal set and form, such that the balance between dynamic and form are geared toward human flourishing. The sacred is the universal set of possibilities available to a community or people. The matters of life and power of lifemaking are interrogated as matters of possibilities, possibilities of freedom, or actualization of potentiality for human flourishing in any given context. I demonstrate that it is in the nature of the sacred as the universal set of possibilities available to a people or community that we can find the red thread that connects most of Africa's sociopolitical problems, that links most of its religious and nonreligious issues, and that contains their possible solutions.

The form is the dimension of organization, the *nomos* of each historical manifestation of the sacred in specific context. This is what I am naming as lifemaking. It is the practices of resoluteness that allow life to successfully express itself. Lifemaking not only supplies the capabilities, virtues, and resources for citizens to flourish but also creates citizens who are sensitive to human flourishing and desires abundant life for all. Lifemaking is the totality (rhizomatic network) of the experiences and understanding of actualization of potentialities, ways of being for potentialities, and strivings for the actualization of potentialities that make it possible for a people to engage the dynamics of life (*zoe* and *bio*). It provides the stratigraphy of social relations, axiologies, epistemology, ideas, and practices a people (a community of practice) crafted to carry forward the changes in the form and substance of their social existence in their continuous encounter with life—a universal set of possibilities. How can the meaning of lifemaking in a given context shine through it?

Lifemaking uses political philosophy as a vestment covering it. Put differently, political philosophy is the skin of the skein of lifemaking. It communicates the inner rhythm of the process of lifemaking to the outside and protects the inner rhythm from the outside. Political philosophy shows lifemaking in its proper form. Lifemaking is the substance of political philosophy, and political philosophy is the form of lifemaking. This relationship should not be construed to mean that political philosophy can fix the meaning (shape or identity) of lifemaking. Political philosophy never does more than trace and repeat lifemaking.

The third aspect of our trinitarian framework is the imperative that drives and balances the two toward their destiny, their socially constructed *telos*: human flourishing. This third dimension of our interpretative framework can also be named as the spiritual character of life insofar as we understand it as the search for human freedom and flourishing in the name of an *ought-to-be*. Human flourishing in this tripartite framework is not defined by accumulation of objects of desire. Lifemaking locates human flourishing in freedom. It is not what those on the right see as the accumulation of objects of capitalism. To those on the left, it is not about the disrupting and decoding of capitalist flows, desires, or compulsions to accumulate as the source of ultimate satisfaction. Human flourishing is located in freedom, the actualization of human potentialities. Potentiality—its contingency, gaps within its chain of signification, and the lack of last actualization that provides its ultimate satisfaction, meaning—is the necessary condition for human freedom. Potentiality is not some preexisting essence that transcends history. A community creates, sustains, or destroys its potentialities. Potentiality is a creation of human sociality, interactions, and so-called social or collective brain. Thus, locating human flourishing in freedom is not a median position between the right and left perspectives, not a compromise between them. It is beyond the opposition between them, transcending the philosophical limits inherent in them.

By focusing on lifemaking, this book attempts to interpret the political reality of traditional Kalabari society by applying all three roots of the trinitarian thinking (the abysmal character, the human flourishing character, and the form character). If the abysmal character of human life is neglected, a technocratic impulse transforms politics into heteronomous subjection to *unfreedom*. If the form (logical) character of life is neglected, politics as death drive transforms human creativity into the "postcolonial incredible"[8] or sheer human destructiveness. If the flourishing (spiritual) character of human life is neglected, politics as record of courage to affirm life and challenge all that thwarts life is impossible.[9]

This book is based on a trinitarian interpretation of human life and its prudent organization as lifemaking in Kalabari to form the basis of new thinking on politics in Nigeria, making the possibility of human flourishing ever more material and alive. It presents a new thinking that converts enjoyment into ethics, subtracts national resurrection from the crushing weight of death and bad governance, and transforms necropolitics into lifemaking. It is a new thinking that *possibilizes* the nation from a vision that promises to make life and to make it more abundantly. It reveals political philosophy to be a commitment to the love of life and human flourishing. This is my thesis for this book. I subscribe to this new thinking that strives to overcome the necropolitics of Africa's largest economy and most populous nation and asks the question: What kind of politics comes after necropolitics?

This is a work in *ananecropolitics*. Ana plus necropolitics; *ana*: after, anew. Ananecropolitics means encountering politics anew, reengaging politics as lifemaking to the citizenry after the loss of focus on life. It is a retrieval of politics from *necro*. Ananecropolitics is a double negation—negating the necro-negation of politics that necropolitics installs. It captures this movement: politics ⇒ necro-politics ⇒ negation of necropolitics, which is lifemaking. Principally, lifemaking represents the possibilities of returning to politics of human flourishing after the derailment, detour, or destruction caused by necropolitics. Ananecropolitics is an interplay between *disclosing* and *disenclosing* politics and constricting necropolitics; that is, it is the possibility of rooting African governance in the expansive deep structures of life after the stormy and destructive wind of necropolitics and moving beyond the kind of politics that set the stage for the emergence of politics of death. Ananecropolitics is provoked by the very (death-dealing) practices that allowed politics to move beyond love and care for life, practices that motivated the thwarting of human flourishing in the first place. Ananecropolitics is a double movement, moving from necropolitics after the denial and destruction of life and moving toward lifemaking, giving thought and light to the deep structures of life in the African sociality. Simply, ananecropolitics is return to life in politics after the death of life in politics. It opens naturally to lifepoetics. In the present postcolonial predicament of Africa, lifemaking will be a deliberate enactment of alternative amid the domain of necropolitics and yet beyond the stealing, destruction, and death of its enclosure. Life and the gerund mak-*ing* speak to the always emergent character, eventfulness, and openness to human flourishing envisioned in the new site of politics.

In this new work I attempt to generate a fresh frame for analyzing contemporary African politics or envisaging its future. The frame is rooted in indigenous political philosophy of lifemaking of the Kalabari people of the Niger Delta, Nigeria. I am hoping to provide an alternative perspective to the one on necropolitics that dominates not only the practice of politics by African leaders but also philosophical and theological analyses of the same. I am not hoping to soon transform politics in Nigeria or any other part of Africa for that matter, but to heed a recurrent realization that it is always incumbent upon us as philosophers, theologians, and social ethicists to put forward alternative ways of thinking even if for now our ideas would not move the needle of everyday practice. We do not want Africans to be caught in the TINA (there is no alternative) syndrome. Thus, this book is a *site* through which an inspiration for an alternative to the current necropolitics can be grasped. Because the book's thesis is an unreserved surrender to lifemaking, it places what is essential about politics within the frame of human flourishing for all.

Nimi Wariboko
Westwood, MA
June 11, 2022

Introduction

Africa is an almost unbearable configuration of death, more death, and life. This insufferable crystallization inhibits actualization of worthwhile life. The problems of this troubled continent need to be confronted in the power of vulnerable life, through a normative political philosophy that taps deeply into the roots of Africans' intense attachment to life, living on, and human flourishing amid anxieties of mortality and finitude. This concern, in essence, will be the task of this book.

Africans' vexing failure to properly engage with life and draw from it the necessary resources to live fully into their aspiration of human flourishing has generally been attributed to two deficiencies: economics and politics. Economic maladministration is not the worse of these two obstacles. Politics is the primary cause of Africa's societal failure. Politics underdevelops Africa, and obsolete political philosophy underdevelops obsoletely. *Regular underdevelopment* holds a people down, moves them backward, and deprives them of the energy to lift themselves up from poverty into prosperity. Regular underdevelopment kills persons, destroys their potentialities, and steals their future.

Obsolete underdevelopment goes beyond all these. It is an *unheimlich* habituation to death, decay, dehiscence, and destruction. Obsolete underdevelopment is deadlier than regular underdevelopment. It tends to separate a people from their potentiality-to-do, rendering obsolete their life, subjugating their lives to the power of contingent, dispersed death. In the regime of obsolete underdevelopment, national economic management is not about disciplining bodies to control them and increasing productivity in the economy. It is about creating zones of death, exercising the power to take life, signifying the ultimate exercise of domination as capability to impose death on the people. Unlike regular underdevelopment that

1

struggles to improve life and living conditions, obsolete underdevelopment "reveals itself in the guise of arbitrariness and the absolute power to give death anytime, anywhere, by any means, and for any reason."[10] Obsolete underdevelopment is a form of necropolitics. It is a "driver of necropolitical principle insofar as it stands for organized destruction of [human potentiality] . . . a generalized cheapening of the price of life."[11]

Today, African leaders have political philosophies that manufacture death instead of supporting life. African politics and its underlying political philosophy and administration of terror have produced hundreds of millions of people who live at the edge of life, precariously standing at the rim of the void of death. As Achille Mbembe puts it in his book *Necropolitics*, these are persons

> for whom living means continually standing up to death, and doing so under conditions in which death itself increasingly tends to become spectral, thanks both to the way in which it is lived and to the manner in which it is given. This life is a superfluous one, therefore, whose price is so meager that it has no equivalence, whether market or—even less—human; this is a species of life whose value is extra-economic, the only equivalent of which is the sort of death able to be inflicted upon it.
>
> As a rule, such death is something to which nobody feels any obligation to respond. Nobody even bears the slightest feelings of responsibility or justice toward this sort of life or, rather, death. Necropolitical power proceeds by a sort of inversion between life and death, as if life was merely death's medium.[12]

Indeed, the situation in Africa is dire. Mbembe bears witness to the depravity of the African postcolony. The powerful witness in his books *On the Postcolony* and *Necropolitics* causes many African readers' blood to boil within them, almost enough to stir up their revolutionary spirit, to nudge them to muster the courage to transform their nations. This is also the hope and motivation of this book—from a different angle of the African predicament. I write to provide a political philosophical framework for the day after the revolution. Not only to provide for that day alone, but also to provide resources for today's need. There is an urgent need for action. Indeed, African leaders have lost their soul and hence the *future* of the continent. Every morning the sun rises, and African leaders behave as if nothing has happened the previous day. To them, bad things must always happen to Africa. But the sun that rises every morning is not neutral. It relentlessly shines its light on the decadence, poverty, and depravity of the race. The leaders hope the sun will bathe their oppressions and injustice in its eternal light. They hope that as men and women hail the wonderful light of the world with joy every dawn, they will celebrate their poor performances, their nonachievements. No, no hope for them.[13]

We must not fold into ourselves, into our being, this grave obscenity. Not in this century, not in these throes of death. Every day, thousands of African children die because of malnutrition and common diseases. No sane leader will ever have his or her country's future carried out in wrapped mats. But our insane leaders see it and say nothing about it. In this century, in this poverty, we (the citizens) should recover our future. If we are in power, we will never let thousands of our children be carried to their comfort of nothingness. In this century—in this horror!—we should never let the world give only a passing glance at our dead children within its exuberant and indifferent celebration of abundance of life. We are worried that our "blackness" will die tomorrow and our unborn will have nothing to say to the world. This is true because they are not equipped to speak! In this century, in this poverty, in these throes of death, we must arise like the sun and no longer pretend that the helpless children being parceled out to their lonely spots are "sheltered by God's hands," sleeping as if in their "mother's house."[14] Frightened to death in the African storm of poverty, they depart without even speaking to us. In this storm, in this horror, we will no longer let them be carried out. For Africa's sake we will no longer hold our peace.

We do not need to wait for the day after the revolution to change our political philosophic orientation in ways that would help the African child. In place of the deadly and deadening political philosophies that underpin and invigorate obsolete underdevelopment, I offer the *philosophy of lifemaking*. Lifemaking is the totality of those practices and ideas that resist death or all that thwarts human flourishing. The measure of politics of lifemaking, then, in general, "is the difference which exists between the effort"[15] of advancing human flourishing and resisting all that thwarts this objective.

In Africa, lifemaking and necropolitics confront each other as opposing forms of politics. The advancement of necropolitics is the retreat or the near obliteration of the other in the zero-sum game. From all indications, it appears the excesses of necropolitics now offer Africans only one choice. This book not only endeavors to clearly describe the alternative of lifemaking but also provides normative principles capable of framing a new perspective on politics and unifying its variety of logics, expressions, and visions within an indigenously generated framework.

Lifemaking: Political Philosophy for Human Flourishing in African Perspective constructs a political philosophy from a tradition of thought that is indigenous to Africa, arguing that there are long-neglected resources within African philosophy to guide African citizens and leaders toward creating African polities that can sustain human flourishing and resist necropolitics. Exploring notions of power, justice, freedom, citizenship, law, and corporate belonging, I construct a political philosophic framework to rethink solutions to the vexing problems of political development. I examine the meaning the Kalabari give to each of these notions. I also interpret the necessary conditions of their giving each notion a meaning. Then I provide an account of how the meanings hang together in a coherent way or relate them to the quest for human flourishing. Basically, it is an account of how life is *made* to produce and sustain a set of virtues, capabilities, and conditions that generates higher levels of well-being, the good life, and prosperity, as well as generating new relations, practices, and realities that support the actualization of potentialities of a person, group, or community. The goal of the drive toward human flourishing is to create community that perpetually permits every human being to be the best that she can be given her gifts, talents, and communal-institutional support for her sake and that of the community—individual and community aiming for the highest good, *lolo*.

Political philosophy is made rather than found.[16] It is made in the power of lifemaking, lifepoesis. Political philosophy is a "property" of lifemaking, a society's particular way of making life. Human beings make political philosophy by making life in which to articulate or phrase human flourishing. Political philosophy tracks or traces lifemaking that is already ongoing, and it makes life that has never been dreamed of before. It brings lifemaking to self-consciousness, frames the countless contingencies of lifemaking entering experience. Political philosophy is the story (a dramatic narrative of self-overcoming) a society tells about lifemaking, describes itself in the act of lifemaking. As a narrative, political philosophy is not a system of general principles but a reminder of, an abbreviation for, a co-traveler of lifemaking and not a justification of it. Lifemaking and political philosophy rejoice in each other's company in their bounded context. Because political philosophy (at least, as conceptualized in this book) is tied to lifemaking in a particular context, to lifemaking in a particular present situation, there is no need to bring particular political philosophy under some general principles. Political philosophy is particular, a product and producer of idiosyncratic contingencies of past and present lifemaking. There is no intrinsic human lifemaking—no lifemaking that escapes from time and chance, no lifemaking that is definatory of humans. Thus, political philosophy cannot latch on or dock with something universal. "To demand more than this is perhaps a deep and incurable metaphysical need."[17]

In the preceding paragraphs I have provided preliminary meanings of lifemaking, human flourishing, and political philosophy, the three key terms in the title of this book. A question arises at this point: What is the social glue that holds these notions together in the Kalabari traditional society? What is the social glue that holds political (social) organizations? The *Alabo* (chief of the *wari*, the canoe house trading and fighting corporation; it was also the basic unit of Kalabari traditional polity[18]) is the quilting or anchoring point for stabilizing or stitching the dissemination of meanings of the three terms. The chief (*Alabo*: wealthy man, creator of wealth; the governor or ruler of the political unit; *omualabo*, the warrior that maintains peace; and free person) is the structured network of meanings, which enables them to take on a precise signification. The *Alabo* (a metonymic assemblage of the community's promise of wealth and well-being) is the nodal element that sews the five major concerns (peace, freedom, economic prosperity, wealth-in-people, and self-creation) of public policy together to perform or illustrate the point of the polity. Collectively the chiefs hold groups of individuals (*wari*) into a political totality, the Kalabari community.

Peace (Dein): The *Alabo* (*imbi saki tebo; dein-weribo*), as the leader of the war-canoe house, with the help of other members of the house, generates, manages, and sustains the capability and financial means to defend his *wari* and community in wars and ensure peace in the community.

Freedom (sibi tombo so te; sibi nyana): *Alabo* is the epitome of a free person, he owns his body and shows his "who" in the public space as subject to freedom (*sibi nyana bara ke angaa*). He also works to ensure that he raises other men to this level of freedom by helping them to become chiefs (see chapter 4 for more discussion on this).

Prosperity (Lolo): *Alabo* by definition is a wealthy person, and the primary goal of his leadership is to increase the wealth and prosperity of the *wari* (house) and improve the well-being of its members.

Wealth-in-people (wari duama): This is about commitment to social worth. It is defined as "the value of people, but also the value obtained through people and the value invested and accumulated in people."[19] Every chief (*wari dabo*) works to increase the number of people in his *wari* through birth, marriage, and absorption of outsiders. The goal of having more people in the *wari* is to increase its labor and military capabilities, enlarge social relations, and build a group with diverse and complementary skills or qualities. *Wari duama* is not just about political strength in number, it is fundamentally about putting human well-being as the front and center of communal life, at the top of society's value-hierarchy, and the *wari* is about people—making life in its physical, economic, social, affective, aesthetic, spiritual, and intellectual dimensions. The normative practice of wealth-in-people is a creative process of nourishing individuals to reach higher levels of self-actualization and human flourishing. The *Alabo* as the leader of the *wari* apprehends the lives of house members not only in their facticity but also in their possibility. *Alabo* is a lifemaker.

Self-creation (*tombo-tombo so*): The conditions and organizational format of *wari* and *ama* (town) are geared to give opportunities or chance to every member for self-creation, for members of the house to be the best that they can be given their abilities.

The *Alabo*, as one at the center of the rhizomatic network of these pentagonal energies, is the lifemaker-in-chief. This is a role he shares with all citizens of the polity. In holding these five public concerns together, he quilts not only lifemaking, human flourishing, and political philosophy but also the polity. The *Alabo* as a signifier "creates" a consistent polity (a unified, structured field) for the citizens. All this is not to say that the *Alabo* (as *point de capiton*) is the point of supreme or ultimate meaning in the polity, but he is a performative tool that gives the appearance, if not the illusion, of a totalizing ideology of the community or unified field that halts the sliding of meanings. He has to perform power to maintain the perception of a quilting point, to continuously knot disparate meanings. He is like the upholstery button that holds the fabric and mass of stuffing together. The Kalabari chief literally wears this "quilting function" on his body as exemplified by the "buttons" he wears on his dress. The *doni*, a full-length flowing gown with long sleeves worn only by chiefs, has four stud buttons. Men (gentlemen of substance) who are not chiefs wear only three stud buttons on their *woko* dress. In the Kalabari-Ijo number symbolism scheme, three stands for men and four for females.[20] The use of four stud buttons by chiefs is a subtle device for them to give themselves a larger-than-life and "spiritual" image. The physical representation of spirits in the forms of sculpted masks and dressings of masquerade players are always made to look like a hermaphrodite (i.e., the co-representation of both male and female features in the same masquerade). The four stud buttons convey the image of the male chief as a quilting point for both feminine and masculine energies of the community.

The *Alabo*—theorized here as the quilting, anchoring point—should also not be construed as the big reality behind the three notions (life-making, human flourishing, and political philosophy) and the five public policy concerns (peace, freedom, economic well-being, self-creation, and wealth-in-people). He is only a pattern of appearance of these notions and concerns that are not suprahistorical, that is, not beyond contingent historical circumstance and institutions. He is not a metaphysical figure.

Perhaps I need to explain why this study is limited to the Kalabari-Ijo people. As I do not have the ability or sufficient time for an in-depth study of the philosophies of many indigenous groups for this book, I have chosen to focus on Kalabari. They are located in the Niger Delta in southern Nigeria. Nigeria is a country of over 200 million people in the throes of necropolitics, poverty, and obsolete underdevelopment but with great potential for political transformation and economic development. As I will demonstrate in the chapters that follow, there are resources within Kalabari philosophy to guide policymakers toward creating African polities that can sustain human flourishing. The indigenous Kalabari philosophy is the opposite of a *planned* academic philosophy; it is a philosophy that grew organically around everyday practices, needs, interactions, and lives of the people. The orientation of this philosophy is to make it possible for all persons to live and develop their full potentials in community. In a previous book, I demonstrated how this kind of Kalabari philosophy could help African leaders to transform their national economies, to craft economies that can positively respond to the existential desire of Africans as it relates to human flourishing.[21] Economics and politics in the traditional Kalabari community are about constructing the practices, norms, values, procedural rules, and institutions that could create the material conditions that not only sustain the production, reproduction, and growth of human life but also enable every person to develop their full potentials.[22] My aim in this book is to capture the inner logic of indigenous Kalabari political philosophy, critiquing and developing it into a form of political theory that can assist the African postcolony to negate necropolitics and affirm life.

With this book, I join with other African scholars and social justice activists with the hope to render to life those that the African postcolony has given over to death—if not directly them, then their descendants or their future. We need to render to life, to bring new bodies to form new communities of Africans to re-create their worlds. Mbembe in his inimitable way expresses this hope in this way: "Rendered to life and thereby different to the fallen body of colonized existence, this new body will be invited to become a member of a new community. Unfolding according to its own plan, it will henceforth walk along together with other bodies and, doing so, will re-create the world."[23]

In this book I offer a new body of political philosophy arising from a fallen Kalabari body of indigenous knowledge, a body in its neglected, traumatized, and colonial existence, inviting it to walk along with other bodies of knowledge to re-create Africa, to *make life*. The abiding task of this book is to posit, postulate, and position human life as the urgent and proper subject matter of African political philosophy. Lifemaking as a philosophy in today's Africa does not forgive intellectual silence.

Let me state some of the intellectual steps I took to (re)construct the inherited African philosophy for possible political development of the African postcolony. The philosophy is crafted from these four sets of raw (or processed) materials. First, the political philosophy in this book is based on or draws from Kalabari political theories, social traditions, history, and political practices. Second, it is based on my interpretation (or theorization) of the Kalabari materials. There is no appeal to nonlinguistic knowledge in my interpretations: they are not based on metaphysical arguments but on sociohistorical data through and through. Third, the first and second steps place us inside the Kalabari tradition, and the proximity can blur our vision, hindering the opening of critical perspective on the materials. So we need to step outside of them, to properly grasp their contours and to reach into their core meanings: "We need to look at [them] from the outside, expressing ourselves in different [but related] language from its own."[24] This need led me to engage non-African philosophies (e.g., continental philosophy) to offer critical and helpful perspectives on the materials I was studying without ceding the animating force of my analyses to extra-African thoughts. Finally, there is the infusion of my ideas (as embedded in my interpretations) into the inherited tradition (nonetheless, an ongoing debate) to create a framework of political philosophy for today's Africa.

What emerges from this methodology of study is that my ideas are simultaneously inside and outside the horizon of Kalabari philosophy. The intake of my political ideas (or, for that matter, continental philosophy) is carefully done to illuminate only core Kalabari ideas, to highlight their extraterritorial relevance, never to put the Kalabari substance in the shadow of my political thought (the thought of a Kalabari man formed by training in Western universities and now living and teaching in the United States of America). I believe that the four intellectual steps I undertook enabled me to open a point of immanence within Kalabari philosophy intended to bring it into deep conversation with ideas, philosophies, and perspectives in contemporary cutting-edge political theories or African studies. Every time we as Africans must tackle twenty-first-century political problems by drawing from the past, our indigenous philosophies or received wisdom must be slightly expanded. As Frantz Fanon put it: "Everything up to and including the very nature of pre-capitalist [indigenous communities], so well explained by [our ancestors and their collective philosophies], must here be thought out again."[25]

The result of this synthesis or expansion is a *hashtag*. The synthesis was created to enable possibilities of thought to coalesce around the key idea of political development of the African postcolony. This is similar to what hashtags do around trending or viral topics. While hashtags do this with memes that have powerful semiotic charges, the quadruple steps as foci of emphasis and concentration of ideas promote and provoke interaction and dialogues across intellectual traditions. The synthesis I have named as "hashtag" is to collect and organize rigorous ideas to instantiate a new framework of interpretation of the political predicament of the African postcolony. The four-pronged methodology or the book, like a hashtag's message, is not about revealing or recovering the supposed objective original meaning but about deciphering dynamic ideas that might work best to uplift Africans from their excruciating necropolitics. The synthesis is an assemblage of ideas that I am floating in the ocean of uncertainty of lived experience to seek understanding, to create islands of promise, and to condition that lived experience of Africans. The synthesis constitutes a critical realistic bundle of methods of analysis that operate empirically, imaginatively, and theoretically to respond to existential situations.

The bottom line is that this study is not necessarily a regurgitation of traditional Kalabari political philosophy, but a Kalabari philosophy spiced and marinated by my intellect and by my vision of what it should be for contemporary Africa. More precisely, I should say I provide pictures of Kalabari indigenous political ideas. These pictures are not photographs of the indigenous ideas. They are also not idealized paintings that project any form of congruence between an ideal philosophical model and the philosophical minds of the traditional Kalabari society. The philosophical picture of each set of ideas that I provide is an "expressionist portrait." I have tried to enter into the deepest meanings of each set of traditional ideas that I studied, to profoundly "participate" in its reality, in its "inner life" to mine the deepest philosophical meanings embedded in its core. In every chapter I will try to take the reader beyond the surface traits of indigenous political thoughts or an idealized version of them (the traits) according to a philosophical model, allowing the reader to experience the "being" of Kalabari political thoughts through a participation in their deepest meanings.[26]

At the end, the portrait that I paint of any set of political ideas, using the expressionistic style, carries the force of realism, impressionism, and expressionism. Realism because the certitude of my interpretations of each idea (practice) are rooted in the inner reality of Kalabari society (culture, worldview)—and not on mere abstract intellectual musings that do not reflect or do distort the *reality* of the tradition. There is enough force in the interpretation to leave the reader with an *impression* of rigorous philosophy in the tradition. Finally, there is a powerful witness to the reality and philosophical impression in the portraits to impact the reader with the sense that an encounter with each of the portraits is an *expression* of a call to social justice or social transformation of the African postcolony.[27] The power of this call is a weak one; it is not a brute force.[28] It summons or calls Africans to their greatness, to the promise ahead of today, and to their forgotten paths to human flourishing through the force of their inherited political thoughts and selective borrowings from other traditions.

This book makes seven contributions to the study of political philosophy. First, it provides a general foundation for future work of scholars of African political philosophy that would make indigenous political thought their point of departure. Second, the book crafts an understanding of political philosophy that puts at its center lifemaking, engendering intensification of social life, putting life's centers of gravity in life, and refusing to define existing life against death. Lifemaking is lived in the expectation of the new and not in the fear of subsumption of life by death. Third, often scholarly works that retrieve African ideas for use today are driven by nostalgic appeal or lost completeness. They locate ultimate enjoyment (satisfaction) in Africa's own past or in the others, such as Westerners, whose enjoyment of life is coming at the expense not only of Africans but also of future Africans' enjoyment. Such works project the idea that Africans might return to a stable relation with past objects (i.e., political institutions or values) with possibilities for harmony or complete satisfaction. This book is not driven by what I believe Africans have lost and needs to be regained but by an investment in the future that carries forward the valuable lessons of the past.

Fourth, this book offers the *lifemaking method* of discovering a community's answers to human existential questions through interpretation of observable practices, ideas, data, and transcripts of the sacred.[29] This method mobilizes a tripartite system of analysis to unlock the answers. The method brings together three vital elements (principles) in philosophical thinking for the interpretation of politics: sacred (the abyss of the universal set of possibilities), form (the form the abyss takes in social existence, dimension of organization), and human flourishing, which unites the first and second principles, the universal set and form, such that the balance between dynamic and form is geared toward human flourishing.

Fifth, Achille Mbembe's work portrays postcolonial Africa as the home of necropolitics (death-making)—and rightly so. This book draws from indigenous philosophy a robust model of being-with, politics, and life's way of being that counter the necropolitical narrative and seeks to provide the resources of lifemaking that might reconstruct the political in the African postcolony.

Sixth, this book demonstrates the nature, logics, and dynamics of "biopolitics" in precolonial Africa—if I may call what I have studied in this book *biopolitics*. What I have loosely named—for the sake of discussion of this book's contribution to knowledge—as biopolitics in Kalabari is different in conception or form from what obtains in the West. Generally, biopolitics in the West is about the administration, monitoring, and survey of human life processes for maximal political control, hierarchization of life, and various forms of discriminations, exceptions, erasures, and violence that place death at the heart of politics or being-with. Biopolitics in Kalabari is geared toward human flourishing, mutual care, communality, and the equipping of every citizen to leave a legacy for future generations. Kalabari biopolitics is not just about legitimation of power as life-protecting but about the philosophico-political logics of lifemaking of the people, by the people, and for the people.

Finally, this whole book is a theory of lifemaking, an innovative framework for comprehending how life hangs together in a polity. This is a theory that is not only concretely correlated with the African predicament of necropolitics but also came out of the lived experience of pain. It is what bell hooks might name as theory of liberating practice. She writes:

I came to theory because I was hurting—the pain within me was so intense that I could not go on living. I came to theory desperate, wanting to comprehend—to grasp what was happening around and within me. Most importantly, I wanted to make the hurt go away. I saw in theory then a location for healing. . . . I found a place of sanctuary in "theorizing," in making sense out of what was happening. I found a place where I could imagine possible futures, a place where life could be lived differently. This "lived" experience of critical thinking, of reflection and analysis, became a place where I worked at explaining the hurt and making it go away. Fundamentally, I learned from this experience that theory could be a healing place. . . . When our lived experience of theorizing is fundamentally linked to processes of self-recovery, of collective liberation, no gap exists between theory and practice. Indeed, what experience makes more evident is the bond between the two—that ultimately reciprocal process wherein one enables the other.[30]

Organization of Chapters

The rest of the book is divided into six chapters. In chapter 1 ("Lifemaking: Poetics of Politics in Traditional Africa") I lay out the concept of lifemaking and show that this notion is key to understanding the political philosophy of Kalabari society. I also demonstrate why it is important to rethink political philosophy, to reconceptualize human flourishing and politics within the framework of lifemaking. Lifemaking as a philosophy and practice can serve as a remedy for the necropolitics of Africa.

Chapter 2, "The Philosophy of King Amakiri: Kalabari as a Political Narrative," explores the various institutions and ideas that a Kalabari king, Amakiri, and his chiefs in the eighteenth century deployed to create and sustain lifemaking as the central philosophy of politics and governance. The range of institutions and practices that were informed by the philosophy of lifemaking was wide and deep. For instance, even the theory of citizenship was transformed. Citizenship moved from being determined by indigeneity to residence, language, and culture. Members of the society were bound together principally by location (their placeness in the same territory) and the institutions, the civilization, and the history they commonly possessed, and not by blood or descent. This was a remarkable political thought. Compare it to how citizenship is generally understood in twenty-first-century Nigeria. Today in Nigeria, "home" is defined as ancestral, and indigenous land is only for the natives. Citizenship is ultimately defined on the basis of indigeneity—whether or not a person can trace his or her ancestry to an indigenous abode. Citizenship is equated with ancestral home in the precolonial period.

The discussions of King Amakiri and his chiefs in chapter 2 portray sovereignty in the Kalabari context as the creative cultural-moral functions of human life oriented toward mass flourishing of citizens. The chapter offers us what sovereign power organizes in Kalabari: the production of a flourishingly humanized people or the excellent self (which we shall treat in chapter 6). In this way, this book offers an understanding of sovereignty that is outside the biopolitical and thanatopolitical continuum in which most Western theories of sovereignty are stuck. Once the reader grasps this insight, she is likely to see the book as a subtle tracing of the category of sovereign power and how it is conjugated in different ways across spheres of life. Thus, this book uncovers an understanding of sovereignty in indigenous Kalabari society as subjugated to the praxis of lifemaking, a symbolic order of meaning and purpose, and not to the (brutal or exceptional) power to "make die and let live" or to "make live and let die."

The philosophies of governance, citizenship, nation-building, sovereignty, and lifemaking that Amakiri and his chiefs crafted were geared to enact and sustain a high quality of human life. Their efforts would have come to naught or accomplished less than what they did without a sense of collective belonging. They created a virtual/ideal entity (non-entity) that (can only) exists as the subjective "presupposition" of engaged or subjectivized Kalabari citizens. This is called *amatemeso*, functioning like a symbol of the nation. It

> exists only insofar as subjects act as if it exists. Its status is similar to that of an ideological cause like Communism or the Nation: it is the substance of the individuals who recognize themselves in it, the ground of their entire existence, the point of reference which provides the ultimate horizon of meaning to their lives, something for which these individuals are ready to give their lives, yet the only thing that really exists are these individuals and their activity.[31]

Amatemeso is a result of collective existence—the people becoming a product of themselves. *Amatemeso* is the people in the process of their own self-actualization. It is often interpreted as a transcendent (supernatural, transhistorical) being. But it could also mean an immanent being, a product of human interactions. And this is how I interpret it in this book for the limited purpose of our study of lifemaking. The discourse and interpretation of *amatemeso* is the subject of chapter 3, "*Amatemeso*, Otherness, and Violence."

The chapter presents *amatemeso* as a form of political imagination of the Kalabari nation. It also analyzes the ethos of masculinity that increasingly came to condition political practice during the Amakiri era, such that political imagination increasingly got more masculine and harbored an ontology of violence. These two were parts of the three major forms of political imaginations that arose from the Amakiri era. The institution of chieftaincy was the third form of political imagination of the state, of the imaginative power of state. The Kalabari state and chiefs were a realization or an unfolding of an imaginative idea of a particular kind of nation building or politics-as-statecraft. The next chapter explores chieftaincy as a form of political imagination.

In chapter 4, "Chiefs: Subjects to Freedom," we see how the Kalabari people embody freedom in persons and institutions, and we consider how the Kalabari political philosophy centers on beginnings (*natality*). Among this people, chiefs symbolize as well as instantiate the freedom to begin a new kind of time and to effect passage to new conditions of being or existence. Our analysis of the Kalabari chieftaincy institution as a locus of freedom reveals that for the Kalabari the political is a form of imagination, a way of being for the new, of representing to the self a form of human existence.

Chapter 5 ("Sediments of Life: On *Poiesis* of Social Immortality") investigates how Kalabari people create and manage an ethical system that harnesses legacies of deeds of both chiefs and non-chiefs to make lifemaking into the highest good in their community. In Kalabari society there is a drive for legacy as a paradigm of transcendence, as a means and hope of going over the limitations of day-to-day existence, death, and transience. There is an opposite of legacy, which is the erasure of the person, symbolically expunging a chief and his war-canoe house from society, from memory. This happens when a chief dies or is captured by enemies in a war. If legacy "let live" a chief in the afterlife, the erasure "make die" a chief in the same sphere. Both states of the dead are part of the symbolic order of meaning and purpose of Kalabari society.

What does this chapter tell us about lifemaking in the Kalabari context? In a certain sense, the value of a person's life in relation to others is ultimately seen in its contributions to her legacies for her own community. The significance and meaning of today's work are sought in relation to how it would be considered in the future as the actual performance moves into the past. Work (as creativity leaving behind legacy) is considered in the context of the *togetherness* of the three temporal modes of the human creativity: past, present, and future. In the same way, lifemaking, which is the context of the drive for legacy, is not limited to the present of the individual's or community's activities but also involves the togetherness of the three temporal modes. Through legacy, past work (actualities) enters the presence of the lifemaking so as to fashion and refashion it. Present ongoing work can actualize itself only as a finished product by taking account of the potential that past work offers and the potential and possibilities for future work. Past work is involved in present work, and future work is also involved as anticipated.

The concern with legacy is not about "timing" the value of one's work or legacy but about the maintenance of the webwork of relationships that undergirds a community's lifemaking. This is the connection between legacy (work as social creativeness, or social ethic) and lifemaking. Chapter 6 ("The Excellent Self: Existential End Goal of Lifemaking") further explores the nature of the link between social ethics and lifemaking, further elucidating deep ethical thinking that informs lifemaking. It establishes the end of lifemaking as the production of the "excellent self," the production of a flourishingly humanized people. At the very end I suggest that lifemaking could be the restrainer (*daasamaye* in Kalabari) of necropolitics in Africa.

NIGERIA'S PROBLEMS AND THE ORGANIZATION OF CHAPTERS

While each of these six chapters is crafted to present a particular dimension of Kalabari indigenous political philosophy, each of them offers resources to reflect on solutions to some of Africa's (Nigeria's) political problems. They are (1) necropolitics; (2) weak cross-cutting foundational political institutions and ethos to properly orient governance toward national cohesion; (3) weak citizens' sense of collective belonging; (4) no clear-cut ideal to galvanize the nation toward human flourishing, an ideal the nation's leaders must embody and endeavor to always actualize; (5) no trans-ethnic value system that moves citizens to engage in deeds and actions that would generate legacies for the betterment of future generations; and (6) no clear notion of the ideal of the "excellent" Nigerian, the Nigerian oriented toward the common good of the nation and committed to creating and sustaining an environment where all citizens can flourish. This list of Nigeria's problems is by no means exhaustive. To address comprehensively and exhaustively all of Nigeria's political problems in any one text is to write an impossible book.

Chapter 1 offers a conceptual rethinking of politics, laying out lifemaking as an alternative to necropolitics. Chapter 2 demonstrates how a team of visionary leaders can craft the politico-cultural institutions that would promote human flourishing in their nation. Currently Nigeria's leaders cannot craft the constellation of institutions that would advance the political development of their nation. They are also struggling to build a sense of collective belonging among Nigerian citizens. There is an urgent need for a viable social philosophy to aid in the reconstruction of ethos in ways that will foster senses and practices of human co-belonging, co-humanity. Chapter 3 provides resources within the indigenous knowledge and spiritual systems of Kalabari to aid the task of crafting Nigerian national spirit. Chapter 4 demonstrates how Nigeria can overcome its leaders' lack of commitment to freedom, the endless actualization of human potentialities. The precolonial Kalabari system of governance demonstrates how leaders can embody the ideals of freedom necessary to sustain human flourishing in their community.

Another problem that plagues Nigerian national politics is the absence of an ethical system that encourages its citizens in one generation to execute deeds that would make the country better for the generations behind them. The ethological model of social immortality discussed in chapter 5, the ethical process of creating legacies as an ideal of good citizenship, offers Nigeria's leaders a way to reflect and create a similar system fit for the twenty-first century. Finally, chapter 6 teaches us that the end goal of lifemaking and politics is to create the *excellent self*, that is, the flourishing citizen, the people living flourishing lives based on actualization of their potentialities as driven and supported by an environment that allows every person to be the best that he or she can be given their natural endowments and acquired skills.

All this has implications for the way we evaluate the political administration or governance of any community and its common good.

A political leadership geared toward creating excellent citizens must aim to create an *excellent nation*. At the minimum, excellence in national governance practice will involve the creation of possibilities for the nation and participation by all its members so that their potentialities can be drawn out for the common good. A nation should be adjudged *excellent* because it allows (creates an enabling environment for them) its people to develop their potentialities in the pursuit of ever greater common good. How well a nation does this will depend on how it allows individuals to develop their unique traits, capabilities, and potentialities and on how well these individual endowments are related to each other in the pursuit of the common good. An excellent nation is the one that is adept at combining these two opposite tendencies or processes: a movement toward uniqueness counterbalanced by movement toward union.

In such a nation the orientation toward the *not-yet* permeates all of its social practices and individual lives. The goal of politics is the creation of possibilities for all to participate in the polity (economy) and to realize their potentialities and in so doing enable the community to realize its potentialities. Science is an engagement with nature so as to fully understand, realize, extend, and create possibilities buried in the potentialities of all beings and processes in the universe. Education (*e-ducere*) is to draw out and lead forth the potentialities of a person. The organization of market competition is also oriented in this way—it is *agonistic*. The Latin root of our English word "competition" is *con petire*, which means to seek together. In competition the participants help each other to stretch their skills as they meet the challenge posed by the other. What each participant is seeking is the actualization of their own potentials and to help the other person come to his or her best.[32] In the same vein, an excellent friendship is the type of partnership and fellowship in which each person aspires to bring to realization the latent potentialities of the other. The friends say to another, "Let your actualization advance as mine does." An individual's life will be adjudged excellent if it is a life that is engaged in the pursuit of ever greater development and creative realization of his or her potentials. This involves, among other endeavors, overcoming challenges to create, manage, and sustain possibilities for responsible personal development.

Chapter 1

Lifemaking

Poetics of Politics in Traditional Africa

Introduction

What is lifemaking?

Lifemaking (*poiesis* of living) is a power of social existence that works on underdetermined possibilities to actualize (realize) them in ways that not only sustain biological life and political life of citizens but also create new possibilities. Second, lifemaking is a mechanism of power that bears on people to believe not only in themselves and others in the community but also in the world created or envisaged by the community in order to *labor*, *work*, or *act*. This mechanism runs on the engine of trust. Community, polity "solicits and produces individuals' trust by appealing to their conscience, their memory, and their representations. By creating an object of identification, it powerfully contributes to their constitution as individuals/citizens" of the Kalabari nation.[1] Lifemaking is, indeed, an artifact of creating and sustaining confidence or trust and acting on new possibilities. "In order to realize the power to act, we need to believe (trust) in the 'moving present,' the present as possibility, that is, in the world and the new possibilities of life that it holds. The power to act is subordinate to an existential affirmation, to a 'yes' that expresses a self-positioning. It presupposes hope and faith, anticipating what has not yet come to pass, making the impossible possible."[2] Third, lifemaking is the explanation (affirmation), production, and control of subjectivity, commanding (organizing) and distributing it to places and tasks in the community.

Lifemaking power of a community operates in two forms: lesser and higher powers. The two forms are complementary. The lesser form is used for ordering and maintaining what already exists; it is an organizing power for the flows of goods, institutions, and practices that already exist. The higher power prescribes and orders the set of possibilities for the future of the community. It does this by affecting and influencing the choices and decisions that condition the direction of future flows of goods and practices. This second-order power contains the capacity to create and destroy, conditioning time as possibilities and their actualizations. It is the capacity to reconfigure existing power relations and range of goods, practices, and institutions. The substance of the first power is history (congealed time, past and present time), and that of the second is time (future time as a set of possibilities).

The process of lifemaking creates citizens who are subject to these two powers through the "mobilization of [their] conscience, memory, and representations."[3] Lifemaking is the process of transforming the social existence of the individual into a debt to her community. This is the original sin of the polity that every generation inherits from preceding generations. The content of this debt is not money but existence, morality, and personhood. Here existence "means the power of self-affirmation, the force of self-positioning, the choices that found and bear with them modes and styles of life."[4] Morality here means ethico-political constitution of the community member. As Laurenti Magesa argues, the individual can become a person only within a community: "The individual can exist as a person only in a community, his or her well-being can be assured only in the context of the well-being of the community. It is in the interest of each member of the community that the corporate body is strong and healthy; at the same time, the health and strength of the corporate body has as its primary purpose the assurance of the welfare of each of its members."[5] Thus, within the credit-debit relationship, the new member of the community is turned into a citizen or brought under the community ethos; its demand to make and keep promises about its paramount goal is incorporated into the member. In turn, the community supports the individual to be the best that she can be given her natural endowment of gifts and skills.

Each person is socialized and supported to live a life that will enable them to discharge their debts, to keep the promise of upholding the paramount goal of the society.[6] Let me quickly add that making and keeping promises of this sort does not imply a life of indebtedness for the citizens. The community is both the creditor and debtor in this relationship. The community gives its members their time of existence (i.e., creation or expansion of new possibilities of life). The community receives from itself the "sacrifices," contributions of its members' physical and intellectual abilities, their sense of belonging, their mode of existence—the production of individual subjectivity. The community mobilizes the ethical action constitutive of its members, their moral existence as the spirit or substance of itself. Thus, to say that community holds within itself the creditor and debtor relationship means that when a community sacrifices itself for one of its members, for her debt, it is none other than paying itself back. The creditor-community "sacrifices" itself for the debtor-member. It is also true for the individual. In her relationship with the community, she is both a creditor and debtor. Her "personal existence . . . flesh and blood . . . social virtue and importance, which constitutes the material corporeal form of the spirit" of the community, is both an object of the credit-debtor relationship and the material on which the community exists.[7] Her trust in her world (community) and its attendant new possibilities of life, her time as set of possibilities, choices, decisions, and actions is the "symbol" of the spirit of the community.

Economy and Lifemaking

Economy is making provision for the future. It is in lifemaking and not in the provisioning that we see the archetype of political organization. The "production" of lifemaking reveals itself to be the primary form of production, the "provision" that goes into the production of all other provisions.[8] The primary dimension of this provisioning for the community is to form a person capable of the promise of natality, someone able to initiate something new, that is, capable of keeping the promise of possibility. This promise is bound up with or animated by the community's "investment in survival," the promise of living on, the ability to live on. The goal of the "investment in survival" is about care for life as a matter of negotiating existential conditions: that whatever they care for is subject to irreparable loss and that whatever there is does not and cannot transcend temporal finitude. The goal of living on is not to overcome temporal finitude for eternal repose or to achieve timeless perfection but how to grapple with the condition of time that is constitutive of every human desire. Survival or living on can take place only in the conditions of time. For in eternity nothing flowers, nothing fades, nothing passes away, nothing is born as nothing lives on in time.[9] What motivates a being to strive for survival, to desire to live on, to aspire to enjoy or change any extant state of being, to care for its sustenance and those of others, is the very impermanence of time—temporal finitude, the susceptibility to change and loss. To live, to be a living being, is to have "a structural relation to loss even in the persistence of the 'same' being across time. Every moment of living on necessarily involves a relation to what does *not* live on, and this negativity already constitutes a minimal relation to death. If one survived wholly intact—unscathed by the alteration of time—one would not be surviving; one would 'always be the same in every respect.' By the same token one would not be susceptible to any form of change, since nothing would happen to one."[10] All this motivates us to care for life. Because we know that life is short, that it could suffer irrevocable loss and is not present to itself, we care for its sustenance. If, on the contrary, we know that nothing can happen to it, that it can go on forever, always the same yesterday, today, and forever, we will not be motivated to invest in its survival.

The Political and Lifemaking

I have just elaborated why lifemaking and not economic provisioning for the future is the archetype of political (social) organization. This begs the question, What is the polity, at least in the way we are using it in this book? The polity in a certain sense is the set of practices to sustain natality in the community, to sustain the promise to living on amid the radical uncertainty and unpredictability of time. The traditional Kalabari polity is a polity of natality (creation of new possibilities) and promise in a specific sense. It means creating and subjecting present and future possibilities to the survival and reproduction of life in society. The polity subject to the uncertainty, fragmentation, and fleetingness of time harnesses the possibilities of time to the promise of living on, the promise of actualizing the concentrations of possibilities of life in a particular space.

The political is that part of society—the network of relations and systems—that grasps and expresses lifemaking as a substance and as subject. Lifemaking (life that is given a purpose by a group of persons) is not true to a community without including the subjective position, the contingent and particular point of community from which it is conceived. The political is the art of weaving life (lifemaking) and subjectivity together in such a way that community requires their entanglements for its becoming; they also need each other for mutual becoming.

Life is equally a substance and subject. Life is purposive activity, and this purpose is self-moving. The purposive activity is the relentless movement from potentiality to actuality. Life is self-moving because it is self-realizing, begins in potential and moves into actualization. Life makes life real. It starts with its purpose and ends with its purpose. Life moves itself. This self-movement is the basis of subjectivity. Life does something because of itself as a "subject." Its action is caused by itself. This self-movement is negativity. As life moves itself it constantly negates its state in order to change or transform itself. The self-movement is what life is. In this self-movement life constantly relates itself to itself: life as a purpose is always relating itself to itself both as its beginning and its end, negating itself within itself, negating its products in the purposive movement of the self. Life is negation of negation. In creating itself life negates itself to be what it wants to be, to move from potentiality to actuality. Life abstracts itself from itself.

The negativity that separates the present state of being from its previous one—the negativity between the two states that differentiates them—is the animating force of subjectivity. This negativity in the very power of life is the source of subjectivity (substance, as Slavoj Žižek would say, is always already subjectivized). The substance of life is in disparity with itself; the negativity is active within it and constitutes it. As Hegel would put it, substance is subject because it negates itself; it has negativity within itself; it splits (differentiates) itself because of its own self-negating power. Substance (subsistence of life) is a static image of subjectivity. Subjectivity emerges from life's abstraction; life creates difference in itself; the oppositions are abstracted from itself. This is the power of self-negation.[11] Life goes beyond itself to return to itself. Life is its own becoming. Thus, life's identity is not self-identical because of its self-movement, self-determination through its self-negation. Substance is only the frozen image of this endless negation of negation. Subject (subjectivity) is the crack within the substance, within being, the void of self-relating negativity. The subject is the constitutive gap around which the substance is structured. As Žižek puts it: "The Hegelian 'subject' is ultimately nothing but a name for the externality of the substance to itself, for the 'crack' by way of which the Substance becomes 'alien' to itself, (mis)perceiving itself through human eyes as the inaccessible reified otherness."[12] In another place, he writes that for Hegel, reconciliation, unlike Marx's conception of it, designates "an acknowledgement that the dimension of subjectivity is inscribed into the very core of Substance in the guise of an irreducible lack which forever prevents it from achieving full self-identity."[13]

The structure of life is thus incomplete, and its negation in the form of reaching out to what lies outside of itself and reconciling it to itself in a constant movement is its motive force. Life is incessantly striving to be something other than itself, ever trying to cover up the hole (the split, the negativity) that is at the center of its being. Lifemaking in the political sense is the passage from substance to the subject, the self-actualization of substance, the substantial whole of society. How will the ebb and flow of substance create the flourishing subject? How do we prepare a society to self-circuit itself, not to become a close and deterministic system, not to ground itself as itself, so it can create a space for human flourishing and freedom? The responses to these questions will involve comprehending how the community performs the destructive and constructive staging of possibilities, the distribution of its universal set of possibilities.

The political is the site of the power to command and prescribe the destruction and creation of possibilities and potentialities. The power is exercised to control possibilities of life, to distribute persons and groups to places in society and to their assigned tasks, and to begin something new—to create new possibilities. The political corrals and canalizes powers of life from all forms of creativity and dimensions of existence—rhizomatic web of social possibilities—in the community to perform or accomplish a particular vision of human flourishing. The political works to unfold human relationality, actualize potentialities, and help the community to realize its potentials. Politics is both a way of being for life and for one's own community. In this sense, politics is one way a community prepares its citizens for lifemaking, for the unfurling of their humanity and being for the whole community.

The political is the network of practices by (through) which a society finds (creates) and engages (cognizes) its constitution, existence, and flourishing as a community in its affirmation of (confrontation with) life. Society or the political is nothing if it separates itself from life. Either of them has no future within itself. An economy makes provision for this future, and politics not only makes the fences to safeguard the future and the provision but also distributes the possibilities of life into places and positions to enhance life. Put differently, the political is the process of protecting, liberating, and enhancing life and on the basis of this flourishment experimenting with expanding, intensifying, sharing, and actualizing of potentialities. Is this not what lifemaking is about? Is this not the elaboration of new relations of life that structure society as a whole? Politics is not merely a mode of sharing power, not merely a mode of distributing the resources of society, but a reduction of relations, ultimately, to relations of life. The relations of life also contain or conceal the mines to explode them. Lifemaking generates explosive possibilities for its destruction, re-creation, and reproduction of potentials for alternative forms of lifemaking. Politics is an instrument of lifemaking; the making of collective life is a two-edged sword. In this sense politics is *plastic*.

The concept of plasticity is about how the potentialities (possibilities) that course through human societies are perceived to give, receive, and explode forms of flourishing in social relationality. The community as a network of potentiality, impotentiality, actualization of potentialities, and material and energetic flows engendered by billions of micro interaction rituals is characterized by plasticity. This refers to three of its properties. Plasticity possesses "at once the capacity to *receive form* . . . and the capacity to *give form*. . . . But it must be remarked that plasticity is also the capacity to annihilate the very form it is able to receive or create."[14] The political is an attempt to name, understand, or interpret the plasticity of collective life or the universal set of possibilities available to a community. Its purpose is to enable us grasp what leads the universal set of possibilities toward metamorphosis; to lay bare the metamorphic structure that undergirds its capacity to order, animate, or articulate transformation; to sustain the alterity of the political with regard to itself; or to perform exchanges with itself. In this sense, the political is nothing but the mutability, the plasticity, of the community.[15]

Political Philosophy and Lifemaking

The political is a form of organization or practices of society to maintain life (*zoe* and *bio*), to preserve, maintain, or perpetuate its conatus, to keep its power, what is to its own advantage in the face of constant oppositions from and resistance of other communities, persons, or beings. Thus, it is the function of the political system to create an environment within which life can flourish by attention to virtues, capabilities, arts, religion, and business (economy). The political, among others, is conceived with the ethical virtues that will enable community members to pursue the common good and flourish in doing so.

A major threat to the common good and mass flourishing of the people is necropolitics. Defeating or eliminating necropolitics is at the heart of the philosophy of lifemaking. The death that is at the center of African politics or governance is directed not only at the good life of the people and their self-actualization but also at their economies. The Grim Reaper of African polities suffocates the desire, weakens the will, and cripples the capacity of Africans to innovate. Innovation—initiating something new amid ongoing social processes, inaugurating new practices—is the character of economic development. Necropolitics is restraining economic development in Africa. For lifemaking to dismantle necropolitics as well as lift up African economies, it must also clear paths for innovation. This is to say that it must deeply operate in ways that engage the people in the processes of production of increasing economic knowledge. The politics of lifemaking must structure African economies for "the exercise of indigenous creativity and pathways from there to innovation—for what has come to be called 'indigenous innovation'" to put African economies on sustainable development timepaths.[16]

Lifemaking, insofar as it is a bulwark against necropolitics and promotes mass flourishing, must concern itself with political development. If we think of political development as a process by which nations deliberately set the conditions of possibility for all their citizens to creatively actualize their potentialities, then it must emphasize the creativity of the people that participate in the economy. This is precisely what lifemaking is about, at least, as we have interpreted it. We have so far interpreted lifemaking as something that happens and breathes new form into the dimensions of the natural, human, and cultural. It symbolizes creativity, serendipity, and a stance opposing the kind of thinking or policy that denies the unfinishedness of all forms of human socialities. Owing to the possibilities of self-realization, the actualization of human potentialities, lifemaking is to an extent undetermined. It must be open to innovations, unpredictability, and how it (or its economy) will develop. This is to say lifemaking relentlessly invites creativity and unknowability, encourages experimentation and exploration, and promotes innovation. This basic philosophical orientation of lifemaking fits with what the Kalabari people call *bekebeke, mbregede*; it is a kind of kairotic openness to the future. To this extent, they reject the formatting of the future, are ready to interrupt the drift of society into a formatted future, and look forward to new possible time, toward a new horizon of possibilities.

For instance, part of the national drum name[17] for Kalabari is *Agbo kuro tereme sugbe kra*, meaning "War starts before sharpening the spear."[18] This idea does not imply a rejection of preparation ahead of time for projects or inevitable challenges before they occur but a deep orientation to the event character of life and lifemaking. And subjectivity is the fidelity to the event. ("Event" here means a rupture in the symbolic order or ongoing social processes; I am using it in Badiousian sense.)

To further support my argument about Kalabari openness to the future let me turn to one of their core beliefs: *Ngei konte*, there remains one more. There is always an unfinished business, one more thing to do. People in the culture are always reminded of this fact, and in Kalabari Ekine Society (an arts and dancing and governing club) this belief is constantly broadcast via drum lore at the times of masquerade displays. According to the religious historian G. O. M. Tasie, amid drumming for the masked dancers, the chief drummer will punctuate "his messages with the conventional *Ngei konte* of the *Ekine*, meaning 'one more.' This is to indicate to the masquerade that there is always an unfinished business in the *Ekine* requiring the *Sekibo* member [dancer] to be on the guard all the time."[19] This unfinishedness or incompleteness is at the inner core of their understanding of lifemaking and life in general. We see this dynamic self-realization or moving beyond in the Kalabari conception of forms of life.

Three Forms of Life and Their Political Implications

There are three forms of life in Kalabari that refer to the biological species, normative species, and transformative species.[20] The first form is *dumo* (*zoe*, biological species life) as the universal element of life.

Second is *dumo* as *bios* (ethical life, "humanized" life). *Dumo* at the level of *bios* in Kalabari is about the aesthetics of life. *Dumo* (*dumo-agabara, dumo-torugbe*) at this level is about a particular form of life as determined by the ethics and morality of the society. *Dumo* is here about *bio*-graphical life of an individual. Thus, Kalabari could say about a man, *O dumo siim*, meaning "Life is bad." This is to say the person is not conforming to community standards. "Whereas *zoe* belongs to the individual qua member of a species, the *bio* of the individual is something that happens 'outside' of the individual and does not belong exclusively to her, but to the *in-between* that Arendt calls the 'world' or the 'public.' To be 'dead to the world,' that is, to be alive but insignificant to those others alone who can judge the significance of our words and acts, is to live a life that 'has ceased to be human life because it is no longer lived among men.' "[21]

Third, we have *dumo* as referring to legacy, transformative and creative life. *Dumo* here actually is a short form of *erefaabia-dumo, warifaabia-dumo*. It means life that keeps the good reputation of the person, family name, or the family itself alive or prosperous. It is about legacy or social immortality. The individual has deftly combined the universal and particular dimensions of life to contribute to the well-being of the community, or to initiate something new amid ongoing social processes. It is a form of life that looks beyond the current life into deeds that would leave good legacies for the next generation of community members so that one's name would still be remembered long after one has joined the ancestors. The citizen combines *dumo* and *dumo-agabara* in an ethico-political constellation that initiates something new or a form of life that constitutes a higher identity of life beyond death.

Politics is *action* (in the Arendtian sense) in Kalabari. And this is not rooted in *dumo*, where the experience of biological necessity dominates, but in the dimension of freedom of life (transformative life species). This dimension of life is not apart from *dumo* and *dumo-agabara* (or, to put it in Arendtian terms, apart from life and labor). Political action is rooted in natality (politicization of *dumo* and *dumo-agabara*) as a new birth but does not escape biological life. "With word and deed we insert ourselves into the human world, and this insertion is like a second birth, in which we confirm and take upon ourselves the naked fact of our original physical appearance. This insertion is not forced upon us by necessity. . . . Its impulse springs from the beginning which came into the world when we were born and to which we respond by beginning something new on our own initiative."[22]

In Kalabari, political action as a new birth (make a beginning, begins something new) metaphorically relates to the crossing of mother (cooking hearth, eating plate, *efere*) and father's name, a movement from physical birth into initiating something new in the public space, the in-between of families. The father's name, the condition of acting in the public space, is itself conditioned by act of birth, "original physical appearance." The condition of action does not lie outside of the biological life itself. Kalabari say the *daeregoabo efere finji-a*. He who does not name his father, his lineage, cannot participate in the public square, the *in-between* of the plurality of human beings. *Efere* (food plate, china) in the saying harkens back to the mother's hearth, which symbolizes the "everyday transmutation of the raw into the cooked, of nature into culture."[23] The father's name transcending or crossing the hearth fire, the female realm, the movement from the processes of biological dependency into the freedom of life, is creative of novelty and signifies an engagement with the plurality of public space. This freedom of life speaks to the nature of politics as a matter of plurality, or, as Hannah Arendt would say, politics is between "man" (isolated single biological species life) and "men" (always in the plural). As she puts it: "*Man* is apolitical. Politics arises *between* men, and so quite *outside* of *man*. There is therefore no political substance [because human nature is different from the human condition of plurality. She rejects the Aristotelian "naturalization" of politics]. Politics arises in what lies between *men* and is established as relationships."[24] The public square where the *efere* is to be opened is a site of relationships between members of the community coming together from various natal hearths. Yet, it is germane to mention that the cojoining of *efere* and father's name informs us that this movement of life into the public square—the transformative life species operating in the plurality of men and women—is no real opposite of *dumo*, biological species life.

The Kalabari answer to the question of politics (life-affirming politics) among plurality of human beings and as transformative life in the community is to conceive politics rooted in the phenomenon of natality (new birth, political natality). The consciousness of natality involves intentional acts of ruptures, which lift off the crust of tradition and habitude over the common world. This act of world (re)making, this act of bringing the world into greater actuality through human inventiveness, is, among other considerations, an attempt to cultivate the self, to actualize one's potentialities. As Kalabari say, *tombo tombo so* (person should become person, be all that the person can be, to become his or her best person, the actualization of an individual potentiality to become all that he or she can be).

Political natality is the actualization of gifts (spiritual and nonspiritual), which makes a space of appearance for one in the shared common existence as a distinguished "who" and a creative transformer of culture. By virtue of political natality, the Kalabari man or woman inserts him- or herself into the pluralistic world where he or she aspires to transform the community or its culture. This insertion, this phase of the ongoing rebirth, may be stimulated by what is happening in the culture at large or the world, but it is never conditioned by it; its impulse springs from the logics and dynamics of lifemaking to which the member is responding by beginning something new, the transformation of culture.

Culture and Lifemaking: Elements of
Participation and Separation in Life

In the above interpretations of *efere finji*, patrilineality presents itself in the form of its opposite, matrilineality. The interpretation might have given you the impression that ideas of matrilineality transmigrated into patrilineality. This is to say that matrilineality as a central axiom of cultural semiotics was transposed from the "home-front" into the political dimension of power in the public square, into a central political axiom. The proper interpretation is to say that matrilineality has been influenced by patrilineality. There is actually a double flow whereby the maternal is paternalized and the paternal is maternalized. The meaning of each of them has been changed by the other, producing mutual effects. These two orientations have overlapped each other for a long time. The political in a limited sense is the performative effect that each of the two orientations causes in the other.

In the act of authenticating a person to speak in the public square, to participate in the in-between of the plurality of human beings, the reference to the *efere* (the food plate) indicates that paternity (the father's name) includes what it has historically superseded. The Kalabari notion of paternity includes maternity inside it "that constitutes both its dialectical driving force and the excluded remainder."[25] It speaks to the wider issue of inclusive exclusion and exclusive inclusion in the culture; some objects or ideas are being included by virtue of their being excluded, but others are being excluded by virtue of their being included.

The dynamic of the political in Kalabari is that of division and unity, or separation and unification. It unifies what it divides and separates what it joins. This machination (dialectic of unity and duality) is discernible on at least nine levels. First, its name Kalabari (precisely, *Prebokalakeibari*) symbolizes the whole that gives a part of itself to the other. But the gifted part and the whole are reconciled under the subordination of the part under the authority of the whole. Second, the proverb *Ama bebe buru, ngeribo buru pakiri* (meaning that the community owns the whole yam and the individual only has a portion of it) offers another perspective.

The *pakiri* is not a piece but a part. Let me resort to Roberto Esposito's comment on Martin Heidegger's distinction between part and piece to clarify this point. "Heidegger talks about the 'piece' (Stück) rather than the 'part,' since 'the part shares itself with parts in a whole. It takes part in the whole, belongs to it. The piece on the contrary is separated and indeed, as the piece, is even isolated from the other pieces.' "[26]

Third, this concerns the matter of the dialectic of unity and duality as I have already analyzed with respect to matrilineality and patrilineality. As I have demonstrated earlier, the political system as an articulation of mother and father involves the element of participation and separation, unity and tension. There is an analogy between political ideas and the basic structure of experienced life in which they are rooted. Political ideas reflect life and demonstrate how life works as a struggle of contradictions. This is the dialectics of life as symbolically applied to political life. Political ideas move divergently and convergently, separating and uniting simultaneously, to fashion sociopolitical life. Political ideas (matrilineality and patrilineality) and their application to or fusing with matrilineality and patrilineality do not form a dead identity. In life, the absence of participation and separation, complete identity or complete separation, is death. Political ideas include in their makeup an element of otherness. The "spirit" of this makeup, the various structural elements in their unity and their tension, represents the absence of complete identity or complete separation.

Fourth is the creation of chiefs in *wari* (canoe house). The canoe house was the most characteristic political and social institution of the Eastern Niger Delta states in the eighteenth and nineteenth centuries. It was not a lineage or descent group; rather, it was, as Gwilym I. Jones puts it, "a compact and well organized trading and fighting corporation, capable of manning and maintaining a war canoe."[27] Similarly, in 1913 the canoe house was defined by the British protectorate administration as "a number of persons grouped together for the purposes of trade and subject by native law and custom to the control, authority, and rule of a chief known as the head of the house."[28] A canoe house continued to function as long as it was dynamic, flourishing, and profitable. A prosperous, senior canoe house would spin off sub-canoe houses, which kept their connections with the parent-canoe house. If a sub-canoe house became more prosperous than its parent, it absorbed the parent house and in turn became the senior house. An unsuccessful canoe house folded up, voluntarily merged with another, or was acquired by another house.

In the eighteenth and nineteenth centuries, the leaders of the canoe house system were wealthy traders who commanded the support of their organizations. A chief (manager) held his position only as long as he was successful in his business endeavors. If he were to stumble or fall, leadership was taken from him and given to any member (slave or freeborn) whose character, commercial ability, and wealth most suited the furtherance of the fortune of the house. The managers were thus primarily engaged in finding and exploiting new business opportunities and markets and maintaining or increasing the wealth of the canoe houses.

The chief controlled the affairs, resources, and members of his house. Every member directly or indirectly worked for him. Some worked directly as traders, agents, paddlers, or soldiers for the war canoes. Others, a group of enterprising and ambitious traders, were identified and permitted by him to trade independently and in return periodically paid a tax in trade goods to him. The chief controlled the funds of the house, including house-tax receipts, "comey" (custom dues paid by ship captains to the king and his chiefs), invested capital, and retained earnings. He used them to maintain the war canoes and their ammunition, support the welfare of the whole house, give seed capital to such traders as enjoyed his favor, and make investments aimed at the growth of the house's business. The house increased in size by birth and by recruiting new members through marriages, adhesion (absorption of members from declining canoe houses), or the purchase of slaves (the word "slave" is not really a good word to translate *nyanabobo*, the alien who was incorporated into the household as a son or daughter). When the population and wealth of the house had reached a certain level it would produce a subsidiary house by planned segmentation.[29]

Fifth, the multiple is what generates the one in Kalabari. As Adolphus G. Karibi-Whyte, a former justice of the Nigerian Supreme Court, has argued, Kalabari do not have a common ancestor.[30] "Unlike many indigenous African ethnic societies who trace their origin either to the benevolence of an all-powerful deity or to the might of a mythical or superhuman ancestor, the Kalabari Nation State has been linked to neither of these origins."[31] Kalabari was formed because different Ijaw/Ijo groups (there were seven such groups/wards) with different deities came together to live on one island. Kalabari did not arise from a common ancestor but from many founders. Kalabari is now a common possession or single collectivity, but it began with diverse groups. When it began, no one learned to be Kalabari; one learned the way of a ward (group) and so became Kalabari in a distinctive and particular style. The Kalabari that became common to all was "achieved only in ways that [were] not common to all."[32]

Sixth, the tension of participation and separation in life is played out with the corpse of an *Iya erebo*: a woman married according to the most prestigious traditional law and custom. When a woman is married to her husband in this manner, she loses all rights in her paternal or maternal families. Her children can now trace their lineage through their father, but this is not so for women who are not married in accordance with this rite. For such women, their children technically belong to their mothers' canoe houses. (Kalabari is technically a matrilineal society, but children, descendants, switch to tracing their descent through the father once their mothers become *Iya wives*.)

Iya marriage unifies a woman with her husband's house (canoe house, *wari*), giving her children full paternal rights. But beneath this marriage machine that unifies her with her husband is a force of her exclusion. This exclusionary force comes to the fore when she dies. Once a wife dies her husband cannot see her nakedness. She has become a stranger to him. There is also a ceremonial ritual fight over her dead body. Her husband's *wari* and her own paternal/maternal *wari* (original house) will fight over the body to determine who has the right to bury her body. The original house will always win the fight.

The struggle is conducted over an empty coffin. The husband's house will make two coffins for her, one for ritual fight and the other for her burial. The coffin for the ritual fight will be broken into pieces to symbolize the intensity of the struggle or the agony of losing her. After her original house has won the fight, they take her body away with the unbroken casket to be buried by her "own people," those who truly own her as their daughter. In the ritualized struggle for the possession of the wife's dead body, the original house members would say to the husband's house, *Meni feebo imgbe faa*, meaning "He who bought (married) the flesh does not acquire the bones." The husband enjoys the living flesh, but not the bones. Bones and flesh, separated skeleton and flesh, usufruct. Here we see that if order is represented by flesh (the smooth run of body-politic meat), then it is forever threatened by divided bones, the strong disruptive powers of division. Once again, we see the elements of life, participation and separation, work themselves out in the culture.

The seventh example we will give to illustrate the tension between participation and separation is the dress (*doni*) of chiefs (*alapu*). Chiefs use four studs on their *doni*, a full-length flowing gown with long sleeves worn only by chiefs. In order to decipher the symbolism of the four studs we have to first understand Ijaw (Ijo) number system (symbolism), particularly in terms of male-female opposition. In the distant past, among the Kalabari, odd numbers in general, and three in particular, were associated with men, while even numbers in general, and four in particular, were associated with women. The number seven (three plus four) was associated with gods.[33] The *doni*'s four stud buttons, which seemingly goes against the tenets of the traditional numerology, is actually part of the narrative and political imagination of the chieftaincy institution. Other Kalabari male dresses below the rank of chiefs have stud buttons ranging from one to three.[34] Four stud buttons on the bodies of chiefs signify that they embody both the feminine and masculine forces of the culture. It is a subtle device of the high-status men to give themselves a larger-than-life and "spiritual" image, a moving physical image of three plus four.

Eighth, at the final ceremonies when a man is being installed as chief, he would be asked to make a choice between a yam and a cannonball. In the traditional society the yam (*buru*) symbolizes his capacity to nourish his house members, to improve their economic prosperity. The cannonball symbolizes his military capabilities, his ability to defend the community against attacks. Chiefs as leaders and rulers carry out both functions, but if an aspirant chooses the yam he will not be installed as a chief. He must choose the cannonball. Here we must be careful not to hastily conclude that *buru* is a real opposite of cannonball. The *buru* presents itself hidden in the guise of the cannonball, its seeming opposite. When all things or enemies are subdued to the cannonball (instrument of destruction of life), then shall the cannonball also subject itself to the yam, and the yam (symbol of life, nourishment of life, lifemaking) becomes all in all, the ultimate existential concern of the polity. The cannonball from which the chief generates his power of defense and control is a power that can subjugate life (citizens, or other contending powers, energies of society) only if it subjugates itself—or rather its welder subjugates himself—to lifemaking, the ultimate concern, which gives the cannon (or chief) this prerogative until lifemaking reabsorbs the cannon (or envelopes the chief's exercise of power) inside itself.

Finally, in the traditional conception of divinity, God has two dimensions, parts, or selves: *Teme-órú* and *So*. *Teme-órú* is regarded as the female creative modality. *So* is the dynamic directing agency, the aspect of divinity that orders the created outcome, the neuter or male counterpart. The *Teme-órú* part is concerned with creation, existence, destruction (wrath). *So* is concerned with destiny and behavior of people, groups, animals, and institutions. The shaping of destiny is done by or, rather, understood via the possibilities that *So* makes available to each person, group, or institution. *So*, when applied to individuals, is called *so*; to households, it is *wariteme-so*; and to communities, it is *amateme-so*.

Teme-órú and *So* work together as creative and directive destiny. The former (a dimension of God) creates, and the latter directs or organizes the possibilities for the created being. *So* is the universe of possibilities from which some are defined as available to persons and institutions and others remain either unfulfilled or simply the set of possibilities excluded to them at any given time. *So* is the ultimate source of possibilities and the principle of limitation or selection. The ideal set of possibilities (destiny) an individual receives from God has to be worked out within history; that is, the person actualizes the possibilities by the way he or she unifies its efficient causes. The person transforms the pure possibilities given to him or her into realizable possibilities under the conditions of the world.

The possibilities that are defined and distributed in any given society are conditioned by the law of the society. Law is used here in a broad sense: as acts of legislature, nomos and ethos, symbolic structures that regulate practices and representations, or specific regimes of interpretations of the religious doctrines, and so on. In every society there are three sets of possibilities: (1) one that is open to all individuals; (2) another that is available to only a few and the rest are excluded; and (3) the universe of possibilities that are yet to be fulfilled or not available to all persons and institutions. The law acts to bring the range of possibilities to manageable proportion and distribute them into the three sets. There are included and excluded possibilities in every existing state of affairs. It is the law that defines the boundaries of these three sets, what is possible and what is impossible. The law is the power that regulates possibilities and access to them. It is the law that tells members of a community what works within a given framework of relations. The operation of the law is always informed by the society's conceptions of justice, freedom, power, and ethics.

Communality and Lifemaking:
Elements of Justice, Freedom, Power, and Ethics

JUSTICE AND FREEDOM

Justice is fundamentally about people having the necessary freedom to fulfill their lives, to act, and to participate fully in the community's life.[35]

This freedom to posit the new, as we shall see later in this study (chapter 4, "Chiefs: Subjects to Freedom"), is tied to the freedom to disclose oneself, the distinctiveness of one's individuality that demands new beginnings even as time chronically marches on. This is freedom for the actualization of human potentialities.

Freedom is about the support the community gives to all citizens to exercise their personhood, to develop their capacities under the ambience of a loving communal fellowship, and to love. It is about developing one's capabilities and using one's personhood and the associated capabilities to work for the community, to maintain the structure of mutuality of life through which a people shape their lives and cope with their day-to-day problems. Freedom is the space the community provides for every member to open herself to others, to fashion communality and have human fulfillment and flourishing. Freedom is, therefore, a communal moral category that depends for its sustenance and progress not only on the moral web of interpersonal relationships but also on capacities of persons to participate and on the right relations that are to be maintained among them.

This view of freedom links it to the Kalabari notion of justice; both are anchored on the being of persons and community within the wholeness of relationships. As with freedom, "justice presses the question of concern for the whole network of relations and persons."[36] This notion of justice rejects the impersonal view that limits it to rules and principles in balancing competing interests in a detached perspective of human relations. This notion adopts the view of justice as right relations and "the practical unfolding of concern in our relationships and activities."[37]

Traditional Kalabari political thought gives justice a central place because it is not only a relational virtue but also related to all other virtues. A person is considered just if the moral impact of her practical activities and her exercise of all other virtues contribute to the good of the community, that is, the preservation and promotion of community, healthy relationships among all members of the community, and flourishing life.

The Kalabari view of justice as rooted in relationships places great emphasis on establishing and sustaining connections between people, connecting self to the other, and making room for the outsider in the inside. Justice is the quality and mode of connectedness in a given set of social relations. Justice is at the heart of all relationality because it asks for the recognition of the value of the other, it regards the intrinsic claim of the other as a person, and it adjusts the relationship toward reciprocity, equality, mutuality, and solidarity. Justice's purpose is to deepen relations, care and nurture, extend the network of relationships, and embody community. Justice is nurturance. Doing justice is "righting wrong relationship,"[38] restoring fractured relationships, and expanding the space for participation in the network of social relations by the poor and marginalized. What is "participation space"? It can be defined as a room in the socioeconomic relations that allows the disadvantaged, poor, marginalized, and outsiders to gain resources for full human capability development without jeopardizing the sustainability of the economy and polity.

In summary, these are the two crucial features of justice in the Kalabari social ethical system. Justice works to bring into deeper communality and fellowship many who are excluded or separated from an embracing community. There is the power of *eros* within justice, which drives the network of relations toward the ultimate goal for all engaged in it.[39] The process of deepening and widening relationships is also one that strives toward higher levels of flourishing, catholicity, and meaning. Second, justice works toward the fulfillment of all humans within the network of relationships. Justice (quality of relationships) is seen as necessary for persons to live and pursue the life of *eudaimonia*, the promotion and preservation of community's well-being.

POWER

It is also in relationships that we can discern the Kalabari fundamental understanding of power. Power is an emergent phenomenon of relationships, and it realizes itself through practices. Even gods arise from or are conditioned by the social practice of worship. The gods arise from such practice insofar as their power of being is in it. The gods are conceived as a source of tremendous power. But the power that the gods possess is believed to depend on the social practice of human worship. Their powers derive from human worship, and as such humans can reduce or completely efface the power of any god by withdrawing worship.[40]

Most Kalabari (in the precolonial period) believe that spirits and gods (except the supreme being) do not have intrinsic powers of their own such that the withdrawal of worship from or worshipful dependence on a god deprives it of power and authority to act on humans or control human activities. Kalabari insist that a god that is not worshipped loses its power. So if a god becomes too furious or demanding, they will tell it from which tree it was carved (*Agu nsi owi baka kuma en ke o kara sin en dugo o piriba*).[41] This means that a community can unanimously annul the power of a god by refusing to worship it.[42] Robin Horton interprets the aphorism this way:

> Literally, if a spirit's demands become too burdensome, the whole congregation can join together to destroy its cult objects, and by this unanimous act of rejection render it powerless to trouble them further. . . . Broadly, then, the more people lavish offerings, invocations, and festivals upon any spirit, the more powerful it becomes both to reward and punish them. And conversely, the less they attend to it the less powerful it becomes—up to the point at which unanimous rejection results in the complete loss of power. Generally, of course, a single man cannot reject a spirit at will; for while he is only one among a congregation of many, it will have the power to punish him.[43]

The relationship, the power dynamics with gods, is such that a human being can bring a suit against a god, and if that god is found guilty, its sculpture (statue, representation) would be given a good flogging.[44] In some severe cases of misbehavior, the god would lose its status as a god. The Kalabari people on September 27, 1857, "killed" one of their gods (Owu Akpana, the Shark-god) and proceeded to celebrate the deicide and its ensuing freedom. This act, which was not metaphysical but historical, involved eating the divine flesh and drinking the blood of the god, incorporating the divine into the human and thus recognizing sovereignty in the people.[45]

It is not only human beings that bring cases against the gods; the deities can also sue human beings. As Karibi-Whyte puts it: "Kalabari legal jurisprudence recognizes the legal personality of 'gods,' 'departed,' 'ancestral spirits,' 'idols,' [and] 'totem gods.' Even these can bring actions in their names. They own property. . . . There have been actions on their behalf for injury done to them."[46]

Kalabari worldview encourages the practices of freedom. As we have already noted, this is very evident in the human relations to gods and spirit. There is an idea of human freedom into which the gods and spirits are not allowed to encroach. If a god oversteps his or her boundary, the penalty is withdrawal of worship and banishment. Horton brilliantly captures this understanding of human freedom vis-à-vis the gods when he describes the relationship between humans and spirits.

> Now any spirit which has become an object of ritual is known as *oru*; and the most general term for ritual is *oru mie*—"making

oru." This phrase carries a suggestion of human power over the free spirits which is borne out in many Kalabari sayings. For example, *tomi oru beremare*—"It is people who make the *oru* important"; and *tomi ani oru ma*—"People, they are the *oru*." Explaining such aphorisms, Kalabari compare the spirits with men of influence, who are only big so long as their followers follow them, and who become nothing when their followers fade away. . . .

This view of man's relation to the free spirits is not surprising, given the belief that every worshipper himself has a spirit which is something of the same order as the object of worship. In the invocation which is the central act of any ritual, a man is said to "put his spirit upon his word," and upon this depends their power. As spirit facing spirit, man does not beg for favours from a position of helpless dependence; he asks from a position of strength.[47]

From the foregoing we can surmise that Kalabari religion and politics have some peculiarities. In most religions, when the relation between god and human beings has been severely fractured because of sin, the adherents strive to purify themselves in order to overcome the alienation from god and restore the relationship. In Kalabari religion, on the contrary, the god is likely to be abandoned, rejected, or killed. The killing of a god and Kalabari/Ijo republicanism (in the sense that political power belongs to no one person) suggest there is a disincarnation of power: political leadership depends on the consent of the citizens, and no leader can function as an incarnation of the divine. A leader can refer neither to an *outside* (to a god or sacred mandate) nor to an *inside*, singular appropriation of the democratic power of the community to privilege his or her authority. Power is groundless and unfounded and thus open to endless interrogation and alteration.[48]

This way of thinking about divine-human relationship or power dynamics is not at all surprising once one grasps the importance of relations as constitutive of both society and personhood in Kalabari communities. Worship is not just reverence, obeisance, praise and exaltation, or appropriate response to deity but the dynamic maintenance of deep, thick relations, a social bond with a deity. All forms of power, be it political or spiritual, are always predicated on the strength of social bonds among persons and the fracture or rupture of the bond or the displacement of harmony in the bond, which means erosion of power and authority. This predication is for the sake of fashioning the web of relationships (in the context of freedom and justice) that would enable members of the community to actualize their potentialities.

Power is the capacity, capability, or drive to actualize the potentialities of a person or group. Every move of power from essence (or will-to-live, power of being) to existence privileges a path, creates a specific process of moods, modifications, and concretizing of existing data or entities to produce and guard its actualizations.[49] The notion of "privileging a path" speaks to the logic of differentiation and differential gearing that every individual needs in order to drive toward self-fulfillment and human flourishing at her own pace and preference within the context of a community that puts a premium on human dignity and equality. To "privilege a path" does not mean that there is a unique path that each person must follow to actualize her individual potentialities. It only means that a person should become what she is essentially and therefore potentially establish herself as a person and a person-in-communion.[50] Every person is a *miracle* of new beginning in the world and has the capacity to introduce something new, something totally unexpected into the world.[51] Thus, ignoring this purpose to do and actualizing what one is essentially and potentially capable of doing is deemed immoral.

Ethics

The individual and her community forge the privilege of a way forward to realization of Tamuno's gifts in the individual. The privilege of actualization of potential is a moral act. Following Paul Tillich, I would say that every moral act is also an act whereby the community and the individual work together to establish the individual as a person capable of answering to the demands of life. And this takes place through the process of actualization of potentialities for the sake of the individual and the community. When an individual is given her due—her privilege—she also gains access to relevant communal-institutional forms in which everyday person-to-person encounters happen that make for human flourishing.

The concept of privilege recognizes the uniqueness of every individual and, accordingly, affirms Hannah Arendt's notion of natality, which nudges us to acknowledge that every human being carries the possibility to act in totally unexpected ways that might constitute a fresh start for our social existence. Every child is a miracle to the world and a potential source of miracle. When the people, a community, regard every child as a miracle, as something that has never happened in the world before, and thus remains open and willing to allow and support her in following the "law" of her own individual development, give her the right of exception to the actualization of her potentialities, and not consider her as a cog in a wheel, they are enacting privilege for her. Here privilege (*privus +lex/leg*) gestures to the "private law," the force of the alternative, the underside of standards that deform and disrupt hegemonies and hierarchies that are proprietary to publicly, widely recognized, institutionally proper practices and appearances.[52]

Kalabari ethics pertains to discerning the appropriate modes of being-in-relationship and is aimed at the restoration of right relationships at every level of communal life (gods/spirits, community, family, person, and earth). These modes are either moral or immoral. Being-in-relationship is moral when it promotes community, equality, mutuality, and reciprocity. Otherwise, it is immoral. Immorality (*si dumo, siamiaye*) is the absence of right relationships at whatever level of manifestation; they are acts that do not serve communion between or among persons. They are acts that fracture and violate relationships of one person to another, to the whole of creation, or to the gods.

The moral life of Kalabari is nothing more than training the senses, sensibilities, and capacities on the maintenance and restoration of communion and living in a such a way that one acquires the constant disposition (*habitus*) of discerning the strongest of objective bonds in the community. Such a moral life is a threefold rhythm and movement. It is remembering and honoring the past and those who lived before, lifting present relationships to the highest possible levels, and anticipating one's future with the community. The moral person accepts that her origin, existence, and destiny do not belong to her alone but also to the community. The moral person is in communion with others. Morality is a mode of *ecstasis*, a means of being for others and self-transcendence. The moral person is also a savior (*dua-boromabo*). The moral act is salvific in that it restores communion; it delivers a citizen or citizens from the side of self-containment, rest (*stasis*), and exclusion to the other side of self-transcendence, continual movement outward to other (*ek-stasis*), and embrace. The moral person, savior, gathers together what has been sundered. This is not all. The moral person is also sacramental: she makes present the reality to which she points. She points to and is an exemplar of communion at all levels of reality, which is the paramount goal of the ethical, virtuous life. She empowers others to live in right relationships with her, with themselves, with others, with the gods and ancestors, and with nature (environment) and the not yet born. She transforms and renews relationships, supports and promotes flourishing of persons, and creates new capacities for relationships in the community so that full personhood can be realized and expressed. Her life is concretely efficacious in transforming deadening impersonal individualism, self-enclosure into lively and life-giving ecstatic, marvelous relationality. The moral life is catholic—as pertaining to the whole community and obviating all alienating patterns of relationship. It invites all to communion. Kalabari moral life is, indeed, not only the capacity for communion but also the orthopraxis of communion.

Concluding Remarks

In this chapter I set out to define and discuss the fundamental ideas and concepts that will play predominant roles in the rest of the book. Together, these concepts and ideas deepened our understanding of lifemaking in Kalabari, demonstrating how institutions, practices, and ideas cohere to sustain life and human flourishing.

The systematic way in which I presented the key concepts that inform or are informed by lifemaking should not lead the reader to think that precolonial Kalabari society first laid out the philosophy of lifemaking in a coherent way and then realized it in practice. The philosophy, which I have described in the preface, introduction, and this chapter, originated through spontaneous means and basic rules of behavior, contingency, and necessity; it is not a product of human design accomplished in a single period of thought.[53] As Friedrich Hayek argues, "All that we call civilization has grown up on the basis of that spontaneous order of actions which is made possible by the delimitation of protected domains of individuals or groups."[54]

This book is a second-order reflection on praxis and can afford to present Kalabari ideas and practices worked out over centuries in a systematic way. This I do with the aim of bringing latent Kalabari philosophic ideas into rigorous conversation with academic philosophical constructs. It is important to set straight what I am doing in this book when I engage the Kalabari materials. I am not producing a work of plain ethnographic descriptions as in reproducing "verbatim" the materials or rendering a pre-theoretical viewpoint. I engage and interpret the Kalabari materials to work out my own ideas or my understanding of certain social phenomena.

The reader needs to be aware that this book is not a report on indige-nous Kalabari thoughts (ideas) but a reading of them as perceived from a particular theoretical viewpoint, that of lifemaking. My presentation or representation of Kalabari materials is theory-laden and philosophically driven. While this book lays out the basic political concept and ideas of Kalabari traditional society, it is also rethinking and reconstructing those very concepts and ideas. This is a philosophical book that aims to work out the conceptual foundation on which politics (political governance) pivots to promote human flourishing in Africa. It executes its task by standing in and standing out of the indigenous Kalabari philosophy of lifemaking.

Now let us turn to the task ahead. In the remaining portions of the book, I clarify how the philosophy of lifemaking I have adumbrated so far affects (or affected) the practical living conditions of the Kalabari people. The philosophy informs practices as it is preformed and informed by past and present practices. The next chapter starts this task of examining the connection between lifemaking and actual living conditions of Kalabari by studying the matter of nation-building as crafted by the Kalabari king Amakiri and his chiefs in the eighteenth and nineteen centuries. Chapter 2 presents the job of creating and sustaining lifemaking as the central philosophy of politics and governance in Kalabari during this precolonial period.

Chapter 2

The Philosophy of King Amakiri

Kalabari as a Political Narrative

Introduction

Dabaye Amachree (Amakiri) was the king (*amayanabo*) of Kalabari in the eighteenth century. He is generally celebrated as the most consequential king in Kalabari history. In the book *Hundred Years of Buguma History in Kalabari Culture* published by Buguma Internal Affairs Society to mark the centenary (1884–1984) of the founding of Buguma, the new capital of Kalabari, the editors write:

> In the history of Kalabari there is one indisputable and out-
> standing fact: that a politically integrated unit with an organized
> line of kingship over it where any man's progeny enjoys an
> uninterrupted succession started with King Amachree I. It is
> on the foundation of his phenomenal outstanding contributions
> which no other leader before him ever made. . . . [He] not only
> succeeded in welding the diverse communities [autonomous
> groups] of Elem-Ama into one people but also enlarged the
> nation by both an ingenuity of internal organization, external
> military prowess as well as diplomatic successes.[1]

Amakiri emerged as a leader after a disastrous fire had destroyed Elem Kalabari, the city-state in the mid-eighteenth century. The heads of the seven autonomous wards (Endeme, Korome, Igodome, Akialame,

Amabiame, Ituruame, and Bukome) sought a person who could undertake the rehabilitation and reconstruction of the city. Their condition was that whoever was going to undertake the reconstruction would be the leader of the town. They approached many wealthy men in the community, but they all turned it down for the fear of depleting their investment capital or for making mistakes in the rehabilitation of the numerous shrines of gods in the town, something that could lead to disastrous spiritual consequences. Seleye Fubura, the leader of the Korome group and the wealthiest Kalabari man at the time, was particularly pressured to take up the leadership of the town. His mother prevailed upon him to reject the offer. Eventually, Amakiri from the Endeme Ward rose to the occasion and was successful in rehabilitating the town. For the rebuilding of the town, Amakiri not only accepted being the leader of the town but also insisted that his children should succeed him in perpetuity as *amanayabo* and that the *kirikiri mine* ritual should be performed at his burial.[2] Before then this rare funeral ritual was done only for two persons considered sacred: the chief priest (*So Alabo*) of *Owamekaso*, the national goddess of the Kalabari people, and *Akwa Alabo*, the drum chief of the *Ekine* or *Sekiapu*, a prestigious masquerade-playing society.

Once he emerged as *amayanabo*, Amakiri used marriages, political alliances, institutional reforms, and friendships to consolidate his grip on power. He was gifted at welding the various groups into one body as a community. He was said to have coined philosophical ideas or pithy statements to encapsulate his fundamental political philosophy to mobilize and galvanize the disparate groups into oneness or inspire their members to pursue the paramount goal of the community. One of those sayings that survives to this day is *Ama bebe buru ngeribo buru pakiri*, meaning "Only the community is tantamount to a whole yam; the individual is always but a part of it" or "the whole community constitutes the full yam, and the individual is half a yam." Later in this chapter, we will return to this aphorism and interrogate what it means in light of the political theory of lifemaking.

Amakiri strategically married women from the other groups to further his aim of consolidating power and the future of his dynasty. He sponsored children from such marriages into leadership positions of his spouses' groups. For instance, he married Ogun of Akialame Ward and had a son named Fubura. He later created a canoe house for Fubara and eventually succeeded in placing him in control of the Akialame Ward. When Fubura died, Manuel, his nephew and son of Adida, Amakiri's first daughter, took over as the head of the Fubura house, which was now in control of the Akialame Ward.[3] Amakiri also gave his daughters as wives to important figures in the other groups. He even gave some of his sons to be raised by the other houses to build political alliances.[4]

By the end of Amakiri's leadership, most of the seven wards had disappeared or declined. According to G. I. Jones, during Amakiri's leadership the Endeme Ward recorded tremendous growth in personnel as it absorbed persons from other wards and brought in people from the Igbo hinterland. The enlargement in size led to the division of the wards into many canoe houses, "some of them separate and some expanded or aggregated into groups and the two largest and most powerful of these groups were those derived from Awo (Barboy) and from Amakiri household."[5] In the course of these structural changes, he transformed the chieftaincy institution, the managerial and political leadership core of the community. He strengthened the chieftaincy institution by raising the standard of accomplishment before any male could aspire to the that position. Chiefs as heads of the groups must be appointed based not just on their ascribed status but also on achieved status or a combination of both.

> Now in the prescribed ceremony of chieftaincy installation, it became necessary for the candidate to publicly pick up a cannon ball indicating his willingness to serve in defence of the State. He must be a man of substance, who will also display at least a fully equipped war-canoe as a condition of attaining the high office. This new chieftaincy standard of the war-canoe house meant that the chief is able to muster into one large canoe at least two operational cannons, twenty-six paddlers (of young men who are his wards) and sufficient supplies of food and other weapons, which must not be counted as provisions that he cannot replenish. It required showing proof that at least the equivalent of this outlay in men and materials is available to him in reserve should the first line of defence suffer reverses.[6]

We will come to back to the Kalabari chieftaincy institution in chapter 4 and examine its underlying political philosophy of lifemaking. The canoe houses (*wari*) exist and relate to each other in common, but in turn their interactions and relationships also produce and sustain the commons. Kalabari was once described by Robin Horton as a congeries of *wari*, which function as singularities linked by the commons they share and not by a strong theory of sovereignty. Indeed, Kalabari is a commons.[7]

Friendship was also one of the instruments Amakiri used to weave the various canoe houses together in Elem Kalabari. The most known friendship during Amakiri's time was the one between him and Chief Iju Jack. There were other famous friendships in Kalabari history in the eighteenth and nineteenth centuries. Some of the most well-known ones were between Chief Igbanibo Will Braide and Chief Dodo West when they were both at Elem Kalabari, and between Chief Braide and Chief John India Yellowe Iyalla from Tombia. Amakiri in particular was deft at using friendships to further his political aims and consolidate his hold on power. Iju (Jack), the head of the Igodome Ward, was known as his closest friend and confidant. They even grew closer after Okrika, another Ijo community, launched a devastating attack on Elem Kalabari. Okrika attacked when most of the Kalabari chiefs and able-bodied men were away on ritual pilgrimage to Obio markets (*Oru fe*). Okrika sent out two war parties: one attacked the town, and the other ambushed Amakiri and other chiefs on the high seas on their way back from the ceremony. According to Tonye Erekosima and his coeditors of *Hundred Years of Buguma History in Kalabari Culture*:

> The town was saved from total destruction by Chief Iju, who had turned back from the pilgrimage on receiving a premonition of disaster when an ominous bird flew across his fleet's bow thrice. He was able to prevent the massacre and destruction of his own group of houses as well as those of persons who were able to run to him for protection. The rest of the chiefs and their crew other than the one ambushed by the Okrikans, and so arrived home unscathed. Amachree took the ambushed route. He was saved, it is said, by a combination of his naval skills and his powerful invocations, which drew protective response from the tree known as *aku*. He routed his second Okrika war-party and also arrived home unbeaten only to face a depopulated and ruined settlement.[8]

The friendship between Amakiri and Iju was so close and delicate that the memories of it survive in the *kirikiri mine* funeral rituals of Kalabari kings more than two hundred years later. One of the rituals before a Kalabari king is buried is the formal cutting of animals and pouring of their blood on the body that lays on a mat on the floor. Each head of the canoe house would come with his animal and say to the dead king,

"Kini-nyanabo, Amakiri" ("Our Lord, Amakiri"), and present the animal to the king's first son who would slice off the head in one stroke of his sword and smear the blood on the dead king. Only Iju comes to the dead king with a fish, snapper (*agbara*), and declares, "Ikiabo, Amakiri," meaning "My friend, Amakiri."

According to a version of oral tradition among the Iju group of houses in Abonnema today, when Amakiri would visit Iju his friend, his scepter would not touch the ground as a way of acknowledging their special friendship and intimacy, as if to say his status as the sovereign ruler of Elem Kalabari should not come between them as friends. So today, whenever a chief of Iju house dies and the youths are performing ceremonial *igira sara* (a war-like stampede, storming around the town with martial songs and sexually explicit gait, to signify the symbolic breakdown of law and order owing to the passing of the chief), they would often hum, "Amakiri Nkpara laa kiri," meaning "the scepter of Amakiri does not touch the ground on our territory."

Let us now take a moment and briefly reflect on the place of friendship in Amakiri's understanding or performance of sovereignty. He cultivated a constitutive community in which the virtue of friendship that makes for stability was fostered, to actualize the necessary political cohesiveness for Kalabari polis. In friendship the Kalabari citizen expands, opens, and transcends the boundaries of the self and seeks the well-being of other persons for their own sake, opening the transpersonal relationship to the possibility of breaking the automatism of social processes, to initiating something new. The coming together of friends and networks of friendship can and do generate political power—exactly in Hannah Arendt's sense of a group of persons engendering power in their being together, cooperation, and acting together—to transform societies. In all this true friendship forms and shapes citizens into a community of character fit for the polis.

We have been piecing together the kind of political imagination that Amakiri had that enabled him to create a united Kalabari nation. We have examined his strategic alliances, friendships, military and economic capabilities, reforms of the institution of the chieftaincy, and negotiating skills that not only founded his dynasty but also gave him sacred privileges reserved only for key leaders of cultural and religious institutions. There are two other actions that he took at the early period of his emergence as king that fed into this narrative.

After the Okrikans had devasted the town's population, most of the houses did not have enough men and women to properly function as compact trading and military units. Amakiri was able to repopulate many canoe houses with men and women from his own house. He also acquired more servants (slaves, *nyanabo-apu*) to rejuvenate the depopulated houses. All these gave him opportunities to restructure the community to his taste. As he increased the population and redistributed people, he also restructured the original seven wards into fourteen.

Amakiri not only replenished the devasted population of Elem Kalabari but also bought new domestic animals to replace the ones destroyed or captured by the Okrikan soldiers. The domestic animals he bought were allowed to roam about the town and could be claimed by anyone in whose house or compound they spent the night. "This is the origin of the expression *ama kiri menji nama*, referring to animals not owned by anybody. It is also the excuse why *Sekiapu* [and youth masquerade groups today] freely kill animals that are found anywhere during their festive periods. It is believed that all domestic animals are owned by Amachree."[9]

The gifts that Amakiri bestowed on the community were a quintessential demonstration of his grasp of lifemaking. Lifemaking is the process of generating, ordering, and sustaining the endless networks of exchanged and binding gifts that constitute a community as community (*munus, kaleke-ibari, diyepriye*). It also involves erecting safeguards against the habits, forces, and events that will pervert the process, that will work against the spread of the *munus*.

Gifts, Governance, and Political Imagination

Amakiri's gifts at the crucial moments transformed thanatopolitics (death and devastation visited on the city by invading Okrikan army) into biopolitics. His gifts represent the fundamental sacrifice of the community, and the gifts bind the community together in moments of anguish and grief, bind its wounds, and (re)constitute its bond. These gifts and sacrifices (*munus*) give us a sense that, for Amakiri, politics was, among other things, a form of "immunization" against material lack. Politics for him was the immune system of the community against lack of being-with, expropriation, and contagion of immiseration. Politics immunizes the community against existential lack (nonbeing), to support the *being* that is at stake in how the citizens' lives hang together, the being of their existence that is always a coexistence. Politics as immunization is about working out the good and the fitting *nomos* to share a polity's abundant being-with and material goods in ways that (can) promote human flourishing for all.

Generally, in many other political systems, immunization refers to curtailing the contagion of the *munus*. Communities set up im-munities against the spread of the *munus*.[10] It appears Amakiri tried to overcome the immunitary barriers to the contagion of the *munus* by his relentless focus on the common. His famous proverb, a piece of his political thought, *Ama bebe buru ngeribo buru pakiri* ("the whole community constitutes the full yam, and the individual is half a yam"), exposes the *munus* as a condition to the flourishing, peace, and security of a community's members. Of course, the original name of the Kalabari people suggests similar interpretation of the role of *munus* (the "fundamental gifts and sacrifices that constitute the bond of com-munity," the contagion of the *munus*).[11] The name is *Perebo-kalakeibari*, meaning "Let the well-endowed, the wealthy, share his or her rewards, gifts, winnings, or resources with me"; "Let him or her give me a little of his or hers." The ethos or princi-ple of *Perebo-kalakeibari* encourages those who are talented or gifted to develop their skills and reap rewards with the understanding that their endowments, rewards, or winnings will be shared with the community, to give a part of their rewards or winnings to improve the situation of other members of the community.[12]

From the foregoing we can discern that in the traditional Kalabari community as crafted by Amakiri and his chiefs, governance and political leadership were never defined to exclude material betterment (*putting food on the table*, kitchen table issues) and security. Political leadership must provide security, including food security, to the people, offer gainful employment to young men and women in the community, and raise future entrepreneurs who will put the energy and skills of future generations into productive use.

This notion of governance is exemplified in the choice of items every would-be chief has to make during the installation ceremony. At the ceremony, the would-be chief is given two objects: a cannonball and a yam. He is asked to pick one. Always, the aspirant picks the cannonball, an instrument of defense. He would not be installed if he picked the yam. The choice of cannonball reflects his commitment to deliver security to his community. Security here includes food security. To directly go for the yam is to miss the point. In the midst of the precarious precolonial existence of slave raids and general insecurity in the Delta area, military security became a metonym for all sorts of security.

Besides, one could not offer oneself for chief if one was not already a successful entrepreneur capable of providing economic and food security to his canoe house members. He must also have demonstrated an uncommon capacity to put the energies and skills of many persons in his *wari* to productive use. He must have already raised successful entrepreneurs who could be chiefs in their own rights in the future.

The concern for food security comes to the fore in another ceremony. One of the rules for offering oneself as a would-be chief is that the man had already married a woman through *Iya* ceremony. In this ceremony the man lays out a variety of foods in abundant quality. The bride is systematically given portions from the different plates (*efere*) to taste, which she must reject. Her refusal is meant to portray her as someone not given to easy gastronomical pleasures. The bridegroom's provision of the sumptuous foods is a testament of food security in his household or *wari*.

The bottom line is that governance was never defined to exclude food security, day-to-day security of life, prosperity, and gainful employment of young men and women in the community. This pragmatic understanding of governance was a technology for managing how lives hang together in the community.

Governance as exemplified by Amakiri was not only about material betterment but also forging a certain kind of political imagination. For him, the political was a form of imagination, a way of being for the new, of representing to the self and the community a new vision of social existence. As he instituted far-ranging transformations of the society and its power structure, his political imagination worked to keep the connections between tradition and change relevant, subtle, and robust for flourishing human life. Political imagination, for him, was world-making, opening up new interpretations of sociality and new horizons of possibilities and creating new meanings.

There are three different political imaginations from Amakiri era that are worth noting. First, the city-state was an imagination based on common residence and culture—and not on blood or land. This simply means that the criteria for citizenship in Kalabari was the possession of the distinctive culture (*amaganganbra*) of the community and residence in it.[13] This understanding of citizenship is a counterpoint to the current Nigerian notion of citizenship that is largely rooted in indigeneity. Where did this Kalabari new thinking on citizenship come from?

Let us not forget that the *wari* (Kalabari canoe house) was established, sustained, and perpetuated by a trading corporation. Kalabari towns and villages are always segmented into semiautonomous units and organized into three levels of hierarchy. There is the house (*wari*), which consists of entrepreneurial households (historically, a merchant, his family, staff, servants, dependents, and relations; all these members who were not necessarily joined by bloodlines had to be brought together by a common factor and transformed into a cohesive group). A *wari* (as in Elem Kalabari) or group of houses makes up the *polo* or ward. The combination of wards makes up the town, *ama*. Kalabari society is organized as thus: individual (household), *wari/polo*, and *ama*. Citizenship in any Kalabari town was based on residence and acceptance of the community culture. Acquiring such citizenship status was only the first step for a man to become a "complete Kalabari man." To acquire this valued distinction, the man had to perform a dance test. This test involved a masked dancer successfully pointing to over thirty shrines as he was being directed via a drum language. Learning to understand drum language is not an easy undertaking; it requires long training and tutoring. Drum language consists essentially of "tone patterns extracted from speech,"[14] and its interpretation and understanding demand the acquisition of the "community's myth and history" and fluency in the ordinary Kalabari language. Most important, drum names "take the form of proverb or metaphor, learning them plunges one deep into traditional attitudes and imagery."[15] Participants in the pointing ordeal are being tested for a particular character trait that the Kalabari community holds very dear—the Kalabari aristocratic ideal. A man imbued with the Kalabari aristocratic ideal is to bring off his achievement with extreme "nonchalance." Robin Horton has posited that there are three main components to this idea: (1) *asa* (stylishness, flamboyance, and youthfulness); (2) *agbo karo tre sugbe kara* (admiration for "nonchalant achievement"); and (3) *bu nimi* ("knowing oneself"; self-control, balance, restraint, decorum, and dignity).[16] Kalabari hold the view that a person must in all circumstances show balance and self-control, nonchalantly breezing and bluffing his or her way through very serious tests of his or her social standing.[17] This character trait is taught and emphasized in a million subtle and not-so-subtle ways. The *Igbo* masquerade, which is an embodiment of all three components of the national character, is a popular and beloved masquerade in Kalabari. "It should be remembered that the *Igbo* play was one way whereby the Kalabari man kept his society the way he wanted it. His strangers . . . all went through this kind of test of culture as a prerequisite to the granting of high status."[18]

Let us now turn to the second type of the emergent political imagination of the Amakiri era. An imaginative ethos of masculinity increasingly came to condition political practice during the Amakiri era. Political imagination got more masculine, and in the Ijo context of the eighteenth century, this means it became more patriarchal (or patrilineality supplanting matrilineality), and violence came to be seen as the ontological basis of society. More precisely, we can say that the violence of the slave trade during the Amakiri era promoted an ontology of violence, and such an ontology shaped the social and political imagination of the city-state (or what became a nation).[19] We will take up this issue in chapter 3.

Third, chieftaincy was developed from the imaginative power of state. Kalabari was a narrative, a certain story, and chieftaincy was both a production and a reinforcement of that narrative about who Kalabari were. The chief as an individual lived in the imagination of the state, played roles in its imaginative projects, and was both an agent and effect of the state. To say all this is not to say that the state or chiefs were phantoms or unreal. It is to say that the Kalabari state and chiefs were a realization or an unfolding of an imaginative idea. The issue is not to choose between reality and fantasy. The contest is between two types of imagination: the Kalabari understanding of the political and that of people outside its culture. The state was an imaginative project. The chieftaincy was the drama of recruiting and retaining bodies to play certain roles in this imaginary, brought to its highest actualization. Bodies were harnessed to the imaginative ideas of the state by playing roles in it, were inscribed with the narrative of the state, and were places for the enactment of its imaginative powers. In chapter 4, we will return to the matter of chiefs and the subjection to freedom as the actualization of human potentialities.

The indigenous notion of political imagination that Amakiri and his chiefs handed over to subsequent generations has as its goal to open up possibilities so that life can be lived affirmatively, to thwart all that threatens life so that people can live a better life in the here and now. This kind of political imagination generated a form of politics that had three major qualities. First, it was about bringing something new into one's world: the exercise of freedom. Second, it was about equality. In the chiefs' sphere (*ala-siri*), as we shall see in chapter 4 ("Chiefs: Subject to Freedom"), hierarchical values were no longer allocated. Third, Kalabari politics aimed to achieve individuality (not individualism) or individual distinctiveness among people in the community. Robin Horton, the anthropologist who studied the Kalabari for about fifty years, compares their culture with that of the Tallensi of Ghana: "Kalabari society, whether in its village or in its city-state variant, encourages aggressive individualism [*sic*] and personal achievement. If the emphasis in Taleland is on 'fitting in,' in Kalabari it is on 'getting up.'"[20] In the traditional competitive Kalabari community, the most vexing problem caused by poverty and lack of achievement was not hunger (*buru-ba*) but social darkness (*toru-pakaa, toru-fa*). This whole idea of coming out of concealment and making an appearance is fundamental to the Kalabari understanding of existence—even in an ontological sense.[21]

These three features of politics we have identified not only are grounded in political imagination but supervene on a kind of political philosophy. The problem of political philosophy in Kalabari is the problem of creating and maintaining an embracing community (reciprocal relatedness). At the foundational level of every political philosophy (as part of the ethical system or theory of a society) is a conception of what a person is, a view of the person-in-the-world, and an account of how persons are related to one another. Therefore, any systematic philosophical investigation of a political philosophy must provide from the beginning a theory of personhood on which the philosophical system it is analyzing is based. Let me clarify this statement at two levels of deconstruction. Each level provides a set of reasons why any systematic investigation of a community's political philosophy must start from an analysis of personhood. This notion is so full of implications for interpreting and understanding any society and its ethics that it is pertinent to reflect on it as the unavoidable point of departure. First, all thinking about the person is ultimately philosophical and profoundly ethical. It seeks to fashion a way of regulating life and human interactions and to present a sociality of a particular type that will best control the inevitable clashes and conflicts among persons in a society. A theory of personhood seeks to gain or maintain a better form of interaction. It usually claims to be grounded on some conception of what is the good. Every theory of personhood is a form of political thinking as it is directed to some purpose as its good. The nature of personhood as a form of political thought cannot secure a strong foothold without specifying the nature of human beings it considers as normative. Paul Tillich rightly states, "The roots of political thought must be sought in human being itself. Without some notion of human nature, of its powers and tensions, one cannot make any statements about the foundations of political science and thought. Without a doctrine of human nature, there can be no theory of political tendencies that is more than a depiction of their external form."[22]

As soon as we engage in inquiring into the nature of persons for which a social system is about, we are confronted with three questions: Who is the ethics-creating person? How is ethics created? What is the result of the ethical system? The answer to these questions is the same in Kalabari. Person-in-community creates ethics. She creates her ethics through her quest to preserve and promote the community's well-being (preservation of life, human flourishing in the community). The virtuous citizen-in-community is the result of ethics. All these issues are usually fleshed out in the community's theory of personhood. Elsewhere I have amply discussed Kalabari theory of personhood, and I will not repeat it here.[23] I will limit myself to commenting about the life that is embodied in a person and how lifemaking deals with the "immanent and transcendent" dimensions of human life in Kalabari society. Kalabari hold that human life is always embodied in a person, but it is irreducible to the person. There is a free transcendence, enigma, otherness in life that is beyond its materialization, incarnation, givenness. Lifemaking as a pragmatic adventure attempts to give cultural forms to this imbrication of transcendence in immanence that is ever opening up to a future that is still to come. What kind of ethico-political task does the Kalabari form of lifemaking call its citizens to? To provide a response to this question is to offer Kalabari political philosophy. Its political philosophy is the possibilizing of human flourishing (*lolo-mie-pakaba*) as both refiguring lived experiences and prefiguring the coming of abundant life, the promise of a new beginning. *Lolomiepakama* calls every member of the community to the fullness of their humanity and full responsibility in the here and now.

Political philosophy is not crafted to produce a community that imitates or represents an ideality, a world of ideas, or transcendental signified. Political philosophy is about neither order nor the arrival of event (disorder) as an absolute surprise or rupture in the order of things. The Kalabari data enable us to reinterpret political philosophy as possibilizing community, as a reflection on the possibilizing power of the community that can transfigure the incapacity of members to new capacity.

Amakiri's Yam and Its Part

This possibilizing power of the community is one sense in which to interpret King Amakiri's famous philosophical pronouncement: *Ama bebe buru ngeribo buru pakiri* ("Only the community is tantamount to a whole yam, the individual is always but a part of it"). Where the individual member—always a finite fragment—reaches the ultimate limit of her effort, the *in-finite* power of the community possibilizes her effort and transfigures it into fullness. The community possibility (power) sub-intends, supersedes, and advances the fragmentary power (possibility) of the individual. The collective power (possibility) that supervenes is not a totality, not a total of all individual powers or possibilities.[24] The whole is traversed by the split between the part (fragment) and the whole. The individual's share embedded in the whole disturbs it from within. The fragment (a structural necessity within the whole) that is an obstacle to the whole claiming self-identity is at once the source of "whole's" wholeness (oneness). The fragment is only possible when faced with the whole, that is, where it is impossible for it to claim wholeness. The fragment is a whole that has to reckon with its brokenness as soon as it becomes a part. "The condition of possibility of [a fragment] is also and at the same time the condition of its impossibility."[25] This is the kernel of the political truth in Amakiri's statement. The possibility of a Kalabari person standing apart, cut adrift from the whole community, requires her to do the impossible of "disappearing" the whole to make the impossible possible. Yet the disappearance of the fragment "un-wholes" the whole. Fragment is not the mere contrary of whole but rather its promissory note. The part is neither whole nor not whole but a future *may-be*. The individual even in her drift-apartness is never part-of-no-part (more precisely, part-of-no-whole), but the whole-that-may-be. The fragment, separated from the whole, represents the openness of the whole toward incoming events.

Amakiri's point could also be comprehended in this sense: If there is no whole, then fragment has no meaning. Where the whole disappears, fragments cease to have meaning. Where all possibility of the whole is lost, fragment withdraws from our grasp. We cannot ascertain if it is a fragment or not. Or, in axiological terms, where there is no value of the whole, the value of the fragment also ceases to exist.[26] The fragment (the relative, the separated) resides in the whole (the absolute, the union).

Amakiri's thought here borders on the absolute and relative, wholeness and fragmentation. Community is absolute; the relative is the individual. Jean-Luc Nancy in *The Sense of the World* writes: "That which, for itself, depends on nothing is an *absolute*. That which nothing completes in itself is a *fragment*. Being or existence is an absolute fragment. To exist: the *happenstance* of an absolute fragment."[27] The existence of Kalabari—or the community Kalabari—is an *absolute fragment*.

There is more to Amakiri's thought. His words are in a sense geared toward counteracting the becoming-autonomous of the fragment. If the fragment (the individual) declares itself autonomous, then it voids or cancels the relativity that it is or it is to affirm in the whole and moves toward a wholeness, a completeness, an absoluteness. In this way the individual sets up him- or herself as an alternative absolute; the fraction is absolutizing itself, absolving itself from its relationships. The desire of the autonomous person (personhood) eventually reverses itself to become a desire for absolute meaning and value, to be whole, a deluded proposal for mythical fullness. Amakiri's *Ama bebe buru ngeribo buru pakiri* captures this tension between wholeness and fragmentation (absolute and relative). The whole yam and part yam are a synecdochic mirror image of each other. The desire for autonomy on the part of the fragment ends up being an absolute, not what the fragmentation intends. The whole is also absolutely relative to the part that is other than itself.

The loaded meaning of Amakiri's statement is therefore this: just as the fragment depends on the whole that is prior to it, the whole is constitutively dependent on its fragments (parts). It is wrong to interpret Amakiri as saying only that the fragment depends on the whole without acknowledging that the whole is also dependent on the fragments. Amakiri's statement dwells in the cognitive space between the absolutization of the relative (the part in total isolation to the whole or to anything outside itself) and absolute relativization (the whole depends on its fragments). In this in-between space, the split between the part and the whole is both internal and external to both of them. This is the ambiguous beauty of Amakiri's thought. At one level the split is external, the whole and its separated parts. At another, it is internal. The *pakiri*, the parts of the yam in their strewn fragmentation, constitute the whole yam. And the "fragment carries the promise that its fractal line will not disappear into a gathered whole, but, rather, will rediscover itself elsewhere, lip against lip of the other [part]."[28] The whole is the other of the fragment that gives rise to the fragment, or for which fragment gives rise to itself, in the spacing of the whole in itself, in succeeding itself as an infinite (good infinity) series of fragments. The whole is also a moving image of the fragments or a collection of fragments coordinated by the *nomos* and *ethos* that precede and succeed them.

The dialectic of part and whole, completion and incompletion, plays out in another sense. Amakiri made the famous statement in the context of discourse about the Good, the good of the whole community. A proper behavior or activity is that which manifests the idea of the good. In the light of the Good, we can imagine that a particular behavior or action has categoric worth as it plays and enjoys its role in the whole order. The Kalabari idea of the Good is expressed in existential condition as the well-being of the community, which is itself the community's paramount, supreme good (the *teleion agathon* in Aristotle's theory). The well-being of the community is the *whole* good life. It is a "complete good" in that the disparate goods of every individual, group, and institution within the community are coherently combined in their right proportions in it. An individual who has all the goods coherently together in proper proportions in his or her single life is called the "complete person" (*krakra-te-tombo*). The good Kalabari political actor who wants to initiate something new amid the continuity of the social processes must comprehend this whole and place his initiatives, his figuration of something new, in it even as he attempts to refigure the whole.

The dialectic between the whole and the part that I have laid out has informed the way I translate *pakiri* into English. I translate it as "part" and not "piece." Indeed, the *pakiri* is not a piece but a part.[29] The Kalabari citizen in the density of Amakiri's political philosophy is not a piece but always a part of an embracing and caring whole, the community that brings unity-in-difference into a perpetual play and also fosters ethical relationality without stifling the citizen's creativity and flourishing. What notion of citizenship, then, was operative in Kalabari community?

Kalabari Citizenship: Between Fragment and Whole

The Kalabari notion of citizenship is located between the whole and the fragment. The citizen is caught, inserted between these two antagonistic forces, and she constantly fights them. The "whole yam" presses her from behind, and the fragment blocks her from going forward or fully into the public square. Dwelling and dwelling well in this space of struggle between two antagonists is the virtue of agonistic communitarianism.[30] Thus interpreted, Kalabari citizens are not just borne along in the flux of traditions but insert themselves between the past and the future of community practices or tradition in order to initiate something new or establish the "who" of their persons (individual distinctiveness).

This insertion constitutes something like an *absolute fragment*—in Nancy's sense. The insertion itself (modality of citizenship) depends on nothing and on that which nothing completes in itself.[31] The insertion (which some may call subjective citizenship) is not dependent on a prior model of indigeneity, of a preexisting community of "blood and soil." The whole depends constitutively on the insertion. This insertion is not *given* once and for all so that after its taking-place the citizens can step out of the fight; rather, it is a constant *giving* and *giving out*, continuous creation. It involves neither a foundational point nor an end. It is a process where the beginning ceaselessly makes the end, and the end the beginning: each into (or by way of) the other, the beginning end, the end passing into the beginning, "turning endlessly back on itself without returning into itself."[32] In the traditional Kalabari community, people do not merely acquire citizenship; they *become citizenship* or the battlefield of citizenship. The "now" of citizenship, the interval between its past and future, the interstices between Amakiri's whole yam and partial yam, is not granted to observers but only persons who in themselves are the "now." Such men and women are the embodiment of the interstices. In a certain sense citizenship (or a dimension of citizenship) is not something that a person possesses, but it is what they become. Changing their historical circumstances is an integral part of *becoming* (exercising) citizenship, which is tied with their capacity for freedom, the capacity to initiate the new. This is what real politics is all about in the Kalabari community.

Citizenship as defined by residence and culture accents *sharing* as the philosophical foundation of the community. In this "sharing" citizens *ex-pose* themselves to one another and express their being. This ex-position needs the play of interdependence between whole and part, absolute and relative in the politics. There are two mutually supplementary models in the politics of citizenship in traditional Kalabari society: sharing and agonistic subjecthood. The latter is the praxis of calibrating and recalibrating the social bond between the individual and the group. This is the site of the tension of agonistic communitarianism.[33] This tension of being-in-relation is captured or expressed in the aphorism of Amakiri as it relates to the notion of citizenship. The aphorism traces out the praxis of the tension and the fragmented cosmetics (or essencelessness) of citizenship. Why praxis? Because the aphorism when properly interpreted is not about citizens engaging in activities that produce something, that is, in poiesis. Praxis is an activity that changes the agent that participates in it, he or she "produces" or "realizes" her- or himself. Essence-lessness? The Kalabari understanding of citizenship is not anchored to a (transhistorical, foundational) substance. It is focused on contingently articulated practices relating to the institutions of the community. It is a *sharing*.

Amakiri's political thought as expressed in the aphorism posits the citizen (the part of the community) not merely as the means to the community but also as the first need of the community's life. Let us recall what Amakiri said: "*Ama bebe buru ngeribo buru pakiri*," meaning that the community owns the whole yam and the individual only has a portion of it. Now take a moment to breathe, inhale and exhale. Listen intensely for Amakiri's voice as he utters these words. It invokes despair along with demand. It shouts its despair over the members turning away from the community (toward the nihilism of citizenship). It shouts out its demand for movement of the community toward the estranged. *Pakiri* (part) names precisely that which is subtracted from the whole, the "there is" of community. *Bebe* (whole) is the name of the demand for the trans- formation of the "there is," the whole into lifemaking, a work of life, or to preserve itself from coalescent disintegration. We need to quickly add that this "there is" is not a fixed substance but a process.

The notion of citizenship as based on residence, culture, and open borders—a rhizomatic network of social relations, practices, and pro- cesses—suggests that we turn to the processualist orientation of citizen- ship. Kalabari citizenship in the precolonial period was "as an ongoing *process*, one propelled by mechanisms and aimed at goals even if always incomplete."[34] This turn to process theory to define the body of Kalabari citizens should not be construed to mean that it is in perpetual flux, a boundless flux without self-identity at any time. There is always something recognizable about it. The body has an internal structure that coordinates the series of events that unfold in it.[35] On the one hand, the events are constituted and governed by practices of freedom, the actualization of potentiality. Freedom is a creative process in the sense that residents are constituted to become a body of people in its practices. (We will talk more about this freedom in chapter 4.) On the other hand, it is the nature of the lifemaking in the community that constitutes the larger context for the pursuit of actualization of human potentialities. And it is this larger context of what human beings can be, their being open to the *novum*, and their willingness to be carried to an unfolding order of communal relationships that coordinates the series of events that unfolds in the body of citizenry or the community.

I think that conceptualizing the Kalabari body of citizens as a process and not as a *thing*, which is completely determined, gives us a better phenomenal description of the body. This view of the body of citizens does not diminish the perspective of those who see it as a thing or substance, as it only requires us to accept that the body "presupposes processes and their constitutive events."[36] Adapting Paulina Espejo in her process theory of people in a nation, let me say: "Seeing the people as an unfolding series of events (a process) is compatible with seeing the people as a stable, identifiable thing. Yet when the people is conceived only as a thing (say, a definite collection of individuals), the conception is poorer and less descriptive. A series of events can include an aggregation of individuals . . . but it also incorporates the changes that occur among and within individuals when they do not aggregate."[37]

Indigenous Theory of Citizenship

Why did the Kalabari largely abandon indigeneity—blood, descent, and inborn rights—as the foundation of citizens? The easiest explanation is that, given the nature of the canoe house (*wari*) as a trading corporation, it dictated certain forms of membership in the community; that is to say, it relates to the way the houses enlarged their membership. Families or canoe houses predominately expanded by incorporating new servants (as adoptees) or absorbing or adopting outsiders. The community was crafted to absorb all newcomers and encouraged them to imbibe its corporate culture. There were three major characteristics of the trading Kalabari community that set it apart from most other traditional African societies.

First, the organizing principle of grouping members was based on the concept of the trading corporation, not on bloodlines and marriages. The boundaries of households were defined not by bloodlines but by firms' sizes. The household or the house was an aggregation of parents and their biological and adopted children, trading assistants, and employees. The household was established, sustained, and perpetuated by a trading corporation. Second, it was the trading corporation (the employer) that allocated land for settlement and provided training for the development of trading skills, mutual aid, and conviviality for the acquisition of the culture of the communities. The individual was therefore totally dependent on the corporation as his link to the society. Third, the trading corporation was the only basis for tracing descent and for enjoying political rights in society. One was not a member of the community if not a member of a canoe house. These three features of the trading community were to determine its definition of citizenship. The criteria for citizenship in Kalabari were the possession of the distinctive culture of the community and residence in it.[38]

In this context and its dynamics, citizenship took the form of a performance of "memory figure" (cultural memory and identity).[39] The borders between the homeland and outside were not drawn by the red bloodlines of descent or delineated geographically but rather by a cultural space and living in the home ground. The borders of the homeland were not conceived as boundaries of exclusion. The crucial element of citizenship that was to depart from indigeneity was prefigured at the origin of the nation by migrancy, itinerancy, and diaspora sentiments at its beginning. We have already noted in chapter 1 that Kalabari was not founded by one person but by different groups. Elem Kalabari as the founding site was not autochthonic. The initial set of inhabitants were constituted migrants and settlers from various Ijo groups—and a group is reputed to have come from a non-Ijo ethnicity. According to Adolphus G. Karibi-Whyte, a former judge of the Nigerian Supreme Court,

> Oral tradition has it that the nucleus of the present Kalabari consisted of seven independent wards. They had no common name. . . . It has been difficult and almost impossible to trace the origin of the six other wards who inhabited the island, but who even in their history had neither a common name, nor origin [apart from Endeme, one of the seven wards, which eventually gave the name of its founder, Prebo-kala-keibari, to the island and subsequent nation]. Each of the seven wards was identified most probably by the place from which they claim to have come, by their totem deities or by the names of the founders of the wards.[40]

It is clear that *Kalabariness* emerged as a form of cultural identity that was not exclusively tied to specific territory. This central image of cultural identity and citizenship was sealed even before they moved to their current places of settlements and thus became (almost) universally valid and extraterritorial no matter which new lands or territories they found themselves in as they moved from territory to territory until they got to where they are today.

The third reason they abandoned indigeneity has to do with their expansive "unwritten constitution." The political project of Kalabari was operated on the basis of unbounded terrain. The political system was decidedly open to expansion, inclusion of new territories. It was a network driven by boundless, inclusive architecture and poised on the pivot that linked the immanence of lifemaking to the idea of sovereignty. The logic of sovereignty or lifemaking is the idea of an expansive power in networks and productive synergies of people in networks constituted on the plane of immanence. Lifemaking and sovereignty stood in as relatives in reciprocal implication. This openness to expansive movements must be distinguished from an imperialist form of expansion; we must separate the expansionist tendency of the political philosophy of immanent lifemaking from the expansionism of imperialist, transcendent sovereignty. The Kalabari form of expansion was founded on the notion of network power and siblinghood (*tera se na amine abile*, three cities and their allied partners or relatives, or satellites). When Kalabari (precisely, Elem Kalabari) expands, its sovereignty (immanent lifemaking concept of sovereignty) "does not annex or destroy the other powers it faces but, on the contrary, opens itself to them, including them in the network. What opens is the basis of consensus, and thus, through the constitutive network of powers and counterpowers, the entire sovereign [community] is continually reformed."[41]

King Amakiri and his chiefs understood the materiality of the frontiers as integral to the open process of the nation in its collective self-making and recognized it as a basis that supported lifemaking and its notion of citizenship (mixed population). Lifemaking, open spaces, and mixed population stand in relationship of reciprocal and dynamic implications. I should add that this history or rendering of Kalabari sovereignty hides harsh subordination of marginal citizens and territories. Overall, was Kalabari imperial or imperialist? To respond to this pertinent question, it might be helpful for me to extend Michael Hardt and Antonio Negri's description of the United States Constitution to Kalabari insofar as it relates to the distinction between imperial and imperialist. "We should emphasize once again that this Constitution is imperial and not imperialist. It is imperial because (in contrast to imperialism's project always to spread its power linearly in closed spaces and invade, destroy, and subsume subject countries within its sovereignty) the U. S. constitutional project is constructed on the model of rearticulating an open space and reinventing incessantly diverse and singular relations in networks across unbounded terrain."[42]

Finally, to understand the Kalabari notion of citizenship that encourages mixed population, we have to interrogate what it regards as the ideal in its cultural system. The ideal type in Kalabari is often a composite of many types. From men to gods, from aesthetics to art, from textile design to ancestral screens, from the living to the dead, the Kalabari idea of perfection is the collage, the composite, the blend. In Kalabari culture, the provocative, the excitable, the lovable, the acceptable, or the ideal does not stand apart at the hilltop or dwell in the valley but adheres at the conjunction of the extremes. This concept of the ideal type principally derives from predilection to borrowing, transformation and reinterpretation of "foreign elements." Kalabari show a bias for the composite or prefer to create their identity by drawing elements from many sources. Elsewhere I have named this cultural preference for the composite (bricolage) as the "synthetic ideal."[43]

Kalabari show a remarkable preference for artifacts, concepts, or ideas that are of a composite nature. We find in various aspects of Kalabari culture that power, danger, excellence, or mediocrity is attributable to conjunctive elements, to an amalgam. Nigel Barley, a British anthropologist, aptly captured this penchant when he wrote, "The Kalabari have developed their own identity and determinedly created for themselves an ethnicity from elements drawn from many sources. Part of the genius of Kalabari culture consists of its ability to ingest and transform the alien by a process of reinterpretation."[44]

Why do the Kalabari show a bias for the composite or prefer to create their identity by drawing elements from many sources? Partly because of their trading contacts, Kalabari have for centuries used foreign artifacts as media to express their cultural beliefs and to reconstruct their identities in their creative adaptation to pressures they faced as a competitive, open, commercial society. In the precolonial period Kalabari had a long history of trading with both European and African societies. As a society that served as an intermediary between European and African cultures and absorbed an incredible number of foreigners into itself, it faced enormous pressure both on the boundaries and margin of its body politic and from within. Kalabari imposed order by continually modifying, enriching, and bringing into the core through a process of selection only those elements that promoted stability or harmony with its worldview.

Kalabari, threatened at its boundaries, pressed at every ingress and exit of the body politic, may well have responded by guarding itself against "pollution danger." After all, Bonny, another state in the Eastern Niger Delta, in a similar situation responded by "sealing" off exits and entrances into its body politic. Bonny, which was also a trading nation, felt similar pressures at the boundaries of its ethnicity and responded with a decree against foreigners speaking its (Ibani) language. In the eighteenth and nineteenth centuries, at the height of Bonny's participation in the transatlantic trade, there were a great number of Igbo who were in Bonny as traders, servants, or slaves in transition to the New World. Bonny felt threatened by the Igbo population and decreed that all foreigners should stop speaking Ibani and that the Igbo language should become commercial lingua franca in the community. The reasoning was that Bonny citizens could then use Ibani as a secret language to keep vital information away from foreigners (Igbo) and competing merchants. The result was that by the beginning of the twentieth century Bonny had virtually lost its native tongue.

Kalabari took a different route. Its leaders decreed that every person within its territory must speak Kalabari and forsake his or her language, and they took drastic measures to enforce this rule. A resident of any Kalabari town who could not speak the Kalabari tongue with the proper accent was made to "disappear" by *koroni-ogbo*, an agency charged with enforcing this rule. Kalabari was interested in absorbing all foreigners. Bonny tried to keep them out. We see in this comparative analysis of responses to moral panic how Kalabari deployed a method that strengthened its notion of citizenship that rejected indigeneity and accented cultural adaptation.

Today in Nigeria, "home" is defined as ancestral, and indigenous land is for only the natives. Citizenship is ultimately defined on the basis of indigeneity—whether or not a person can trace his or her ancestry to an indigenous abode. Citizenship is equated with ancestral home in the precolonial period. An Igbo man might be born in Yorubaland and live all his life there, speak only Yoruba, be married to a Yoruba woman, and pay taxes in Yorubaland, but he would not be considered an indigenous Yoruba man. When it comes time to authenticate his citizenship for the sake of getting benefits from the Nigerian state or occupying a major political office, he would be asked to go to his local government area where his parents or grandparents hailed from to get his "clearance papers." The man is always considered a non-indigene in Yorubaland. Of course, the same fate awaits a Yoruba man born and bred in Igboland, Hausa-land, or Ijo-land. Nigerians do not truly have Nigerian citizenship. What they have are rafts of indigenous citizenships floating together in a common political space. A person is a Nigerian only as an isolated traveler on any one of the rafts. Nigerian citizenship is based on indigeneity. Citizenship derives from an ancestral connection to a territory. National citizenship is mediated through ethnicity and not through the law and the state: indigeneity is the litmus for Nigerian citizenship. And Nigeria is not Nigeria as long as it is hamstrung by nativist definitions of national belonging.[45] The constitution of Nigeria, among others, states that Nigerian citizenship comes through belonging to a tribe (ethnic group) indigenous to

Nigeria through the individual parents or grandparents.[46] Residency is a qualification only for foreigners waiting to naturalize as Nigerian citizens.

The Amakiri Apparatus

We have come a long way from the beginning of the chapter where I introduced Amakiri and proceeded to deepen our knowledge of his political philosophy as it operates across and between various spheres of lifemaking. The discourse has portrayed his philosophy of governance, citizenship, nation-building, and lifemaking as an *apparatus*.[47] Giorgio Agamben defines apparatus as "anything that has in some way the capacity to capture, orient, determine, intercept, model, control, or secure the gestures, behaviors, opinions, or discourses of living beings."[48] In this sense, the Kalabari nation became a sort of apparatus for lifemaking in the hands of Amakiri and his chiefs. But let me quickly add that the nation as an apparatus does not have an independent existence apart from the social practices of Kalabari themselves trying to enact and sustain a high quality of human life; it is not a mega-entity, a transcendent substantial reality, aware of itself and controlling them as puppets.

What this means is that while the apparatus has the power to ground the social practices of Kalabari, it is a virtual/ideal entity (non-entity) that (can only) exists as the subjective "presupposition" of engaged or subjectivized Kalabari citizens. Borrowing from the words of Slavoj Žižek from a different context, let me end by stating that the nation (the city-state of Kalabari)

> exists only insofar as subjects act as if it exists. Its status is similar to that of an ideological cause like Communism or the Nation: it is the substance of the individuals who recognize themselves in it, the ground of their entire existence, the point of reference which provides the ultimate horizon of meaning to their lives, something for which these individuals are ready to give their lives, yet the only thing that really exists are these individuals and their activity, so this substance is actual only insofar as individuals believe in it and act accordingly.[49]

This substance in Kalabari political philosophy or worldview is known as *amatemeso*—at least this is how I intend to interpret it in this book for the limited purpose of our study of lifemaking. *Amatemeso* is a result of collective existence—the people becoming a product of themselves. *Amatemeso* is the people in the process of their own self-actualization.

Amatemeso is often interpreted as a transcendent (supernatural, transhistorical) being. But it could also mean an immanent being, a product of human interactions. I have made this statement for two reasons. First, the sacred, according to the Kalabari who can tell a god from which wood it was carved from, is neither some kind of a transcendental spirit who controls human history nor something that ossifies possibilities. It is none other than the human process of dealing with life's possibilities—reflexively shaping and reshaping potentialities in the midst of obstacles—through which the process of knowing *So* takes place and human consciousness of mega-Spirit thus arises. Out of the foaming ferment of human creativity in dealing with the entangled possibilities of coexistence, *So* arises fragrantly, as Hegel might be tempted to put it. (Let us not forget that the very emergence of the sacred is in itself mysterious or adds to the "sacredness" of social intercourse. An "objective order" emerges out of the interactions of individuals, and once it appears it cannot be reduced to interactions; it stands above or is viewed by them as a substantial agency that now determines, controls, or conditions their lives. This is what Slavoj Žižek calls "the ultimate mystery of the so-called human or social sciences."[50])

Second, history as a certain concrete ethical life that is open to the new is both conditioned and conditioning: an outgrowth of prior human activities that in turn condition future activities. This conditioning power of history may function in the manner of Hegel's "reflexive determination." This means a community treats history as a hyperobject ("reification") of its own, while it is only a collection of their activities, and effectively it is a hyperobject because they treat it as one. Let me unpack all this. History is the collection of human actions and activities, an embodiment of the substantial contents of human beings, a manifestation of their creativity, but in certain periods persons or citizens arise who embody in their particular selves the history of their people, or, more precisely, the "soul," the *disciplining power*, of the community's history. The person or citizens presuppose history, posit the substantial contents of past activities as their own presuppositions for their actions. In a sense, through them history as "substance" becomes a subject in the community.

I will explore this notion of *amatemeso* in more detail and how it is put to use in the lifemaking practices of Kalabari in the next chapter. But before we move to the next chapter, we need to interpret the connection between sovereignty and lifemaking. The discourse on King Amakiri and his chiefs in this chapter exploit the Kalabari data for the imbrication of sovereignty and lifemaking in the community's political philosophy.

Concluding Remarks: Sovereignty and Lifemaking

In Kalabari sovereignty is the power to make *excellent self*, the fundamental power to create the society in which human life can flourish and become excellent self (a notion we will treat in chapter 6). It is not the power to make live and let die. Sovereignty is not conceived as the barest or easiest level of power to kill or to let live, which is what even any head of an animal pack can do. It is not about the power to decide on living and nonliving or recognizing who exists, lives, or does not live because the Kalabari see life as a continuum from the living to the dead, to the living-dead, and to spirits and gods. Kalabari, therefore, do not maintain that any human power or institution can arbitrarily decide ontologically or politically the existence of another being or decide if a being (person) has never lived or died. A sovereign cannot grant life, which exceeds and precedes him, to another person. He can inflict death—take life and not give life.

Sovereignty for the Kalabari is about making whole, doing better, and creating beautiful life within life. Sovereignty is the power to create a state of well-being that is outside the biothanatopolitical capture—life that is life—that exceeds the power to kill or nullify life in advance and exults the power to make live with the construction of flourishingly humanized people.

The capacity to create and sustain flourishing human life, excellent self—lifemaking—is what sovereignty is about. Sovereignty is not so much about the power over life and death (Michel Foucault), the capacity to nullify life in advance (Roberto Esposito), the power to produce "bare life" (Giorgio Agamben), the capacity to mark some lives as grievable or not (Judith Butler), or unbearable, neutrally suspended between life and death (Arthur Bradley) as it is to make and sustain excellent self. Sovereignty in the Kalabari context cannot be understood as a biological process (whether "make die and let live" or "make live and let die"). There is a striving toward a particular order of meaning and purpose. What I am calling "sovereignty" is a power of creativity (*ktizo*, Greek for creativity). It is a *ktizonomic* power, a directedness and attraction of human cultural life toward relentless self-actualization, the excellent self. Sovereignty as revealed (implied) in this chapter is about how the creative cultural-moral functions of human life are oriented toward the mass flourishing of citizens, which is at least as important as the biological grounding. The *amayanabo* is no pure transcendental figure "outside" of lifemaking but an immanent effect of lifemaking itself. He is produced and maintained by the cybernetic feedback loop of lifemaking, the creative cultural-moral functions of the community.

This book traces the category of *ktizonomic* power and how it is conjugated in and interlocked at different dimensions or spheres of existence (individual, community, subjectivity, collective belonging, ethical, ontological, political, or conceptual). In all cases, we see sovereignty—though through a glass, dimly—as rendering all human life flourishable.

Chapter 3

Amatemeso, Otherness, and Violence

Introduction

In the previous chapter we discussed the Kalabari notion of citizenship and proceeded to examine how the interactions of the citizens creates a supra body over them. We call that supra entity *amatemeso*. *Amatemeso* is self-unfolding, not an absolute entity external to subjectivity (spirituality) of the citizen-believers. What displays, manifests, expresses *amatemeso* is nothing other than the citizens' collective self-consciousness. For instance, when Elem Kalabari split into three towns (Bakana, Abonnema, Buguma) in the third quarter of the nineteenth century and moved into different locations (*ama*), each town "created" or instantiated a different *amatemeso* (the spirit, god, or destiny of *ama*, land). Each of the three *amatemeso* came to signify the totality of each town's creative interpretation of itself or its moral life. Put another way, it refers to the principle of its self-consciousness or subjectivity. The political ethics of each of these towns came to involve an awareness of the *amatemeso*, that is to say, a knowing of the moral self-interpretation of a historical community of persons who are (or think they are) the bearers of the principle (*amatemeso*). The group of Kalabari that founded Abonnema (a British colonialism's imposed name) gave themselves the name "Nyemoni" (meaning covet what is yours), and their *amatemeso* became *Nyemoni-na amatemeso*. Their political ethics and engagements with other communities must be appropriately grounded in the specificity (*nyemoni*) of their collective spirit, "which acts as the normative sieve that strains, sifts, and negotiates [their] orientation to the future."[1]

The split and the multiplication of the spirit/god of Elem Kalabari into three (in Buguma, Abonnema, and Bakana) suggests that an *amatemeso* is not set apart from its community's practices. It is a different story whether or not members of each community recognize their participation in creating the aura, the transcendental matrix, the representational entity they have come to call *amatemeso*. It is also a different matter if members largely do not reflectively grasp the fact that it is their beliefs, norms, practices, and institutions that also generate and sustain the "shape" of the spirit or the community of self-conscious believers. Their failure to immediately recognize the fact that *amatemeso* is nothing without their collective identity does not mean it could not be used to create or sustain a standard of governance and ground the normative authority of political leadership. At minimum, *amatemeso* constitutes one of the two important features about the citizens that traverse the functioning of the Kalabari polity or the political: the people as *demos* as well as *spirit* that is a disruptive, interruptive power. (The community of organized citizen-believers as divine, sacred energy is what the spirit is, and it is that feature that I have named as *amatemeso*.) As I have already argued in this book, *demos* and the spirit are themselves each marked by (a) *the capacity to begin*, to initiate something new amid ongoing social processes,[2] and (b) *natality* as a political notion that haunts all claims of exception and givenness.[3] These two features are keyed to the Kalabari notion of the sacred. The sacred is the constellation of possibilities and impossibilities in any given community—it is centered on the experiences of subjects in the community. The sacred is the universe of possibilities available to a community.

Notion of the Sacred and *Amatemeso*

In Kalabari worldview and philosophy, the notion of the sacred as a set of possibilities is encapsulated in one of the words for God, that is, *So*. The word *So* refers to both destiny or directing-destiny and the sum of possibilities available to the people. In a sense, the two meanings of the word are not different. Destiny in Kalabari understanding refers to the set of life possibilities allotted to a person before his or her own birth. *So* in the sense of destiny refers to the dialectical outworking of the *telos* of individuals, communities, and the world. It is an unfolding world process that is not confined to follow a fixed groove. The shaping of destiny is done by or, rather, understood via the possibilities that *So* makes available to each person, group, or institution. (*So* when applied to individuals is called *so*, to households is *wariteme-so*, and to communities is *amateme-so*. We will refer to this application of the notion to particulars—the matter of destiny—as lowercase *so*.) The directing concept of *So* is not just about working out a preassigned *telos*. The concept of *So* directs the people to note their limitations, the set of possibilities opened to them or excluded from them, liberatory potentials for the transformation of selves and structures of society, and the sum total of possibilities conceivable given their level of social, technological, and economic development.

Let us call *So* as applied to the sum of possibilities as uppercase *So*. The uppercase *So* is the set of possibilities excluded to individuals, cultural institutions, and social structures. More precisely, it is the universe of possibilities from which some are defined as available to persons and institutions and others remain either unfulfilled or simply the set of possibilities excluded to them at any given time.[4] When lowercase *so* and uppercase *So* are taken together, we get the sense that *So* is the ultimate source of possibilities and the principle of limitation or selection. This combination of infinity and limit defines the structure of the sacred as lived experience in Kalabari worldview, shedding important light on our idea of the three sets of possibilities that mark the sacred.[5]

I would like to note that the uppercase *So* and lowercase *so* are not opposites in Kalabari. Thus, what is not part of uppercase *So* is not confined to extinction. The uppercase *So* is the ground of lowercase *so*. The lowercase *so* is only a set of appropriated or available possibilities at any given time. For instance, a person may have the *so* to be a good dancer from all the possibilities that are available to members of the community and even beyond. If the person dislikes being an artist, he or she can go to a diviner and ask for it to be changed (in a process called *bibibari*, recanting the spoken word, the allotted possibilities before birth) and thus draw another career from that unlimited urn of possibilities that the uppercase *So* can give, and it is a pool that can never be completely realized. A person can literally ask for any set of possibilities, but *So* has the right to defer or "project into the future whatever may be too much for any community or society [or the individual] fully to experience or acknowledge in the present."[6] Because an individual can be given or allotted only a part of the set of all possibilities available to the community at any given historical moment, what he or she has "always points beyond itself to the full range of possibilities for either salvation or destruction."[7] As Richard Fenn puts it: "At some level, societies know that they are based on the foreclosure and postponed fulfillment of possibilities for both life and death. Every social system . . . creates an index or prohibited satisfactions. . . . The sacred always offers only a very limited embodiment of unfulfilled possibility."[8] The individual may encode within her the possibilities allotted to her by the social system (or the gods), but she always stands to look upon the uppercase *So* as the embodiment of unfulfilled possibilities. Humans can imagine alternatives not currently available to them and can take steps to attain what is denied to them. In fact, this is the whole impetus and impulse behind *bibibari*, recanting of destiny.[9]

In the Kalabari-Ijo world, a community never appears without its *amatemeso*—the soul of the community.[10] The living community is its embodiment. A body, communal or individual, does not appear without its soul. The characteristic gesture, the principle of recognizability of the *amatemeso*, is indissoluble from what constitutes its body—and vice versa. Although the *amatemeso* cannot be said to exist apart from the people (its flesh), it nevertheless cannot be reduced to the group, the embodiment. The collective is not only the actuality of the *amatemeso*; the *amatemeso* is also the historically specific regulatory ideal under which the society is materialized. The *amatemeso* is "the normative and normalizing ideal according to which the [communal] body is trained, shaped, cultivated, and invested."[11]

The communal body is also trained to maintain and secure its sovereignty and somewhat separate identity, from the inauguration of nomos as in the old sense of sharing, mutual sharing and apportioning of land.[12] The instantiation or enactment of *amatemeso* by each of the Kalabari towns upon their departure from Elem Kalabari was also an invocation of their sovereignty or autonomy as individual bodies of people. The Kalabari notion of *so* always involves a recognition of an autonomy of body and spirit of a person or group. Hence, every person has their own *so*, groups have their own *waritemeso*, towns have *amatemeso*, and nations have *se-temeso*. Persons and groups may come together to form a collectivity with its *so*, but it does not involve the total surrender of each person's or group's sovereignty. This is in line with the fundamental politics or virtues of democratic republicanism that traverse politics in Ijo communities (in the sense that political power belongs to no one person).[13]

Amatemeso is the source of normative power that derives from the delimiting appropriation and possession of territory or land (*nomos*-ordering). This presupposes that there existed a sovereignty (popular or otherwise) that protected property. Indeed, Thomas Hobbes argued that in the state of nature there was no partition and distribution of lands because there was sovereignty. Does this mean sovereignty, governance structure, or collective belonging preceded *amatemeso*? Or does *amatemeso* go beyond land, the physical territory, and is it what first defines a land as owned collectively by a people before it has to ordered and shared?

Amatemeso is not only connected to the land but also to natality. One is intimately connected to the land because one has a descent that is tied to specific territory, is born into a specific territory (land), or resides in a specific territory. Natality subsumes the fixity of the territory through the burial of the umbilical cord of the newborn. It is the tradition in Kalabari to bury the leftover umbilical cord of every child, the sign and miracle of new beginning into the land. This not only affirms the child's tie and commitment to the good and protection of the land but also indicates the seeding of the territory with the capacity to begin. The land, the territory, the *amatemeso* constitutes (reconstitutes) itself anytime a child is born into it, when hospitality is extended to it, toward it as the "perfect stranger," the "miracle." The placenta is also buried after the birth of the child. The "land" would not be such if it does not "accept 'whoever' and 'whatever' comes out of the womb and onto the face of the earth."[14] In a particular sense, natality gives space to action—a site to initiate something new amid ongoing (inherited) social processes—within the land. It gives space to where the individual, her well-being and opinion, matter to others. Natality gives space to a common political space within the territory where the biological life (*zoe*) of the individual has an innate right to have rights and to actualize one's potentiality. In this synthesis of territory (land) and natality, we see the juris-generative properties of *amatemeso*. Natality opens up the *nomos* based on division and sharing of land into a space citizens can exchange actualizations of potentiality, and from this exchange of actualizations they can generate different creativities for development (*ama-ibi*) of the town (nation).

Amatemeso is also the collective capability of the members of a given community to transform their being-with into a specifically human mode of existence. It refers to their power of sharing, sharing the exposition of one another. As Jean-Luc Nancy argues in his *Inoperative Community*, a community entails the exposition, the presence, of each self to all. The presence of self to self precludes thinking of the community as an essence or effecting its own essence as something beyond the exposition of self to self. A community is this exposition: the co-appearing of finite selves, ensembles of selves, and each self is exposed to an outside. This outside is only an outside of another ensemble of selves. The "being" of community is the exposure, exposition of selves, which "are themselves constituted by sharing, they are distributed and placed, or rather *spaced*, by the sharing that makes them *others*: other for one another," and "whose relationship—the sharing itself—is not a communion."[15] Thus without this exposure and sharing the community would not exist.

The argument here pivots on Nancy's notion of "sharing" (*partage*) in communities under conditions of finitude.[16] He argues that there is no common substance that characterizes a community. Members of community only share of themselves, share in their exposure to each other. Each member is an other to others because of the sharing; each singular being shares in the sharing of others. It is this sharing that constitutes the community and the members as singularities and resists their fusion into one subject or communion. "Community is the community of *others*, which does not mean that several individuals possess some common nature in spite of their difference, but rather that they partake only in their otherness. . . . They are together, but togetherness is otherness."[17]

Community as a community of others speaks to the notion of pluralism that underlines the Kalabari view of citizenship, mixed population, and open borders that we have discussed in the previous chapter. Pluralism (or the human condition of plurality) is a way of sharing of Being, the being that is at stake in how our lives hang together, the being of our existence that is always a coexistence. Pluralism is a way of sharing our being-with, our coexistence in a common polity, our living together in political space. It is about working out the good and fitting *nomos* to share a polity's abundant being-with and scarce goods in ways that (can) promote human flourishing for all. Pluralism in this fostered a sense of collective belonging in the precolonial Kalabari community.

Amatemeso as Collective Belonging

Amatemeso is the sense of collective belonging in its imbrication with the *nomos* of the community. *Nomos* is the historicized and contextualized situatedness and the limit of a particular social existence in time. It is the nexus of relations, laws, habits, and apportioning of property and responsibilities that makes a common world possible.[18] The moral institutions of the community work to translate the domain of moral values into the bonds of the community, co-belonging. These institutions transform the law (norms, *nomos*) into the community's spirit, that is, the individual internalization of the expectations and requirements of the law. In this manner, *amatemeso* sustains the congealed and fluid loyalties and affections of the community members in in the name of an *X* (i.e., justice, freedom, friendship, human flourishing, belonging, abundance, fantasy, etc.).

Whatever that *X* is, it is always in play with a conception of *amatemeso* (*ama-teme-so*). To decode this properly we need to understand the Kalabari theory of the sacred. As already noted, the uppercase *So* is the set of possibilities excluded to individuals, cultural institutions, and social structures. More precisely, it is the universe of possibilities from which some are defined as available to persons and institutions and others remain either unfulfilled or simply the set of possibilities excluded to them at any given time. A community realizes its *amatemeso* by not only realizing the possibilities believed to be allotted to individuals within it and to itself as a group but also straining toward realizing possibilities currently excluded to it.

As per the foregoing, we can define *amatemeso* as a movement toward openness to future possibilities, dislocating human lives and situations toward their future forms, nudging them toward full actualization of their potentials. In its dislocating movement, it has a *novum* character, signaling it as a response to the current order of things whose potentialities exceed the current structuring of individual and social existence. *Amatemeso* expresses as well as transcends the hidden potentials of a situation, existence, or life-in-the-community.

Amatemeso also implies a consideration of the nation as a common instrument, a shared political roof for individuals and groups who own (claim) it to pursue human flourishing, abundant life, collective belonging. Collective belonging is an inclusive table of sharing, the sharing of mutual energies that community members cogenerate and give to themselves in focused interaction and intersubjectivity.

Indeed, *amatemeso*—collective belonging—is sharing. It is the ecstasy of sharing, the *jouissance*, enjoyment of sharing. This is the form of sharing a community's extant set of endowments that continuously replenish its social fabric. It is a sharing that *radically* opens new spaces for sharing friendships, justice, and natality. It symbolizes the dynamic of coexistence that disrupts institutions to open new avenues for real, substantial life, opening them up to play as an endless power to begin. How did traditional Kalabari people allow this power to actualize itself in them and through the common institutions of their communities? Pluralism is the sharing demanded or necessary for lifemaking in a community without a common being or essence. Rituals of politics are also deployed to make provision for the future of this sharing and, indeed, the *amatemeso*.

Amatemeso and Ritual of Politics

Elsewhere, I have argued that the economy makes provisions for the future by securing material needs of a group of people.[19] The political system makes provisions for the future by orchestrating the collective unity and survival of the group, the union of power and meaning of a people. If we name this union the *soul of the community*, then politics constructs and sustains it for the flourishing of people and conserves it as a provision for the future of the group. Ritual for inaugurating the *amatemeso* is part of the political process of making provisions, spiritual provisions, for sustenance of the Kalabari people, especially the young ones. The African scholar Malidoma Patrice Somé captured the provision-making aspect of rituals when he wrote: "The abandonment of ritual can be devastating. From the spiritual viewpoint, ritual is inevitable and necessary if one is to live. . . . The young ones are the future of the old ones. To allow the future to happen, the old ones must work with the Other world. When an elder fails to perform his work with respect to the spiritual, the future of the elder is threatened, not the present. Where the ritual is absent . . . the future is dim."[20]

The *amatemeso* arises out of the collectivity (communion) that is created, invoked, or renewed by such rituals. *Amatemeso* is the split within the "communion" of the people, within the ethical substance that animates and binds the community. It cleaves it into substance and spirit, opening a critical passage from ethical substance to ethical subjectivity. Rituals of politics or enactment of collective belonging raises, even if momentarily, the collective consciousness that seems to come from beyond history—transformation of substance into subject, so to speak. During rituals when the "spirit" grasps a person, the person not only locates herself in (or identifies herself with) the thick unity of her community's ethical substance but also grasps herself as subject. The spirit (*amatemeso*) is the foaming mass of a ritual. It is the ritual of inaugurating the *amatemeso* that produces the *amatemeso*. It liberates the spirit from its immersion in the communion of the people or in the natural land. Ritual forms the people into a group, and it is this subjectivation—the fidelity to the future survival of the group—that liberates the spirit from the land.

Before the ritual the land is an undifferentiated unity of nature and spirit. The ritual that formally inaugurates the communal consciousness transcends the here and now and projects the community and its flourishing into the future. The ritual makes the distinction between the individual and the community and the distinction between every person and their essential universality. Through the ritual, the *amatemeso* emerges as an other higher being than the community's being or the individual selves. The power or communal spirit, *amatemeso* as a higher being, can thus restrain arbitrary wills, reconciling the desire for self-creation (self-re-alization) and autonomy and desire for community (human solidarity).

Through the ritual process the spirit that is "implicit" spirit becomes manifest; the community comes to its own self-knowledge. The self-conscious communion emerges from the unity of the people (nature) and spirit. The ritual is the fulcrum that uplifts the people out of their immersion in the unity (land) and spirit and reconciles them into a higher form of unity of nature (people) and spirit to embrace self-conscious communion. The *amatemeso* that thus emerges is part of something essentially universal, the *So*, the universe of possibilities. The ritual establishes a political space governed by possibilities, actualizations of potentialities. *Amatemeso*, the sovereign power over and above the people, undergirds politics based on the consciousness of ritual, which is a law of possibility. Kalabari stage and restage the distribution and redistribution of possibilities for human flourishing via rituals.

The multitude of arguments in the fabric of *amatemeso*–human relationality as presented so far in this chapter, and when considered as a synecdoche, represents the substantial involvement of *amatemeso's* lifemaking of the Kalabari people. Here, "lifemaking" is deployed in the double sense of *bio* and *zoe* as the *amatemeso* is the ground, ideal, and destiny of the Kalabari community's ontological and ontic life.[21] Simply, the *amatemeso's* lifemaking (life-*poiesis*) is both *biopoetics* and *zoepoetics* as the *amatemeso* unites power and meaning in every concrete life. The Kalabari notion of nationhood (collective belonging, agonistic communi-tarianism) speaks to this double function, the double helix.

Our discussion of *amatemeso* so far might have given the impression that *amatemeso* as relatedness might suffocate otherness (*kiri*). But it should be noted that the relatedness is not necessarily heteronomous or an offense to independence and freedom. I need to discuss the Kala-bari understanding of the law of being to make this point clearer. The substratum that animates all life has movement and plurality at its core, such that it does not remain the same in all manifestations and modifications. The conception of persons-in-relation who maintain their connectedness together as constituting one community also establishes the distinctiveness (otherness) of the persons. *Amatemeso* itself is rooted in the difference and otherness. The *Temeso* (God) part of the name (*ama + temeso*) speaks to a composite force, unity-in-difference. This god is conceived as a composite force, a combination of creative-destructive force and destiny, a combination of person and directing concept. It is both *Teme-órú* and *So*.[22] *Teme-órú* (this word metamorphosed into *Tamuno*, and the new word is now exclusively used for the Christian supreme God in post-missionary Kalabari) is regarded as the female creative modality. *So* is the directive modality, the aspect of divinity that orders the created outcome, the neuter or male counterpart. *So* is concerned with destiny and behavior of people, groups, animals, and institutions.

The distinction between *Teme-órú* and *So* is not a speculative one. The distinction is based on an acknowledgment of freedom of divine decisions as well as that of human beings in dealing with such (divine) decisions. It correlates with the religious anthropology of the people. *So* represents the fixed point (or rather the variable constant) in human dealings with the divine, and *Teme-órú* is the fluid point. The individual is believed to have a two-part personality. The component parts of this personality act as separate "persons." One is conscious; the other unconscious. The unconscious part (the soul) before birth of the person decides the destiny (*so*[23] or *fiyeteboye*), the life course, of the whole person on earth. Before a person is born, the would-be soul of the person goes before *Teme-órú* and speaks the entire course of the life of the individual it is going to inhabit. The other (the conscious, the physical being) only works out its fortunes on earth. The conscious part is generally believed to be aggressive and competitive and desires to excel. The unconscious, depending on what was spoken before *Teme-órú*, may be amiable, noncompetitive, and disposed to failure or, alternatively, cantankerous, competitive, and disposed to success. If a person does not like the course of her life on earth, she goes to a diviner to change her *so* or *fiyeteboye*. The process of changing destiny is called *bibibari* (altering or nullifying the spoken word, recanting). The person visits a diviner to let *Teme-órú* (the fluid concept, the part capable of effecting change) know that the person would like to change how she wants to live her life course on earth. Once the change of destiny is made, the new *so* (which becomes a new point of fixity) determines the whole course of the person. This process of reconstructing *so* also applies to the *wari* (*waritemeso*) and to the town (*amatemeso*). *Amatemeso* carries the tension of the composite force of *Teme-órú* and *So* and of a social construct and divine creativity. It is a conglomerate and admixture of parts.

We learned in chapter 2 that the synthetic ideal of inclusiveness and making room for others is at the core of Kalabari identity. The narrative of Kalabari identity formation not only fosters the affirmation of others but also intensifies the experience of embrace. They are constantly remaking, remixing, and remeasuring the matrix of their culture with materials from within and without. Borrowing insights from Mark Taylor, I would say that "at the heart of [Kalabari community] formation, there is both an affirmation of the other . . . and a de-centering, co-intending of strangers that takes [them] into spaces with unformulatable boundaries."[24]

Otherness and Ascent of Love: From Mother's Mortar to Father's Name

In a certain limited sense, Kalabari politics is about the exploration of possibilities of the human fundamental experience of estrangement, responding to the problems of strangers in their midst, how to understand and accommodate the alterity, experiences of strangeness that refuse or unsettle harmony. Kalabari have used various means to understand or respond to the problem of strangers, otherness. They have used religion to comprehend the gods and spirits, which easily exceed their everyday grasp because of their numinous power and mystery. They have used economics to handle the strangeness of the future by making provision for it.[25] Arts in form of images, sculptures, and dances offer therapy and relief and a hermeneutic model to cope with strangeness.[26] They have used "talking-cure" and attentive listening to manage some of the excesses of the existential situation. Their worldview and philosophy also offer ways of responding to the experience of fundamental estrangement. Politics is another tool, technique, or orientation to exploring or getting a handle on the possibilities of responding to fundamental estrangement. Politics or political institutions are the codes, coding, and decoding of a society's hermeneutics, ways of being, or practices of building and sustaining bridges between the self and others, us and others, for the purpose of human flourishing.[27]

The other in Kalabari is always the relative other (other-than-me), not absolute other. Motherhood is a horizon of fatherhood and vice versa. Otherness is also part of siblinghood. This is captured by the saying "Damina ikiyamina," meaning the siblinghood based on sharing the same father is equivalent to having siblinghood by friendship (or a friend who sticks to one as a sibling). Even God is not an absolute other. God in traditional Kalabari community was not equivalent to self-identity and sameness but the interplay of exteriority and identity, alterity and familiarity. For instance, the all-pervading force of existence, *teme*, spiritness, is shared by God, the spirits, and human beings alike. The characteristic *force* that determines godness, the divine nature of gods, belongs not to the community of gods alone but also to human beings, indeed, to all modes of being. *Tamuno* has a higher degree and intensity of the spiritual power (*teme*) than any mode of existence.[28]

Since the foundational power is counted as part of any being or god, the community of gods does not have any ontological priority in its possession of the spiritual stuff.[29] "This power of being is the *prius* of everything that has being. It precedes all special contents logically and ontologically. It precedes every separation and makes every interaction possible, because it is the point of identity without which neither separation nor interaction can be thought."[30] This common stuff makes humans identical with the gods, "from which they can never be separated completely." In the depths of both humans and gods there is a point of coincidence. The spiritual stuff is continuous, and there is a quality that differentiates stuff as imbued in any particular being; the quality sets off where one being ends and another begins. There are three categories of the spiritual stuff. There is the *primary*, fundamental stuff (spirit, *teme*); then there is *secondary* stuff (kinds of the spiritual stuff: gods, humans, animal, trees, etc., which reflect intensity and degree of the stuff); and finally, *relation* (qualities or properties that a being possesses in relation to another at the same level of degree and intensity of the spiritual stuff) to another being at a different level of intensity and degree of spiritual stuff.

The "subordination" of humans to the community of gods in worship does not imply an ontological subordination in which humans would be seen as of a different substance from gods. The categories of divinities and humans do not apply to their substance but to their relations to each other. Whatever differences exist between them (between gods and humans and between the gods themselves) are only punctual differences; differences are local. This is not to dismiss any suggestion that there may be differences in intensity and degree of the spiritual stuff in a being or that it may "grow" in a person. Older persons, as they age, are said to grow in intensity and degree of the stuff in them. Hence, Kalabari say that as one ages one comes closer to the gods who are believed to have a higher "quantity" of the spiritual force.

This particular Kalabari relation to otherness (the relative other, other-than-me, not absolute other) provokes a summons to relentless lifemaking, *auteuring* life. People not only create their collective life but are also the sustainers of their coexistence. In filmmaking there is a view that considers the director as the primary creative force. This is the auteur theory. In lifemaking, the community plays such a defining role. We would get a deeper sense of the auteuring life, communal creativity, the actualization of their potentiality ("essence") under the conditions of existence. We will do this through the lens of love. Kalabari have five notions (features) of love, which progress from one level to the other and represent a movement to overcome estrangement, emotions contributing positively to the sustenance of the community or the strengthening of the *amatemeso* as the creative self-interpretation of the community. We will now probe the particular shape in which this spirit manifests, displays itself, or auteurs life by interpreting the modes of love inherent in its political philosophy. The Kalabari word for love is *belema*, meaning sweetness, extreme happiness, the "inside is sweet for the other." Love here is not about sentimentality but about the fulfillment of the desire for flourishing of the other that results in vital self-fulfillment, and it is conjoined with power and justice. Love is the apprehension of the other as actualization of a different potentiality.[31] Power is love implementing the demands of the actualization of potentiality. Justice is power correcting obstacles against the actualization of human potentialities for every member of the community. The justice of love in removing the obstacles operates to unite the individual to the community (social body) in ways that promote the flourishing of the individual and the social body.

FORMS OF LOVE

There are five qualities or structural elements of love (*belema* in Kalabari). These qualities are presupposed in every love encounter. They are as follows:

1. *Gboloma* (*eros*, fellowship, solidarity) is what holds a community together. The word *gboloma* is used to refer to mixing, interpenetration, and communion. The word is also used to refer to sexual union between a man and woman,

the *eros* toward another, the ecstatic movement toward the other. *Gboloma* ultimately does not just refer to the glue that holds the group together but also the community itself and the capacity for relationship, ectasis, and inclusiveness. It is the unity that is the community in its fullest sense.

2. *Teme-belema* means love that flows from the heart, the soul of the person. This is love that affirms the other unconditionally, irrespective of status, equality, birth, or special relationship.

3. *Ikiya-belema* (friendship, friendship network) is the love of friends. Excellent friendship is the type of partnership and fellowship in which each person aspires to bring to realization the latent potentialities of the other.

4. *Opoli-belema* means desire, drive toward self-fulfillment for food, sex, pleasure. The focus here is on that which fulfills one's desire.

5. *Gborufuro-belema* is love based on familial connections, between those who emanated from the same womb or the same "mouth of the penis" (*tongo-bibi*). The mother's love (considered the purest form of love) for her children falls in this category. In terms of the ascent of love, it appears one moved from the *gborufuro-belema* to *gboloma*, the love for the community. But each level or, more precisely, form of love is imbricated in the other forms. Love is a weaving together of these five distinguishable but inseparable parts, and each part drives beyond itself in which it finds itself. Love is incomplete without the parts appropriately unified. Love and life are an integral component of lifemaking, of the good life.

Some scholars may argue that the five qualities are partial (and do not ever come together), relative definitions of love, and none of them is capable of grasping love, *belema*. If this argument is accepted, then the interlocutors can proceed to maintain that we cannot have knowledge of love in Kalabari "in itself." If they deny knowledge of love "in itself," we can equally posit in a Hegelian fashion that the relative definitions of love do not block our knowledge of love "in itself" and that the different conceptions or definitions of love are inherent to love itself. Love is split from within. The contradictions between these conceptions constitute the very love that Kalabari want to grasp and comprehend. "Here is the fundamental wager of the Hegelian strategy: 'inappropriateness as such' (in our case, that of opposing definitions) 'gives away the secret' . . . whatever presents itself initially as an obstacle becomes, in the dialectical turn, the very proof that we have made contact with the truth."[32]

The truth of love is not given out there. As our knowledge of the relative conceptions changes or adjusts, the truth itself is transformed. The movements of the partial definitions toward the truth of love change not only them but also the truth of love itself. The relative definitions are our partial contacts with the truth, and as our knowledge changes the truth of love itself must change. These partial definitions are not mere asymptotes, progressive approximations of the truth of love itself. Their movements constitute the truth.[33]

Every quality of love encompasses itself and the other four qualities; that is to say, it sheds light on and informs all other qualities. Every one quality is, in a way, the whole of love. It is actually not a partial quality of the whole of love but love itself apprehended in a specific modal quality.

Behind the multitude of partial loves, the infinitely more embracing and enduring love passion of the mother's love must show through so that all other forms of love take up new dimension and become windows into maternal love. All forms of love become manifestations of mother's love. The "miracle" of mother's love retroactively changes the character of all forms of loves. Thus, mother's love is present in all other loves and opens up a split that can never be filled up. They are always truncated, marked, and disturbed by mother's love. The communal love (collective belonging), the *gboloma* of the polity, is always threatened or haunted by the possibility of "to your tents, oh Kalabari" (*oru wariwari-ye gbokigbo*), by the potential of its constitutive parts returning to where they sallied forth into the common, to return to the originary site of pure (mother's) acceptance.

Mother's love relates to the communal love, the love of country (polity), in four ways. These relationships are at the root of the disturbance or the haunting. First, communal love could be seen as a mother's love writ large. Second, the relation between mother's love and the communal love could be compared to profit and lack of it, akin to + and 0. Communal love works to remove mother's love as an intermediate sphere or power between it and the citizens. The state aspires to directly bind citizens to it, forsaking any attachment to their particular hearths. Third, the relation between mother's love and communal love could take the form of + and – (plus and minus). Both exist but are in opposition. One is positive or negative with regard to its place in the poles of oppositions.[34]

Finally, mother's love lies as the coiled serpent (*ouroboros*) at the root of society, whether we view society as an organic whole or an atomized assemblage of individuals. It is both the fundamental antagonism (wound) that constitutes society and the balm that heals the wound it inflicts. The serpent that can bite, incise a society into disintegration, is the only one that can bind the broken parts.

THE MOVEMENT OF LOVE

The five types start with mother's love and end with communal love, and the movement is akin to the transition from substance to subject. Communal love is mother's love emptied of the wealth of a particular womb and has become a self-relating negativity. In the course of its movement, its character changes; so does its ethos. At the communal level love releases itself from its wombic nature and liberates it (the wombic nature) from the burden of knotting communal bonds. Communal love becomes *daeregoabo efere finji-a*, meaning "He who does not name his father, his lineage cannot participate in the public square," the *in-between* of the plurality of human beings. *Efere* (plate) in the saying harkens back to the mother's hearth, which symbolizes the "everyday transmutation of the raw into the cooked, of nature into culture."[35] The father's name represents the transcending or crossing of the hearth fire, the female realm, the movement from the processes of biological dependency into the freedom of life that is creative of novelty and signifies an engagement with the plurality of public space. Besides, Kalabari moved away from indigeneity (descent, blood, womb) as a basis of citizenship to the "name of the father."

The accent is on the *name*. In order to live into the community, to participate in that *gboloma* that holds the community together, one does not need to trace a route to a womb but wherever there is love between residents of the community; citizenship itself becomes transformed into residence, language, and passion for the culture. These three constitute the name of the father. The love of the mother is now transmuted as the living community in the triad matrices of residence, language, and culture. Mother's love is dispersed, displaced into the matrices. Community is this dialectical reversal. The triad of residence, language, and culture is the formal structure of this displacement. *Daere* (Name-of-the-Father) is the symbolic appropriation of the mother's love, the transubstantiation of the empirical mother's love into a form of appearance of the conceptual mother's love, which is the *Daere*, name of the father, the symbolic mandate of the mother. The supposedly "dead," "noncommunal love," "downgraded," or apolitical mother's love returns as the father's name. Here is a case of the negation of negation. Failure is transformed into success.

There is always a gap that separates the empirical mother's love from the conceptual mother's love. This fissure haunts the polity such that there is no ultimate consistency of the political order, only contingent, partial spaces of stability. As I noted earlier, the *gboloma* of the polity is always threatened by the possibility *oru wariwari-ye gbokigbo*, "to your tents, oh Kalabari." The name-of-the-father *Daere* serves to paper over the inevitable gap that exists between the particularity of the various wombs' claim to the citizens' loyalty and the universality of the state's demand for growing the in-between of public square or *amatemeso*. There is a reason why *daere go*, declare your father's name, is associated with festivals, public events, or gathering. Festivals constitute a way in which the special ideology of the (communal dimensions of) governance or mechanisms of mutuality that transcends the particularity of the mother's womb or love unfolds in time, even as it celebrates the glory (*ibi*) of community (or even *wari*, *wari-ibi*). *Daere go*, declare your father's name, is an acclamation for power, the glory of power. Italian philosopher Giorgio Agamben has recently taught us that modern democratic power needs not only administration and execution (governance) but also glory (the liturgical, ceremonies, and acclamation) to function and sustain itself.[36] One way this was done in Kalabari was the public declaration of the Name-of-the-Father in festival. Let us not forget the role of festivals, liturgical acclamations, and doxologies in the structures and functioning of power. *Daerego* might have been at the center of the political apparatuses of Kalabari kings and chiefs (who were and are still all men) to build public consensus for their political leadership and for the sustenance of the collective belonging that the *amatemeso* represented.

Daere is a unitary conception of the family, of the family in each *wari*. The typical Kalabari family in the precolonial period was characterized by different mothers, *furo*-segments (offspring-group), or cooking-and-feeding-together units (*mumbu*, mortar), but *daere* eliminates or reduces the differences and diversities to unity and compels a single identity for all members of the household, exemplary of households at the state or communal level. For both the immediate family and the polity as a whole, which are functioning below the structure of the *Daerego*, the population remains plural and multiple. In the chief's home (*wari*), the offspring units, the feeding-mortar units (*mumbu*), remain singularities below the *Daerego* structure. The polity consists of the plural singularities of canoe houses (*wari*, the component parts of the community) whose differences cannot be reduced or synthesized into sameness. It is important to mention that though the canoe houses remain as component parts, singularities, they are not incoherent or anarchical. They have common shared values and elements, things the *amatemeso* fashions, supports, or renews.

Daerego is a political concept—at least, a political concept as much as a biological (familial) one. It is determined by political struggles. It is a resistance to the fissures or power of the *mumbu*, mortar units. *Daerego* as a political concept not only reflects the suppression of the internal difference of the womb units but also points to or proposes future lines of their convergence into a common identity. It is a way of subjectivizing community members into political citizens, into a way of being that is faithful to units in the polity larger the *mumbu*, and subtraction from the path of *buugebu*. (*Buugebu* refers not only to extreme selfishness but also to a set of desires condemned to the self, meaning autarkic love, a self-desiring desire that reduces others to nothingness.) *Daerego* creates not only a polity for the subject but also a subject for the polity. Citizens' subjectivity is created in the agonistic communitarianism of the competing houses.

The foregoing discourse on the political nature of *Daerego*, the Name-of-the-Father, should not be construed to mean that mother's love is not political at all. Mother's love in *mumbu* is not just emotionalism, filial sentiment, or maternal enduring warmth toward offspring. It is political—its love is a political concept. This derives from how power is understood and exercised in the *mumbu*. Power is not the ability to force one's will on the other members of the womb-unit. It is akin to communicative power: the members deliberate and agree to act in concert, to pursue a common purpose in the husband-father's household or the public sphere. The power of love that orders the social space of the *mumbu* is emptied out of sovereign-like power, the will to mastery, the ethic of domination of individual members, and is replaced with love for the members of the *mumbu*, with love that works for the human flourishing of all its members for its common good. The basic (social) ontological impasse of love in the *mumbu* is how each person can intentionally extend themselves to sustain or expand the well-being of others in the group. Love is a force for action, for good, exerting power for human flourishing. Love is about giving—giving *convenantly* to sustain goodwill, justice, and joy. Love in the *mumbu* is a form of kenotic outpouring. Politics in the light of the *mumbu* is about how members of a group or community engage the forms, structures, and controls of power for the sake of creating the commons that nurture human flourishing and the common good. The politics of love in the *mumbu* appropriates, accents, or enacts different configurations of power. "The power of love . . . is not a way of getting others to do things but a way of doing things individually or collaboratively for the wellbeing of others. By this measure, authority is inherent in the quality of the life and behaviour of the individual or community that loves."[37] Thus, mother's love is not antithetical to the Name-of-the-Father. This confirms what I stated earlier: the other in Kalabari is always the relative other (other-than-me), not absolute other. Motherhood is a horizon of fatherhood and vice versa.

My effort to interpret Kalabari political theory as grounded in love should not be construed to mean that its politics is the "politics of love." Its understanding of politics is not a mere translation of "love one another" or "love thy neighbor as thyself." Politics is about creating and sustaining a community that supports the human flourishing of all its members. The notion of love, or, rather, the trinitarian union of love, power, and justice, funds this notion, not from the viewpoint of sentimentality but from hard and concrete work of love that anchors, authorizes, and authenticates individual and communal flourishing.

In this chapter, we have made two major argumentative movements. First, we described and explained *amatemeso* as a social construct. Second, we analyzed how otherness is built into *amatemeso* as collective belonging, demonstrating how the two principles of mother's hearth and father's name function as political principle of organizing the Kalabari polity. The polity is organized without some fantasy about returning to some primordial harmony between masculine and feminine "principles." Polity is something they are constantly working out under the existential conditions they create for themselves.

The Kalabari polity could be described as a proto-existentialist society whose existence precedes their essence—to put Sartre's philosophy into use. Though the Kalabari believe in destiny (*fiyeteboye*), the strong inclination to *bibibari* (to change their prenatal apportion of possibilities of life) suggests that they do not believe that there is an essential nature, a fixed nature of a person, "except in the one point that [she] can make of [herself] what [she] wants."[38] The Kalabari person creates what she is. "The essence of [her] being—the 'should-be,' 'the ought-to-be'—is not something which [she] finds; [she] makes it."[39] Kalabari men and women may talk about existence as working out destinies given by *So*. In reality, this mystical concept of being or existence has no real significance in the way they desperately seek to make themselves and existence into some-bodiness, *tombo tombo so*. They work as if nothing is given to them to determine their creativity. To put it differently, they pursue their existence without mystical restriction. They work to make themselves what they want and only read their "essences" from what they make of themselves.

Note that *fiyeteboye* as a prenatal text, which sets a Kalabari person's engagement with the whole of her existence, is forgotten at birth. The text is the experiencing of herself as a consciousness striving for human flourishing in the tension of existence. To put it differently, for *fiyeteboye* as text, existence is its own essence. The text—rather, the substance of the text—is the subject. Its truth is the real only as the deeds of the subject.[40] Kalabari people say *tombo tombo so*, meaning let a person (human being) become a person (human being). A person is both her own subject and predicate. A person is a person as she actualizes her potentiality. This is given as an imperative. The indicative of being a human demands the imperative of personhood. Destiny is practically a notion of subjectivation that carries the idea that a person becomes what actually he or she is essentially, and therefore potentially, in the contingency of time. Becoming a true person is thus a moral imperative. It is deemed immoral not to do and actualize what one is essentially and potentially capable of doing. This idea also applies to groups and communities as each of them has their *fiyeteboye* (*waritemeso*, *amatemeso*, and *setemeso*). Ethics of personal or group development or societal transformation is in a sense internal to the subjectivation process founded on the Kalabari philosophic notion of destiny.[41]

Ontological Violence and *Amatemeso*

We have seen how otherness traverses *amatemeso*; it remains to see how violence adheres to *amatemeso* itself. The dark shadow of violence runs through all of the male-female oppositions in Kalabari number symbolism in its deep connection with *amatemeso*. In the traditional Kalabari society, numbers were descriptions of the world and provided a terrain for gendered political claims. In the life of numbers and changes in their symbolic meanings, the *amatemeso* is imbricated in the history of domination of one gender over the other.[42] As we have already argued, *amatemeso* (irrespective of the religious, transcendent claims some Kalabari natives make about it) is socially constructed and historically produced. Violence is woven into the fabric of this constructed and historically conditioned outcome.

There is no clear and identifiable agent or subject inflicting this violence on the society. In the language of Slavoj Žižek, it is an invisible objective violence—that is, a background of accepted worldview and practices—that does the work.[43] *Amatemeso* is interpellated by violence, by an almost ontological violence, which has made it its habitation. The Kalabari city-state emerged or began its ascension to political, military, and economic glory at the time of the transatlantic slave trade. The emerging state was not only interpellated by the profits of the oceanic slave trade and internal long-distance trade but was also hailed by brutal violence of the slave trade. It responded to the interpellation of violence by successfully internalizing and incorporating this hailing from outside. If *amatemeso* is the soul of the Kalabari community, then that soul was formatted by centuries of their participation in the violent slave trade. This further exacerbated the cleavage between the mother principle and the father principle or, rather, the feminine and masculine distribution of power in the pre–slave trade community as captured in its number symbolism or number system.

The number three, which represents masculinity and violence (aggressiveness) in the Ijo number system, became singularly significant in the operational, social interaction sphere of Kalabari society. In the distant past, among the Kalabari, odd numbers in general, and three in particular, were associated with men, while even numbers in general, and four in particular, were associated with women. In many Ijo communities that were not heavily involved in the transatlantic trade and internal long-distance commerce, which created a more domineering role for men than was hitherto possible, three is not the predominant number.[44]

But in Kalabari there is a remarkable pervasiveness of tripartite schemes. From organization and "design" of society to gods, from worldview to business strategy, from the celebration of life and womanhood to the care of the dead, from construction of homes to the number of days for masquerade display there is always a scheme of three. To give some quick examples, there are three categories of spiritual forces (ancestors, community deities, and water spirits), three types of sculpture and marriage, tripartite hierarchy of textiles, and three-course meals. The question is why the number three is significant in the operational, social interaction sphere of Kalabari society.

My data and historical analyses suggest that the transformation of Kalabari society from fishing village to city or trading state altered the gender balance in favor of men. With their newly found dominance in long-distance trade that relied on violence and military force for success, the reproduction of social relationships was structured in various ways to produce and maintain the worldview that what was masculine and strong was good for the governance of various facets of society. The transatlantic trade transformed the number symbolism, particularly in terms of male-female opposition. Centuries of long-distance trade gave rise to increased domination of men over women, compared to a baseline culture, and effectively diminished the role of even numbers, which were associated with women in Kalabari traditional cosmology. The prominence of the number three in Kalabari social relations is, therefore, an enduring tell-tale sign and "archaeological" evidence of historic transformation of gender relations.

It was not hard to imagine that with the involvement of Kalabari in the violence-laden transatlantic trade, men's actions would come to overshadow those of women. In the transatlantic trade, where the strong dominated and raw strength meant intelligence and privilege, men's numbers (odd numbers), which were already associated with strength, agility, and chief divinities, became increasingly privileged and connected to the sacred domain. And women's activities, associated with supposed weakness, docility, and peace, were relegated to the profane category.

My study of Kalabari number symbolism has shown that numbers (particularly three) contain and reveal hidden stories about gender relations. The number three captures how social interactions are ordered and objectified to the disadvantage of women. The number three can be seen as reflecting either social-political or religious categories or hard evidence of gender inequality. Either way its story is a story of the *amatemeso*.

The story of the number system as repository of gender relations offers this scholar a way to imagine *amatemeso*'s characterization as the high form of political being-together of the community. How Kalabari citizens chose to live ethically in the polity and how they construct the *amatemeso* depend on the kind of narratives in which they make meaning out of their communities and social bonds, how they understand themselves, and how they make sense of their lives and relationships. They can answer the question "What is our *amatemeso* is all about?" only if they can answer the prior question: "What stories constitute the *amatemeso* or what story or stories does the *amatemeso* find itself a part?"[45]

In sum, the analyses above suggest that the transformation of Kalabari society from fishing village to city (trading) state altered the gender balance in favor of men. With their newly found dominance in long-distance trade that relied on violence and military force for success, the reproduction of social relationship was structured in various ways to produce and maintain the worldview that what is masculine is good for the governance of the various facets of society. Economic competition assumed the character of warfare and paved the way for the ascendancy of the odd number denoting strength and power, the number three. The predominance of the number three cosmologically authenticated and legitimized a reality that was already firmly established. It was not merely the cultural and historical identification of odd numbers with strength and festival days of chief divinities that caused the dominance of three; rather, it was the character of economic competition that engendered the "monopolistic" rise of three by degenerating into warfare, inevitably propelling the specialist number of strength and power to the lead role. By all indications, the singular dominance of three in the number symbolism system and the attendant conceptual devaluation of women must be understood as a consequence of history, not gods.

Concluding Remarks

What our various, multifaceted analyses of *amatemeso* have demonstrated in this chapter is that lifemaking is socially constructed and historically produced at the intersection of local, trans-local, international, religious, socioeconomic, and political forces. Besides, it is clear to the careful reader that *amatemeso* is a form (or part) of the political imagination of the Kalabari state. In chapter 2 we stated that there are three political imaginations from Amakiri's era that are worth noting. First, we stated that the city-state was an imagination based on common residence and culture. Second, ethos of masculinity increasingly came to condition political practice during the Amakiri era, such that political imagination increasingly got more masculine and harbored an ontology of violence. This ontology shaped the social and political imagination of the background and legitimizing culture of the city-state. It was a particular imagination of politics-as-soulcraft.[46] Third, I stated that chieftaincy was an imagination of the state, of the imaginative power of state. The Kalabari state and chiefs were a realization or an unfolding of an imaginative idea of a particular kind of nation building or politics-as-statecraft. The next chapter explores chieftaincy as a form of political imagination.

Chapter 4

Chiefs

Subjects to Freedom

Introduction

In the last chapter we studied *amatemeso* not as a supernatural being but as a social construction, a form of the political imagination of the Kalabari state. The institution of chieftaincy—the subject of this chapter—is another imagination of the state, and it is an integral aspect of statecraft that King Amakiri prioritized in the lifemaking processes of the Kalabari people. The last chapter also revealed that a crucial work of sustaining lifemaking is creating and maintaining freedom to do something new. Now we want to examine how this freedom is conceptualized, enacted, and embodied in chiefs in the Kalabari community. What is the political theory (institutional philosophy, if you like) that undergirds its notion of freedom? We want to specifically investigate what the Kalabari were doing with their chieftaincy institution (the *locus* of real freedom) in the nineteenth and early twentieth century with respect to creating a public space where the freedom to initiate the new in social processes could thrive. The goal of this effort is not to write a history of this institution but to offer a historical interpretation of it. As I contemplate this institution, examining its workings and its place in the politics of a traditional society, I will be continuously rising from "particular facts to exploratory reflections"[1] so that we can see things in new ways and illuminate the political theory behind it or, rather, grasp the political theory it produced.

My interpretation of Kalabari chieftaincy (which is open only to men) may be termed "Arendtian" in the sense that I draw my central philosophical inspiration for it from the work of the German American philosopher Hannah Arendt. The purpose is not to find Arendtian categories in the Kalabari material but to reread the Kalabari data with unfurnished eyes, with the vision of a newcomer grafted on the understanding and sensibility of a native-born. I am reading, reinterpreting, reunderstanding the Kalabari chieftaincy institution to " 'give rise to thought'—to give rise, that is, through tension and transformation, to greater philosophical understanding"[2] as to what they were doing. I have reintroduced myself to the " 'cultural treasures of the past, believed to be dead,' so that these cultural gems were 'made to speak . . . (proposing) things altogether different from the familiar, worn-out trivialities they had been presumed to say.' "[3]

Arendt's insights into politics and freedom help me to excavate the cultural gems and uncover the concealed dimensions (hidden behind decades of distorted scholarly focus) of the Kalabari chieftaincy institution. These uncovered dimensions constitute the philosophy of the chieftaincy institution. I have called them philosophy not only because there is a definite (or disguised) way of thinking and thought behind the experience of chieftaincy but also because I have formed a philosophy out of them by interpreting creatively and transforming our vision of the inherited horizons of meaning. My hope in this effort is that the Kalabari (Ijo) people will come to understand something better of themselves, something, perhaps, about their unfolding narrative identities. More important, for our limited purposes in this book, this effort will show their notion of freedom as forged in orientation to lifemaking.

Arendt's Philosophy of Politics

According to Arendt, politics is an arena of humans living together where a man makes his appearance as a free man (liberated from the necessities of life and also free in civil status) in the public realm through speech and action. Politics in this pure and simple sense as participation in the *polis* takes place in interrelationship with other men. "Freedom needed, in addition to mere liberation, the company of other men who are in the same state, and it needed a common public space to meet them—a politically organized world, in other words, into which each of the free men could insert himself by word and deed."[4]

A good entry point into Arendt's philosophy of politics is to start from her model of the ancient Greek *polis*. According to her, there were two realms in Greek: the private household (*oikia*), the realm of necessity, and the public space, the public realm of the city, the realm of freedom. The dominant cares in the private realm, the realm of the economy, are those of biological life, the care for survival, the necessities of life imposed on the human species by nature. As she puts it:

> The most powerful necessity of which we are aware in self-introspection is the life process which permeates our bodies and keeps them in a constant state of change whose movements are automatic, independent of our own activities, and irresistible—i.e., of an overwhelming urgency. The less we are doing ourselves, the less active we are, the more forcefully will this biological process assert itself, impose its inherent necessity upon us, and overawe us with the fateful automatism of sheer happening that underlies all human history.[5]

But in the public space of the *polis* humans act free from their nature and its necessities and escape this automatic process that afflicts them in the private realm. The private realm is natural, and the public realm is unnatural. Only men who are liberated from the necessities and urgencies of life, the realm of nature and bodily needs, can afford to play in the public space, where men become true humans. Their lives have transcended the slavery to and metabolism with nature that is the plight of the human species to reach the vindication of freedom and individual spontaneity. In the private sphere every human being is uniformly a part of the human species bound together by their common needs and desires of natural life, by common tasks of production and consumption and reproduction, by shared features of biological existence. In this reduction to the commonality of just being human species, the plurality and distinctiveness of individuals are not manifest; each can be considered identical and interchangeable. But in the public sphere that exists between and outside of households, there is space to allow them to be plural and diverse individuals. In political speech and action, a man can distinguish himself in significant ways from others, "can communicate himself and not merely something—thirst or hunger, affection or hostility or fear."[6]

The private sector is organized for the sake of freeing men to act in the public, for free citizens to pursue the higher call of action, and hence it is "pre-political." It is organized and administered so that some people would participate in the processes of nature and history not as automatons but as free citizens who act spontaneously, who can disrupt ongoing processes to bring something new, something extraordinary. It is in the public space that men actualize their freedom; politics is the "locus" of freedom. It is through politics that men appear to one another as unique individuals capable of original actions.

This public space, an in-between of men who are free and equal masters of their households, excludes force, sovereignty, and rule. In this space men meet as equals and act together for the common good of the *polis*, absent the hierarchical relations between rulers/masters and subjects as in the household. They appear to one another as distinct individuals in a common world (an in-between that at once relates and separates them) and as persons of merit gained in the *polis*. It is the realm of the political.

Arendt's political theory is centered on a constellation of four interrelated concepts: public life, freedom, action, and natality. This constellation is deeply informed by her philosophic thematic embrace of the notion of human beginning as the key to understanding politics as an event for novelty and the belief that humans can unleash their potentialities for the new to reshape communities. "Beginning, before it becomes a historical event, is the supreme capacity of man; politically, it is identical with man's freedom. *Initium ut esset homo creatus est*—'that a beginning be made man was created,' said Augustine. This beginning is guaranteed by each new birth; it is indeed every man."[7] So far, we have examined the public-private life distinction and freedom. We now turn to action.

The essence of freedom, of transcending the necessities of the private, is for men to show their individual distinctiveness and appear to each other as unique beings. The medium or the means of doing this is through actions (innovative deeds and speech). Actions enable men to distinguish themselves from mere bodily existence. It is through actions that men achieve individuation, distinction, and outstanding achievements. It is through actions that they rise up to the level of heroism and outstanding performance, which are recounted in generations to come and thus achieve social immortality. It is by action that a man becomes a "who" (in contradistinction to "what") and attains identity. "In acting and speaking, men show who they are, reveal actively their personal identities and thus make their appearance in the human world, while their physical identities appear without any activity of their own in the unique shape of the body and the sound of the voice."[8] To act in this way, to appear before others to actualize one's freedom, is what politics is all about in Arendt's reasoning.

To act, to initiate something new, to exercise the capacity to begin, is to be born again. It is like a second birth. This notion of beginning in the physical world and in the political world Arendt calls "natality." She writes that "the miracle that saves the world, the realm of human affairs from its normal, 'natural' ruin is ultimately the fact of natality, in which the faculty of action is ontologically rooted. It is, in other words, the birth of new men and the new beginning, the action they are capable of by virtue of being born."[9]

One other point about the private and public distinction that is important for understanding the norms of the public sphere, the space of appearance in Arendt's model of the Greek *polis*, is the form of rulership or leadership in the private and public realms. Behind the walls of privacy where the Greeks hid activities concerned with the survival and needs of the body the paterfamilias reigned supreme, regulated and "normalized" members' conduct, and represented only one opinion and one interest.

In the private sphere relationships were always hierarchical. There were always those who commanded and those who obeyed. This order-obedience relation had two forms. First, the household head was a "despot" who exercised uncontested power over the slaves and the members of his family. The head was vested with powers of violence, force, and coercion. In simple terms, their relation (the masters and his household members) was based on violence. "Wherever he ruled there was only one relation, that between master and slaves. And the master, according to Greek common opinion, . . . was not free when he moved among his slaves; his freedom consisted in his ability to leave the sphere of the household altogether and to move among his equals, freemen."[10] The second form of rulership in the web of hierarchical relationship is authority. The relationship between the ruled and the ruler was based on authority, which Arendt argues was different from persuasion, which was obtained in the public realm. She argues that since the Greek political realm was a space of appearance of equals, its form of rulership was persuasion, a process of argumentation.

Authority as a form of government was ill-suited for the free men of the *polis* who appear to each other as equals because "it incorporates inequality and distinction as its all-permeating principles."[11] The characteristic image of authoritarian rule is the pyramid wherein those with most power and privilege are at the top, and from there power filters down to those below. The source of authority for the pyramid lies outside it—in the past, tradition, foundation, law, external force that is beyond and above the political realm.

Where authority or violence (absolute rule) was the basis of governance or relationship between citizens, there was always a clear distinction between those who ruled and those who were ruled. There was always a huge power distance between the two. The matter is different in the *polis* as a community of equals. Those who appeared there to become the best that they could be in the community were masters of their own lives. They were not slaves to the necessities of nature and were not subject to domination by other men, whether by sheer violence or by authority. Arendt writes,

> The free man, the citizen of the polis, is neither coerced by the physical necessities of life nor subject to the man-made domination of others. He not only must not be a slave, he must own and rule over slaves. The freedom of the political realm begins after all elementary necessities of sheer living have been mastered by rule, so that domination and subjection, command and obedience, ruling and being ruled, are preconditions for establishing the political realm precisely because they are not its content.[12]

Discerning a Space of Appearance in Kalabari Chieftaincy

If we view Kalabari chieftaincy with an Arendtian lens, we see that it also emphasizes a space of appearance among chiefs, the heads of house (*wari*). The precolonial institution of chieftaincy has been principally interpreted as concerning only administrative, legislative, legal, and economic management affairs of the city-state. It has not been discerned as a matter of appearance in the public space. But *ala-siri* (chiefs' sphere) could be considered as a space of appearance where a man shows himself in the presence of others who are his equal and displays his distinctiveness. As Kalabari say, "Ala-siri ane oyiapu asawo ti ari," that is, "It is in the chiefs' sphere that men display their individual excellence [*asati*]." Appearance, as Arendt informed us in her book *The Human Condition*, is the being of politics. To focus on chieftaincy as a "space of appearance" is not to deny the administrative and economic interests and power in the institution but to highlight a neglected aspect of it.

Chieftaincy in Kalabari had three parts: rulership, administration of house-corporation, and experience of action amid community of equals. The first and second parts refer to the setup and working of political institutions and organizations to serve the purposes of biological life. They are the sustenance, security, reproduction, and well-being of life. The rulership and administration of the *social* is about government. Governing is characterized by hierarchical relationships between leaders and their subjects. The relationships in these aspects of the chieftaincy are often characterized and/ or dogged by violence, status differential, and hierarchism. The third part is about the space of freedom and dignity where fullness of being can be displayed. It is a space of politics, where men act and initiate something new. Kalabari possess two verbs meaning "to act," one of them meaning "to start" and the other "to carry out": *saaki* and *ye*. *Saaki* means "to begin, to take up, raise up, to rise up." On the other hand, *ye* means "to carry through." To ask a person to begin a task and carry through, "to act," they will say, "meni *saaki* te ye," meaning "to start and carry through."

The Kalabari chief moved and negotiated his leadership in these three areas with different styles. Among his slaves (*nyanabo-apu*), servants, and lower members of the house, he was a master. He had uncontested mastery of house affairs. He ruled with *coercion*. But among the ranks of the gentlemen of his house, the men and women with means, he led by *authority*.[13] The chief was obeyed by men and women who still retained their freedom (only in the sense of being freeborn or given some independence by the chief and having some economic resources). He who commanded was obeyed because both parties recognized the hierarchies in the house and the rightness and legitimacy that pertained to them. They all had in common the hierarchies of the house and the necessity to keep the house economically viable on which the continued power of the chief and the prospects of the promotion of the gentlemen to the rank of chief depended. Both parties also needed political unity in the house if they were not going to be broken up and absorbed by rival houses. The chief and the freeborn had these concerns, the obligations to the spiritual realm, greatness of ancestors, the traditions as the source of authority, and these represented a power or force superior and external to them. This source is a focal point above and beyond them and against which the power the chiefs claimed or exercised could be checked.

In the council of chiefs (*alapu ogbo, alapu siri*), members led by persuasion of arguments, by reason. Membership in this group presupposed equality, which is incompatible with force and violence or authority.

Members were by definition free men (a slave, *nyanabobo*, becomes a free and self-owning person once he becomes a chief). The king was the leader of chiefs, the heads of their various houses, and he was *primus inter pares*. He could not be a despot or tyrant. He could not rule other chiefs by sheer brute force. He was not by definition vested with power of coercion and could not rule by sheer violence. He did not even have a national standing army or police force. He relied on the house heads to supply them when they were needed for internal control or for projection of the city-state's might abroad.

It was in the sphere of chiefs (*ala-siri*) that a man was truly free. In it he was neither embedded in a master-slave relationship nor ensconced in order-obedience relationships, hierarchical structures of inequality and distinctions. Outside of the chiefs' sphere the house heads were always in settings constituted by those who ruled and those who were ruled. The sphere of chiefs served as a space of appearance for a man to emerge as truly a free person in the public realm. He was moving neither among slaves (servants, dependents) nor among subjects (those who retained their freedom and who operated within parts of the system of inequality between the ruling and the ruled). The public realm (belonging to everyone) of the city-state or the town was the place in which the essence of an individual freedom was displayed. Here persuasion is obtained by exercise of that supreme human capacity: the Kalabari language used as vehicle of the compelling power of reason. *Ibi ekwen* (excellent speech) was used to express the highest idea of the good (the promotion of the well-being of the community, which is the measure of all things) and let it shine forth most as one's self-interest. *Ibi* means both good and beauty. A truly *ibi ekwen* has both beauty of expression and illumination of the common good in a matter.

The Principle of Natality

Kalabari theory of politics or action stands in and stands out of its understanding of natality. Chieftaincy, as we have shown, is a form of appearing in the world, but this is only a "second appearance." Human beings, men and women, appear in the world through birth and through chieftaincy so that new beginnings will be made. In its deep meaning, the forms of new appearances are attempts by the Kalabari to transcend the opposing forces of the past and the future that through the power of fatalism want to crush the present into eternal recurrence. In every appearance in the public space a beginning is made, or a provision is made afresh for new meaning. Every appearance, be that of a new chief or a new child, represents the possibility of new beginning.

Natality is about the opening, birth, of a new horizon for the future. It is based on a belief that progress is perpetual—the world never comes to an end. There is no doctrine of bringing the temporal mode of the future to a close—there is always a relevant open future.

There are three forms of birth or beginning as a philosophical thematic in Kalabari society: *biological natality*, *factual natality*, and *political natality*. They see in "the experience of birth the human capacity to relate to one's own potentiality for beginning, that is to say, the capacity to *be* in vital relation to one's birth as an event of novelty and unprecedented potentiality for the new."[14] The birth of a child signifies the opening of new horizon for the future. The newborn is important for the hope it bears or contains for a generation of the future of the community.

The birth of a new child signifies the potentiality of the world for the capacity to begin afresh to improve the *ama*, the *world* (the shared common existence), the sphere where residents in an area "act together in the pursuit of a common concern."[15] *Ama-ibi* (literally the well-being of the common existence/world, *amor mundi*[16]) is not really about the betterment of a physical locale but about improvement, durability, and futurity of the shared existence.

"Factual natality" is the formalized fictional birth of a slave or adopted person in the Kalabari community. For instance, when slaves/adoptees were brought into a *canoe house* for integration, they were given fictional kinship ties to all members of the "family."[17] The chief became the "father," his wife became "mother" to them, and the children were "brother" and "sister." These fictional ties were heavily invested with drama. As Robin Horton states:

> When the newly bought slave arrived in the community, the breaking-off of all his previous kinship ties and the assumption of a whole series of new ties was brought home to him by means of a dramatic *rite de passage* in which his new "mother" shaved his head clean and then gave him a ritual meal. From then on, the "mother" was supposed to live up to her title in the fullest possible sense. . . . There were severe penalties for referring publicly to the fictional nature either of a man's

kinship ties to his fellow house-members or of his descent from his house-founder. Publicly calling a slave a slave was a heinous crime. The use of kinship idiom, then, did a great deal to ensure that the slave was assimilated into the house on the same footing as the freeborn and to instill in him the same loyalties.[18]

The child and the adoptee (slave) are forms of "primary natality," and birth of the chief and his new house is "political natality." "The experience of political natality is the supreme actualization of the capacity for beginning inasmuch as its singular orientation is directed toward the world of human affairs while its special concern is to uphold the experience of plurality as that condition which distinguishes a community of political actor."[19] We are getting ahead of ourselves. Let us step back a bit and discuss the process of birthing a new chief and the attendant new house.

The founding of a new chieftaincy stool was accompanied with the birth of a new house or sub-house. The canoe house (*wari*) was founded and headed by a wealthy merchant. By the eighteenth century the house was no longer primarily based on bloodlines as it was in the fishing village era before the emergence of long-distance trade and it had become a cooperative trading company of a wealthy trader and his relatives, trading assistants, servants, adoptees, slaves, and followers.[20] For a canoe house to continue as a subsidiary (i.e., to maintain its charter), it had to be dynamic, flourishing, and profitable. A prosperous canoe house would spin off other canoe houses, and these houses kept their connections with the mother canoe house. But if a younger canoe house became more prosperous, it absorbed the mother house and became the senior house. An unsuccessful canoe house folded up, voluntarily attached to, or merged with another house or was acquired.

Promotion and headship of a canoe house was based primarily on commercial ability, drive, and wealth. This "open criterion" meant that any man, even a slave, could, by dint of hard work and accumulation of personal capital, rise to head his house or found a new house. An enterprising young man, native-born or slave, would start by building his capital. When the young man had accumulated sufficient capital, he would begin to populate his household either by marriage or by purchase of slaves. This was done because one of the qualifications to head or found a house was an ability to fit a thirty-two-man war-canoe with his men, trading goods, and war ammunition.[21] The formal ceremonial recognition of the man as a chief proceeded in three steps, and at each stage his hand would be raised by a relevantly qualified chief from his house or compound and presented to the members of the community.

Elem Kalabari (headquarters of Kalabari in the eighteenth and nineteenth centuries) was segmented into semi-autonomous units and organized into three levels of hierarchy. There was the house (*wari*), which consisted of entrepreneurial households (a merchant, his family, staff, dependents, and relations). A *wari* (as in Elem Kalabari) or group of houses makes up the ward (*polo*). The combination of wards makes up the town (*ama*). Kalabari society was organized as thus: individual (household), *wari/polo*, and *ama*. In the first step of a three-step process to be formally recognized as a new chief, when a man deemed himself qualified, he presented himself to the head of his house (*wari*), and if the head approved, he then presented the aspirant to the whole house in a general meeting. Thereafter he was presented to the head of the *polo* that would in turn present him to the *amanyanabo* in council. In sum, in nineteenth-century Elem Kalabari a man aspiring to be a chief had to be presented to the *wari*, *polo*, and *ama* before the whole community accepted him.

The newborn child, the newly accepted member (authenticated by *sibi-kiri*, shaving of the head), and the new house (headed by the new chief, *waripakama*) symbolized the "power to begin something new out of [their] own resources,"[22] the capacity to begin. All three forms of natality—birth, *sibi-kiri*, and *waripakama*—are connected to the idea of beginning in another sense. They are linked to the idea of communal identity: oriented to the source of their beginning and that of the community, to their shared communality under one *amatemeso* (destiny of town), to their identity as coming from one source, *Teme-órú* (creator-spirit), which conferred vitality and liveliness to members of the community. This referring back to the origination of life and community—to the beginning as a way of coming to be is very obvious in the *sibi-kiri* exercise of slave or adopted members. By shaving the hairs of the would-be new member and taking him or her to the common river to take a ritual bath, he was connected to the beginning of the community. The slave/adopted person, the newborn, and the new house (chief) became a (renewed) member of the community through the process of referring back to the origination of life. Each person was now appropriately reminded as coming from the *amatemeso* (or *Teme-órú*) and he or she was going to it, and it was between the two ends that he or she comprehended his or her presence in the community.

This referring back is not a "throwness" into the past. These people were referred back in order to acknowledge a new beginning; to acknowledge becoming newcomers in a particular community, a particular class; to acknowledge becoming embedded in a particular web of relationships that antedates their insertion into it. This new birth, the fact of their natality, offered a promise to the community: it guaranteed futurity as represented by the new beginning that each of the three types of persons represented. More important, this referring back was, in a sense, a celebration or at least a recognition of the principle of beginning, the human potentiality for beginning, the inherent potentiality for novelty that exists in the in-betweens of any community.

The child, the adoptee, and the chief represent the principle of beginning. Each of them represents the beginning of somebody with the capacity to initiate the new. But the beginning of the chief has something more to it. It is not only the beginning of somebody but also the beginning of something. The other two only represent the condition for further beginning in the temporal structure (gap) of existence; the chief alone initiates actions (in the strict Arendtian sense), exercises the capacity to continue to begin. The child's or adoptee's beginning happens in a pre-political circumstance. Their births are a "man's first birth," initial premier into the Kalabari society. In politics, in the chiefs' sphere there is a second birth, so to speak. By virtue of this birth a Kalabari man inserts himself in the chiefs' world where he can truly act as a free man (which is not the same thing as a free born), showing that he was liberated from biological necessity in the presence of peers.

> With words and deed we insert ourselves into the human world, and this insertion is like a second birth, in which we confirm and take upon ourselves the naked fact of our original physical appearance. This insertion is not forced upon us by necessity, like labor, and it is not prompted by utility, like work. It may be stimulated by the presence of others whose company we may wish to join, but it is never conditioned by them; its impulse springs from the beginning which came into the world when we were born [and when we are adopted into the house] and to which we respond by beginning something new on our initiative.[23]

In the Kalabari society there is a drive for legacy as a paradigm of transcendence, as a means and hope of going over the limitations of day-today existence, death, and transience. This was a society that put an accent on social immortality. The living wanted to be remembered after death as a reaction to the ceaseless flow of time. Helplessly caught in change and decay, resentful of other persons' incredible capacity to forget their good deeds, and feeling lost and insignificant in the vast universe, they looked for ways to achieve some permanence, some recognition, and to hold time, as it were, in the present.

Leaving a legacy by acting in the public, common interest was a veritable pathway to social immortality.[24] Life in the public sphere, in the realm of chiefs, had the greatest potential for earthly immortality. Insofar as a man had left the demands and burdens of life necessities and stepped into the public realm for excellence in words and deeds, inserting new possibilities into the common world of human affairs, and acting for the common good, he had better chances of his story being weaved into the history of the community. As Patricia Bowen-Moore argues:

> The public/political realm of human affairs holds out the possibility of achieving political immortality to the extent that the actor exhibits his uniqueness in public where his deeds and words have the occasion to be seen and heard, judged and remembered by those who witness them. The political actor commences a biography of excellence when his actions and speech assume the character of the political and when these experiences are judged worthy to form part of the chronicle of history.[25]

HOUSE SYSTEM

One of the beauties of the Kalabari house system is its openness to augmentation and amendment, that is, an inclusive expansiveness. The house system is an open and expansive project undergirded by open architecture.[26] It is an expansive movement that renews and re-creates its founding and the logics of its order through production and appropriation of new houses. The city-state's political base expands by opening itself to new houses and new chiefs and including them in the network of powers. This concept of open space or open sovereignty was manifested not only in the constant augmentation of houses but also in the expansion of the geographical limit of the city-state. What was known as Kalabari started with the small town Elem Kalabari and expanded into what, as of today, numbers up to thirty-three towns. Kalabari was an open and continuous process before British colonialism froze the expansiveness.

The idea of citizenship is the third area where this conception of openness and open space manifested. Members of the society were bound together principally by location (their placeness in the same territory) and the institutions, the civilization, and the history they commonly possessed, and not by blood. Blood is a kind of common entity internal to members of a group and thus very private. But institutions, history, civilization, and rootedness in a common environment are a set of in-betweens, external to the individual, and thus open and public.

The organizing principle of grouping members was based on the concept of the trading corporation, not on bloodlines and marriages. The boundaries of households were defined not by bloodlines, but by firms' sizes. The household or the house was an aggregation of parents and their biological and adopted children, slaves, trading assistants, and employees. The household was established, sustained, and perpetuated by a trading corporation. The criteria for citizenship in the Eastern Delta states were the possession of the distinctive culture (*amaganganbra*) of the community and residence in it.[27]

It is important to show how this concept of citizenship sheds light on the theory of action and public sphere that we have identified in this chapter. By not tying citizenship strictly to blood, to an unchangeable feature of the past, it signifies the freedom to begin. Citizenship focuses on the future, belonging together. It is an identity beyond the one given by nature. The city-state, *ama*, is space constructed by men and women as the in-between amid residents in a territory. The town or the city-state is a space of appearance in a macro sense of the phrase. Chiefs are the concrete embodiment of this public ideal.

Meaning of Freedom

Following the predominant model of freedom in contemporary social sciences, scholars have often interpreted freedom in traditional African societies as something an individual possesses in private. It is viewed as something internal, being left alone, and as an attribute of will—as *liberum arbitrium*. It is analyzed as sovereignty over one's actions and their consequences, as the free will of a person that cuts him away from others or has its ideal of prevailing over others. Freedom is also narrowly conceived as just a matter of exercise of the will against the force of nature, circumstances, obstacles, and burden of tradition.

But if we consider the notion of freedom in the light of the tradi-tional African spirit of communality, then it is something enjoyed not in private but in the public: concerted participation in public action for the common good with one's peers. Freedom is the power to act together, to initiate new possibilities in the community, to think and act in new ways. It is about appearing to others as a distinct, irreplaceable individual in the public space, the shared world, and performing immortal deeds. In the traditional Kalabari society life was very political and this-worldly. Living together was political because its focus was on participation in public (common) affairs and existence in the memory of others. Life hangs together principally for this-worldly pursuits, for social immortality, for actions in the public arena. The community was not just a *social* organiza-tion for the satisfaction of the ceaseless demands of the body. It was also to provide (to guarantee) a space of appearance for those who had gone beyond life's biological necessities to place their unique individuality and distinction in the service of the community and to initiate common enter-prises among their peers. From the perspective of Hannah Arendt, this is precisely what freedom entails. To be free is to act. As an astute interpreter of Arendt's thought, Margaret Canovan, writes: "It is only in action, in initiating undertakings and interacting with one another, that men, these unique individuals, reveal what they personally are. . . . Action alone is free, for it consists above all in the capacity to initiate, to alter situations by engaging in them, to perform continuous miracles of unpredictability that can be put together to make an intelligible story after the event."[28]

Freedom, in a related sense, "consists in being able to do what one ought to will ([as Montesquieu puts it] *la liberte ne peut consister qu' à pouvoir faire ce que l'on doit vouloir*—(the emphasis is on *pouvoir*)."[29] Thus it is not a matter of the will succeeding against the force of nature, circumstances, obstacles, and other burdens. For Montesquieu what is relevant is the *capacity to do*, and "it is irrelevant whether this failure is caused by exterior or by interior circumstance."[30] The chief, *alabo*, is also an *opubo*. Opubo not only connotes a highly placed personality in the social hierarchy, but it is also someone who has the power, the capacity, to achieve the improbable, who can bring something new into an already existing situation. One way this capacity to do is rendered in Kalabari is *I ye gbeye ye*. This is the pure capacity to do—the "I can." The focus is neither on the will—"I will," which can be defeated by interior (mind versus body struggle) and exterior circumstances—nor on the intellect, which can be paralyzed by analysis of future desirability of aims. *I ye gbeye ye* is pure doability—it is sufficient to act, to manifest one's being in the presence of others, to manifest the human character as an acting with initiative to begin again, to establish a new reality. *I ye gbeye ye* demands doing or acting to bring in the new, even the unexpected. Usually, a series of events is ongoing, and action is needed to interrupt it. It is always this freedom to act, to begin afresh that is the quality of the intercourse among men. The man is free if he can disrupt automatic political, historical, and religious processes by persuading other men to act collectively with him rather than be a slave to them.

Even the humans-gods relationship is not free from this requirement. In Kalabari traditional religion, people are willing to start afresh with the gods. If a god starts a process that is not conducive to human beings, they can disrupt the process to start something new. If a god becomes too furious or demanding, the withdrawal of worship from or worshipful dependence on the god deprives the god of its power and authority to act on humans or control human activities. On September 27, 1857, Kalabari discontinued the Owu Akpana (the shark cult) because sharks that they worshipped had embarked on a course of attacking more humans than they could bear. Below is the record of a Liverpool trader, Mr. William Oates, who was in New Calabar (Elem Kalabari) when the community decided to "disrobe" the shark as a god.

Monday, 28th [September 1857]

[I] went up to [New] Calabar town this morning and while there heard that the chiefs had a meeting in their palaver house yesterday, in consequence of several of the natives having been killed lately by their big Jew Jew [juju, god], the Sharks, they came to the conclusion that it no be use for have wowo jew jew [useless god] all same shark no more and it is therefore no longer held as such, but the natives are catching them as fast as possible and now allow "white men" to do the same if they like which of course we shall do whenever we have a chance as the shark is the sailor's greatest enemy.[31]

So, chieftaincy in its principal sense, as has been developed in this chapter, is about the *real*. Chieftaincy as a means of political administration is different from chieftaincy as a form of politics, a way of concerned engagement with the political. In the chiefs' realm, politics is about unfolding being as a consequence of subjects' decisions about liberatory and life-enhancement potentials, not about positing being as a manipulation of institutions and bureaucratic practices. It is about encountering the *real*. To be free in Kalabari is to become a chief. For it is only as a chief that the nineteenth-century Kalabari man is said to be free, and free he was in all dimensions.

Quintessential freedom of the individual in Kalabari involved three dimensions. First, the person was not a slave to another human being. (A slave got his freedom and was no longer beholden to his master or the one that bought him the day he became a chief.) Second, he was not a servant of necessities of life. Finally, he could act (*ori ine o ye gbeye ye ba*), exhibiting the capacity to begin, to do and act, to start something new in the midst of others (world). To be free is to thrive on the basis of the unprecedented. Kalabari say, "Ala-okolo poku pilamaa," which literally means "a chief's feces do not pollute [desecrate] the sacred." It is generally understood to mean a chief is above the law. But the inherent meaning of the saying goes beyond seeing chiefs as above the law. Law in general imposes limitations of action, and such containment is founded on precedent, but every action (which law is attempting to police or contain) is inherently boundless and unpredictable and thus thrives in the realm of the unprecedented. As Shiraz Dossa argues:

> Law imposes limitations, however imperfectly, on the boundless consequences which flow from action. In this sense, law safeguards "political existence" in assigning responsibility to actors for their deeds. But against the inherent unpredictability of action, men are *politically* helpless because actions affect, influence and inspire other actors in ways in [*sic*] which cannot be foreseen with any degree of certainty. While the law may contain the effects of an action by a particular individual, it is impotent in the face of further actions which the original action may lead to. Law cannot forestall or limit actions of certain kinds universally, nor can it do so prior to the occurrence of the action. Law arises on the basis of precedent; action thrives on the unprecedented.[32]

Finally, the freedom that chiefs represented and enjoyed was to be displayed in the public, in the presence of other men where their individual excellences are displayed, or as they say, where "oyiapu asati-ari." This combination of freedom and public concern and the importance of a forum in the traditional society for the actualization of freedom, the capacity to act, is well tested in the process and rigor of becoming a chief.

Becoming a Chief

The sphere of chiefs is a gathering of equals for the life of the community. As a public-political realm, it is preceded principally by the economic sphere. Households are concerned with preserving physical life and the biological survival of the city-state (town or nation). It is in its sphere that a man masters the necessities of sheer living (including child-rearing and education) and gathers the resources for the defense of the city-state. Domination of the biological and defense necessities of living together is a precondition for appearing in the public realm, in the chiefs' sphere, to be admitted into equality and politics, to be accepted into the public affairs of the *polis*.

There were two very important conditions a man had to fulfill before he could be recognized and celebrated as a chief. Both of them emphasized the public nature of the office and the capability of mastering the biological necessities of life. First, the possession of private property was a condition for participation in this sphere of the city's activities. He had to be rich, wealthy. Second, he had to have men and women as dependents or under his control. This means that the man had persons who could take care of the demands of nature. He had shown by taking care of a huge number of persons that he had mastered the necessities of biological life, that is, as one who is liberated from nature. He also demonstrated that he was engaged in sustaining the flourishing of other citizens in the society, playing a prominent role in the lifemaking processes of the community.

On the actual day of recognition and elevation he was made to choose between a yam and a cannonball. He was presented with the choice and asked to select. Usually, the cannonball was selected—no one can become a state (*se* or *ama*)-recognized chief without choosing the cannonball. As soon as a man selected the cannonball, his house supporters shouted to high heavens his praises and those of his ancestors.

What does the choice between a yam and a cannonball tell us about the public nature of the chief's office? One represents service toward his own house members, and the other toward the city-state. It is really not an either/or choice; rather, the person was asked to transcend the house, the private realm, but not necessarily eliminate or negate it. The presence of the yam points to biological necessity, the care of life necessities, and the administration to support economic and political life. The cannonball relates to public action. The cannonball is not really—or at least not only—about the military defense of the city-state. As good as this explanation is, it does not fully take account of the dimension of Kalabari chieftaincy that we have exposed in this chapter. The cannonball signifies a concern with immortality of the city-state. It stands in the clearest contrast to the issues and necessities of the private domain; it is in contradistinction to the individual interest and concerns of the household. In the face of the city-state that came before the individual and is to outlast the individual (the chief), what should occupy the mind is the sustainability and freedom of the city-state. The chiefs' sphere—and the cannonball as a pointer to its duty—was to create the public space where free Kalabari men could appear and act, where their freedom could be actualized.

It was in the public space where the man could join his cannons and guns with those of others to act together, initiate new possibilities, and make a name for himself among his equals. The cannonball was not only about defense of the city-state but also signified a willingness to step in to a more spacious life, the public realm. This has great significance: no private realm, canoe house, existed wholly free of the rest of the community. The yam conflicted with the meaning of public life. In the deep philosophical context of chieftaincy, it presupposed a kind of deity of the hearth—the warmth and well-being of friends and intimates, the potential to treat members of one's private realm preferentially.

The question about the cannonball came only after another question about his ability to control his urges. The aspirant was asked if he was capable of resisting libidinal impulses to promptly leave for community services when he heard a clarion call for action in the face of a new naked lover who was alone with him in the room. The man was questioned so the community could learn something about his willingness to consciously move from the private realm to the public. The condition of love of the kind they were concerned with is very private, a countercurrent experience to the condition of public (political) action. The lover and beloved (man and woman) behind closed doors at that moment are intensely preoccupied with themselves. Lost in the promotion of self-interest, they no longer belong to the public realm and show no active concern for the world, the space of appearance of where men relate to one another. As Arendt once put it: "Love, by reason of its passion, destroys the in-between which relates us to and separates us from others. . . . Love, by its very nature, is unworldly, and it is for this reason rather than its rarity that it is not only apolitical but antipolitical, perhaps the most powerful of all antipolitical human forces."[33] The question about willingness to ignore the urgent demands of his swollen member was put to the man to remind him that chieftaincy was a concern for the world, about world-creating.

In addition to these questions, the aspirant was presented to the public at three levels: *wari* (house), *polo* (ward), and town (*se, ama*). No one could become a full-fledged chief without the tripartite public recognitions. Once again, the question needs to be asked: What is the meaning or significance of the multiple presentations in the political thought of Kalabari? There are four significant components of the public presentation of the candidates at the three levels in the light of our limited purpose in this chapter. First, individual candidates were not just thrust into the public realm but sought to explicitly enter into it with public recognition. Second, they had to commend themselves to the agreement of others. Political actions are never enacted in isolation: they take place in the presence of others and aim to solicit their consent.

Third, this process reflected the fundamental understanding of power as generated and sustained in a network of persons and within the internal and immanent social dynamic of the city-state. The raising of the hands at the various levels pointed to a mixed constitution of democratic power, aristocratic power, and "weak" monarchic (king-in-council) power linked together in networks. Power is not sourced from a transcendental source but is made by and within society, and the would-be chief was raised to the level where this immanent power produced the space of appearance in society where freedom could operate.

Finally, in his appearance in the public realm, others were expected to concur. This once again tells us that in the chiefs' sphere intercourse was based on persuasion instead of coercion. Reaching decisions (judgments) as a chief involved being able to "think in the place of everybody else."

Judgment, Decision, and Beingness of Chiefs

In this section, we intend to examine how the powers exercised by Kalabari chiefs, the notion of judgment and decision making, and the "ontology" of being of chief operate within and extend the notion of politics as capacity to act, openness, and argumentation. By studying them we will gain further insight into the nature and dimension of politics that chieftaincy represented.

JUDGMENT AND DECISION IN THE CHIEFS' SPHERE

Judgment and decision are what is at stake in the chiefs' sphere, the space constituted by many and where men appear to each other in the presence of others. In this sphere of public life and common world, a man's acting and speaking appeal to common sense (*le bon sens*). The thinking process is different from mere reasoning (where a man dialogues with himself), as a person here tries to put himself in the place of everybody else (what Immanuel Kant called "enlarged mentality") in order to reach some agreement with others about what manner of action is to be taken.

This insight dovetails into the deep philosophical meaning of a popular Kalabari proverb: "Ama bebe buru ngeribo buru pakiri," meaning "The whole yam belongs to the town and the individual has only a part." It can also be translated thus: "The community is the whole yam, and the individual is only a part of the yam [community]." The part can only exist because the whole (the *we*) exists in which it is a part, and it is such only through the whole.

Let us try to exegete this aphorism more deeply in the light of this chapter's subject matter. First, the proverb is teaching that the part is properly assessed and understood only in light of the whole to which it belongs. Second, the whole creates the space for the part to appear. Also, the single actor has to make him- or herself understood by the community that acts as the spectators of his or her actions. The community, as the presence of others, validates the actions of the individual. Third, in Kalabari thought, once a person has lost the capability to communicate with the whole, to converse with the known community, he or she has lost the space for the manifestation of even his or her humanity. Communicability is the touchstone of humaneness. This is so important that Kalabari say to speak their language and converse with them is *to be* human. To speak Kalabari is to speak the language of humanity (*tomina-ayi-fie*), and not to speak it is to communicate in nonhuman, subhuman, and animal tongues. Kalabari language is the property of belonging to human community.

Finally, what the eighteenth-century King Amakiri, to whom the proverb is attributed, is believed to have meant is that one should always act as a member of the community, taking one's bearing from the community sense. The part separated from the whole, from the *sensus communis*, is deranged. The community has the *community sense*, and the single individual has the *sensus privatus*. It is community sense that actions and judgments appeal to for validity. If the part were to insist on its acceptance only on its own terms, it would be considered inconsiderate (in its original meaning) and out of the realm of "sound understanding." Without the whole, the part has no way of comparing its judgment to others and knowing its limitations. The community, with the whole yam, the collective reason of the people, can make better judgments, can abstract judgments from private conditions, circumstances, and inclinations that easily beset the individual qua individual. Not that two or more heads are always better, but there is the benefit of *enlarged mentality, general standpoint*.

The import of the philosophical aphorism attributed to Amakiri in light of the current discussion is that it sets out two principles of individuals acting and judging in the community. The individual can be an integral part of the whole when he or she combines her particular interest with that of the general. He or she can do this either by subsuming the particular under the general (universal), or if the general is unknown and the particular given, then he or she is to derive the general from the particular. The movement from the particular to the universal can be done by aiding one's judgment with the virtue of the idea of community present in all its members, the property of being human. It can also be aided by focusing on village heroes, exemplars of goodness who in their particular feats reveal the generality of community life.

Progress of the whole community is the standard according to which all individual actions and events are judged. Any particular action must be related not to itself on its terms but to a larger process or whole in which it may or may not play a part. The whole or the community is designed or at least seen as designed to develop the capabilities of all members. There is the notion of *amatemeso* that can be properly understood in the light of the idea of perpetual progress. *Amatemeso* (in one valid translation) means the destiny or destination of the community. It means that the community fully achieves its destination, that is, the full development of the human capabilities of its members.

Each individual in every generation develops his or her own capabilities but can never fully express and communicate his or her potentialities. It is only the community that can approach this limit—albeit asymptotically since history can never be completed. And thus, the value of each individual existence and progress through life can be revealed only in this perpetual march of the community.

FORMS OF FULLNESS OF BEING

We have stated that the chiefs' sphere is the space of freedom and dignity where fullness of being can be displayed. The Kalabari chief is often a site of answers to ontological questions. Fullness of being or most characteristic form of being is approached from two angles of view. First, a person reaches his or her most characteristic form of being when the person is close to death at old age. It is by approaching mortality, by disappearing from the presence of others, that a man or woman approaches the fullness of being and becomes an authority for others. There is a second concept of fullness of being where being and its fullness coincide with a person's full appearance in the public as a man or woman of capability. The individual has become the subject of his or her own flourishing, faithful to emerging possibilities. The process of emergence always has a *subject*; he is committed to the emerging possibilities and founding of something new, even if it is about enacting a new identity in an unfolding narrative of identities.

The "subject" in Kalabari language is *laabo*. It is the idea of an individual who rises to an occasion, to an event. It is an event that makes or turns an ordinary *tombo* (person, individual) into *laabo*. For instance, when a man is able to rise up to an occasion, an event, and is faithful to the demands of the event (this may involve not calculating interest and benefits), he is even said to have become a man, a real man, in that moment. There is a moment in which a person decides his or her identity. Kalabari will say, "Ori oyibo late," meaning "He has become a *man*." Not that the man was not a male before, but the event to which he faithfully responded has made him a man. He has become a male-man. Similarly, when a woman rises to an occasion, then she has reached womanhood.

Not that Kalabari do not recognize age and biological progress that turn children into adult males or females, but they insist that is the run of ordinary development. It is in the crucible of the extraordinary that true maleness or femaleness emerges. It is only then that the person can be said to have taken his or her personhood seriously, which is *bukebusin*.

In fact, true personhood also emerges from an individual who is subject to an event. When a person is called to rise up to an event, to be faithful to its expected and unexpected demands, the Kalabari will say,

"Tombo tombo so," "Let a person become a person." This practical notion of subjectivation carries the idea that a person becomes what actually he or she is essentially and therefore potentially in the contingency of the moment. Becoming a true person is thus a moral imperative. It is deemed immoral not to do and actualize what one is essentially and potentially capable of doing. Ethics is in a sense internal to the subjectivation process.

The chief in Kalabari represents the fullness of being from both sides. As an old person or approaching old age and in the process of disappearing, he acquires the fullness of being that comes with age. As a subject in the unfolding events of his time, he struggles to make being coincide with appearance. This idea of the chief being a site of two onto-logical contraries or propositions is not unique to the pursuit of fullness of being. The chief in Kalabari wears a gown (*doni*) that combines two opposing numbers in Kalabari numerology. Among this Ijo community, odd numbers in general, and three in particular, are associated with men and strength, while even numbers in general, and four in particular, are associated with women and weakness. The gods and spirits are represented by number seven (three plus four).[34]

The *doni*, a full-length flowing gown with long sleeves worn only by chiefs (always only men), has four stud buttons. Other Kalabari male dresses below the rank of chief have stud buttons ranging from one to three. This combination of three and four on the body of the chief reveals something about the theory of politics we are trying to develop in this chapter. The chief was existentially superior to the male/female, phallo-centric/gynocentric divide. The chief was an embodiment of plurality and freedom. He was a man marked by the number three and wore four studs on his body, which made him seven, the number for gods. The chief's body (as locus of agonistic numerology) was symbolically a site of freedom and of power as cooperative action in concert. The peculiar four buttons also say something about their high status: a larger-than-life and "spiritual" image. The physical representation of spirits in the forms of sculpted masks and dressings of masquerade players are always made to look like hermaphrodites (i.e., the co-representation of both male and female features in the same masquerade). Typical Kalabari masquerade players are strapped with a narrow cone (*igoli*), which projects horizontally backward from the buttocks. This represents a penis. "A large stomach-pad (*furo pomaye*) strapped at the front represents the protruding womb of a pregnant woman. These two projections give the player the characteristic body-shape of water-spirits."[35]

Revealing the "Who" of a Chief

Kalabari have a saying: "Daeregoabo efere finji-a," meaning "Whoever does not introduce himself through his or her ancestors should not begin his or her speech or act in the public realm." The declaration makes it possible for the person to occupy the place of a son or daughter in the public. The "declaration filiates the declarant."[36] This is one of the ways members of the community fight against losing the memory of their ancestors. A refusal to introduce oneself through one's ancestors is a refusal to "stand in" the memory of one's "living dead" in the public realm. It is interpreted as stepping away from one's story, which defines the "who" of the person in Kalabari. One can explain what a person is by pointing to his or her work. What is he? He is an excellent drummer. One can further identify where the drummer comes from by identifying a place of nurturance, his origins. But one cannot know who the drummer is without knowing his family (*house*) and its particular story, without placing his story within the bigger narrative of his people. In Kalabari, the question "I yeri tubo?" ("Who are you?") is not answered by "I am Professor so and so." It is "I am Professor Dagogo, the son of Iju," followed by a short story about Iju's family. The Iju (Ijumangi) mentioned is not usually the immediate biological father but often a storied eponymous ancestor.

One thing is not lost on the person who introduced him- or herself through an ancestor or answered the "who" question by telling a story. As we will learn in chapter 5, legacy is a mode of narrative and narrating; it is both a story and the continuous narration of a story to keep it alive in the ongoing, unfolding narrative of one's people. The striving for legacy is part of the cultural shaping of biographies and social immortality. In the narrative, a man's achievements and deeds in the community are recounted. The narrative is a medium through which those who come after can experience the lives of their ancestors. As the ancestors' names are mentioned it is believed that the "living dead" (the departed whose names and deeds are still remembered by the living) are called into communion with the living.

The aphorism that applies to chiefs as they open their speech acts points to a unique combination of speech and deed undergirded by communicative interaction. An action (*efere finji*, the metaphoric phrase for the public appearance) without speech risks appearing meaningless. It is by speech that a person articulates the meaning of his action, and such action is then coordinated with the actions of them. A speech without action lacks the crucial means to verify the sincerity and veracity of the speaker.

Another point to note is that the action (speech and deed) happens in the presence of others, the presence of a plurality of agents. The action that is enacted—*eferefinji* (the opening of the china) and talking—are not in isolation from others. They are done in the midst of other chiefs who can judge its quality in much the same way as a performer needs an audience to evaluate his or her performance. Without the presence of others who can judge and acknowledge the performance, the actions risk being meaningless. The action is a form of appearing in the public. In such a performance the man is making himself known and soliciting the consent of others so as to reach decisions on matters of collective concerns. In the combination of word and deed amid the plurality of agents (each equal and distinct) is the power of the political community. This power that is only a potential comes to life, is actualized, when the members of the public sphere act in concert. It happens when the chiefs "stand up" together, *alapu saaki te* (to *saaki* is not just to stand up but to rise up as one body, to act in concert for some common purpose). This rising up always presupposes a consensus—*bibi ogbo sua*. With these two, *saaki* (standing) and consensus (*bibi ogbo sua*) in the presence of equals, leadership is realized not by force and hierarchy but by persuasion and argument. Persuasion and argument have the potential to generate communal political power, and such a power is actualized "only where word and deed have not parted company, where words are not empty and deeds not brutal, where words are not used to veil intentions but to disclose realities, and deeds are not used to violate and destroy but to establish relations and create new realities."[37]

In this public appearance—of opening china and making speeches, so to speak—the speech is predominately about telling stories about one's origin and ancestors. In the weaving of a narrative of the actions, performance, and sayings of the ancestors, their own (the living actors, the speechmakers) identities—as rooted in those of their ancestors—become fully manifest. The telling of the ancestors' deeds in front of the living is also to assure the storytellers that when they are gone their own stories will be told. By such narrations the significance and import of the lives of the ancestors (heroes) are conveyed to the storytellers themselves and their audience. It is believed that such retrospective articulations tell the living more about the reasons and qualities that made the ancestors great than any product or object they made or acquired with their hands. The true significance of a subject's deeds and speeches, doings and sayings, lies in remembrance, memory of the living, and being a source of inspiration and instruction for the future.

The Kalabari chief, in manifesting himself in public, makes himself not only one standing in succession of past community leaders and heroes but also one "contemporaneous" with them. In his manifestation he brings together two noncurrent movements of history: namely, his presentness and the historic acts, community-upbuilding endeavors of the past village heroes (including *ama-oru*). And yet in that moment of *bara-saaki* (when he is celebrated and recognized) he mediates the two moments such that the past acts and future endeavors are experienced and taken as seriously as the present. The essence of this Kierkegaardian contemporaneity is not about simultaneity of time; it is a task and a demand that confront the person who has chosen to manifest himself. He is to participate in the heroic lifestyle, and in so participating, he extends it.[38]

Acting and Revelation of "Who" through Masquerades

The philosophy of politics we have described permeates several aspects of Kalabari society, and it appears that it culminates only in the chiefs' sphere. We have already shown that it is discernible in the community's notion of social immortality. Now we want to show that its forms are also visible in one of the most characteristic institutions of the Kalabari: dance and masquerade arts. The Ekine Society (*Sekiapu*) is a public organization open to all adult males in the community. Unlike the *ala-siri* (chiefs' sphere), both chiefs and commoners can be members of this club. Even though it is lower in political importance as a public space, we can see an emphasis on equality and search for individuality (which is different from individualism).

The Ekine Society is a club for the production of art for art's sake. Males are removed from the concerns of house administration and everyday survival and placed in the public space constituted by the club members. Men gather and work in this space only to enjoy arts, in this case, dance. Robin Horton, who wrote about the Ekine Society in the 1960s, highlighted it as a community of equals and a space for the appearance of the "who" of a person. "In *Ekine*, everyone is equal to everyone else. Whatever people say on the path outside, it is not our business who owns whom, or whose father is greater than whose. We are here for the laughing, drinking, and for the play."[39] Individuals go beyond just this absence of comparison and grading of status that is paramount in the houses (*wari*) and social spaces constituted by them (the houses) to use masquerade for the enhancement of their individuality, individual distinctness, and uniqueness. "[A] man's special masquerade is not only a symbol of this individuality in this life; it is also a means toward posthumous survival in the community that gave him birth."[40] Horton argues that the Kalabari way of judging the worth of a person is "an absolute and uncompromising type." Either a person is a "man," or he is not, and this sets up the need for people who have no status or have not distinguished themselves to use dance skills to reveal their "who."

> In this taxing situation [that is the hierarchy system of a person's worth] the particular masquerade which a person has chosen to adopt assumes a specially weighty significance. Skill in its performance is not just something which compensates to some extent for lack of political influence in the community—though it may do so. It is something much more. For various masquerades played by any *Ekine* society are by and large incommensurable with one another: they are different. Hence, by deciding to specialize in a particular masquerade, a man both makes a free choice and at the same time involves himself in an activity that is not fully comparable with the activities of others. This element of non-comparability looms very large where, in other things, the individual's sense of worth is almost totally vulnerable to a relentless measure based on his influence or lack of it. In such circumstances, the adoption of a special masquerade becomes almost a guarantee of the individual's sense of secure identity.[41]

Among the masquerades played by the Ekine Society, there is one that holds a special place in the hearts of Kalabari. This is the *Igbo* masquerade, which epitomizes recklessness and nonchalance in the face of trials and the unknown yet will come out a winner. Kalabari say *Igbo* is the "bending mangrove that always seems about to fall but never does." It holds a unique and popular place in Kalabari esteem. The character of this masquerade is believed to reveal something about their national character and the *aristocratic ideal* both commoners and chiefs aspire to attain. *Igbo* shows how a man can reveal the "who" of his actions and initiate something new in ways that are compatible with the national character. *Igbo* shows that a man who is accumulating a large surplus of wealth, exercising general influence over other men and women, and enjoying a great deal of leisure should appear to have pulled all of this off with carefree nonchalance. He must appear "cool" and unfazed by what he has achieved, especially in the face of trials.

A man acting in the chiefs' sphere must do so with a high degree of aristocratic ideal, with certain panache. A person imbued with the Kalabari aristocratic ideal is to carry out his most important achievements with extreme nonchalance; he is to always live with style and grace and must *know* himself, mastering restraint and self-control (*buu nimi*).[42] As part of this self-control and act of exercising ultimate control over one's life and its circumstances, a person is expected to stoically hold his nose to cut off his or her life instead of suffering indignity. As the Kalabari say, "Buruba gote tombo olo meni bia"—"A person should not eat his phlegm because of famine."

These qualities of the Kalabari spirit are manifested or displayed by the *Igbo* masquerade dance. The *Igbo* masker performs virtuously in dance the principle of freedom that is the Kalabari spirit. *Igbo* displays a kind of recklessness that shows that actions are not guided by intellect or dictated by the will. It seems unshackled from motive and aim. The *Igbo* spirit and idea capture the essential Arendtian meaning of actions. As Arendt argues:

> Action, to be free, must be free from motive on one side, from its intended goal as a predictable effect on the other. This is not to say that motives and aims are not important factors in every single act, but they are its determining factors, and action is free to the extent that it is able to transcend them. Action insofar as it is determined is guided by a future aim whose desirability the intellect has grasped before the will wills it, whereby the intellect calls upon the will, since only the will dictate action.[43]

A Kalabari chief responds excellently to all that chance throws at him without appearing fazed. He strives to be his best and all that he can be while bluffing his way through life. His response to the challenges of life and the test of his social standing springs not from necessity, constraint, or fear but from the sheer sense of freedom. And to act, to respond to chance, fate, in this way is to be free.

Concluding Remarks

In this chapter I have shown how Kalabari live in and perpetuate lifemaking by exercising freedom, the capacity to initiate something new. We carefully examined how freedom is embodied in persons and institutions and how their political philosophy is geared to the idea of starting something new amid ongoing social processes. The Kalabari story has demonstrated to us one of the possible myriad ways actual societies orient themselves to lifemaking. We clearly saw how ethics is internal to the orientation.

In particular, our investigation of Kalabari chieftaincy revealed the fine-tuned interactions of politics, ethos, and the freedom to initiate the new in the polity. The chiefs are the paradigmatic actors who inaugurate new openings in the time gap between the past and the future to declare their individual distinctiveness in the public space. The existence and functioning of the chiefs' sphere demonstrate how the Kalabari social system strategically allows the initiation of the new into its ordered *nomos*. Our next task is to investigate how Kalabari people create and manage an ethical system that harnesses legacies of deeds of both chiefs and non-chiefs to make lifemaking into the highest good. This will be an elaboration of the notion of social immortality, which I have already mentioned in this chapter.

Chapter 5 investigates how the drive to leave a legacy in the community, the drive to live in the memory of future generations, and other forms of social immortality interact, affect, and shape social ethics in Kalabari. The drive to leave a legacy shows one of the ways citizens attempt to contribute most fully to the work of lifemaking. The study of legacy in the next chapter will be primarily undertaken in the context of the pragmatic and existential concerns of living in a society where religion is integral to culture and in light of a worldview and philosophy grounded in an indigenous religious thought system.

Chapter 5

Sediments of Life

On *Poiesis* of Social Immortality

Introduction

The appeal of legacy as a pathway to social immortality has been long recognized by Kalabari communities, and they have used it to undergird social
ethics. From the hard-bitten merchants of the eighteenth and nineteenth
centuries to the professionals of today, the desire to avoid "bad death"
is strong. Among other factors, a person who does not have the halo of
glory over his or her spirit as cast by good deeds, moral uprightness, and
appreciative close relatives has not died well. He or she would not live in
the memory of future generations. The concern with social immortality
interacts with the absence in the traditional religion of a doctrine of
immortality of soul through an afterlife and with the structural pressures
generated by the canoe house system.[1]

This chapter investigates how the drive[2] to leave a legacy in the
community, the drive to live in the memory of future generations, and
other forms of social immortality interact, affect, and shape social ethics
in Kalabari. This study will be primarily undertaken in the context of the
pragmatic and existential concerns of living in a society where religion is
integral to culture and in light of a worldview and philosophy grounded
in a traditional religious thought system. This chapter will also show how
the encounter between the traditional religion and Christianity has affected
the connection between the quest for legacy and social ethics.

In this opening section of the chapter, it is germane to clarify certain issues, especially the place of memory in this study. The connection between drive for legacy and ethics, which I am investigating in this chapter, is not the same as that between memory and ethics. While memory and ethics are about how the past, the remembered past, affects conduct of relations, behavior, and attitude, the drive for legacy and ethics is about how the future (basically a certain kind of hope) affects the conduct of human behavior. This is not to say legacy and memory do not cut into each other. On one hand, the use of memory may be directed toward the future. The remembered past can be useful in planning for the future. On the other, the person driving for legacy is hoping that their legacy will become memory enough after their death so that a tradition of loyalty to their name (work) could be built and sustained. This is not the only issue. Second, the pursuer of legacy needs memory to keep track of their achievements before even they die and also to follow through on their drive. Third, both the drive for legacy and memory can adhere only in a community where *sense* and *sensibility* reign. Neither the quest for legacy nor memory is about only the events and the people that enacted them (*the sense*); both are also about what emotions should appertain to them as they are recollected, what kind of participatory perception of the events of the deceased person's effort are appropriate (*the sensibility*). It is because of these entanglements that this chapter may weave in and out of the discourse on memory and ethics as we attempt to decipher the sundry ways the drive for legacy shapes social ethics in Kalabari. Nonetheless, we will try as much as possible to keep the focus on the connection between the drive for legacy and social ethics—that is, how attitude toward leaving traces after death informs and undergirds ethical conduct.

The first section of this chapter will explore the general role of the drive for legacy in society. The next section provides background information on Kalabari: its history, religion, and notions of "bad" and "good" death. The study moves on to examine the grounding of social ethics, showing that ethics is grounded in *thick* relations. The discussion in this section is important because the drive for legacy, securing of a social form of immortality, is ultimately a relation-maintenance mechanism in Kalabari. Then I will analyze the interaction between the drive for legacy and social ethics in Kalabari society. Driving for legacy is a kind of searching for a name that will not drop down into oblivion by sharing life with others. The chapter will then examine the case of erasure of legacies. When a Kalabari chief is killed in a war there is symbolic expulsion of the chief's name and his war-canoe house from the society, erasing his name and his house from the community. The Kalabari will take measures to act as if the traumatic event of the chief's violent death never happened. Summary and concluding remarks bring the study to a close.

In general, I argue that the drive for legacy has become for the Kalabari person a paradigm of transcendence, a means and hope of going over the limitations of day-to-day existence. Insofar as there is a future for those who had gone, in the sense that they shall live in the memory of future generations, the present generation gains courage for the future. Because of this magnificent hope for transcending death and transience, their other mundane hopes for a better tomorrow for themselves and their families gain strength, and they do not easily fall victims to despair and cynicism. In this way, the future blows its wind, its breath, its *energia* into the present so that the dry bones of today can live.

The General Role of the Drive for Legacy in Society

The drive for legacy is one of the primary motivating forces in human beings, but it is not usually regarded as a potent force for shaping social ethics and social creativeness. The few that pay attention to it treat it as secondary or tertiary, not worthy of first-class treatment. But even a cursory examination of all human societies, from the traditional to the sophisticated, from ancient to modern times, will reveal that it is common to all persons, influencing their energies and intellect.

One can dare to say that drive for legacy has the same power as the overrated sex drive. In a particular sense, the sex drive is subordinated to it. Legacy drive is the human search for immortality, a bold attempt to mock death, and a calculated venture to live in the Now. Perhaps ever since humans first walked on the face of the earth, they have sought ways of perpetuating themselves, reproducing their ideas, and passing on their genes. In the preindustrial societies, men and women achieved immortality, kept their names in the consciousness of society, by rearing children. Ask the African village woman why she wants children, and she would not hesitate to mention lineage continuity, the perpetuation of her name or family name. One thus sees the sex drive of humans, which has received more scholarly attention, as serving the purpose of the legacy drive. The attempt of a man to pass his genes to the next generation, to keep forever his "person" in the gene pool of society, may be interpreted as only a biological mechanism to achieve the social function of ensuring the sustenance of his "name position" in the social interstices that constitute society.

Men and women everywhere do not like to be forgotten or neglected by their children, spouses, relations, friends, or society.[3] Human beings are, by nature, social animals and want to participate in the web of social relationships directly in the present life and, if possible, by proxy in the afterlife. The need to be recognized in the Now often overrides the extra utility of increment in financial assets and even raising a family. Behavioral experts have long known that workers can be motivated to reach lofty standards by giving them due recognition and by acknowledging their worth instead of just increasing pay. Stories abound of persons who have abandoned raising families to pursue their own more restricted goals. People go to extraordinary lengths to put their names in the *Guinness Book of World Records*. The recognition the man or woman is looking for today is only part of the series of tangible and intangible memorials that would ensure that in the long run he or she is not forgotten.[4]

In terms of the drive for legacy, persons in modern societies of luxury like the United States are not really different from the nineteenth-century African farmer barely eking out a living from the recalcitrant earth. The difference that exists between them is not in terms of the presence or absence of the drive but in the forms of its expression. The modern person goes about the business of ensuring his name in ways beyond biological reproduction. The nineteenth-century man expresses his legacy motivation by siring many children. This way some would survive to carry on the family name. Having many offspring is one of the ways he knows best to beat death and the associated forgetfulness of society. Occasionally, he might have aimed to accomplish a rare feat so that the memory of his deeds would become part of the corpus of his society's oral history. But he did not really trust this way of going about the business of perpetuating his name. He knew his fellow men were fickle, and he did not have a corner on achievement. There would be men with greater achievements, and his would pale in significance. He expected that with time the memory of his deeds would fade and so would his name—and then comes his real death. His best option, he figured, was to secure his genes in the society gene pool.

Something happened to the traditional idea of legacy as writing developed and economies got sophisticated.[5] Writing, which provides society with a better and more permanent means of preserving its culture and the records of achievements, altered thinking on creation and sustenance of legacy. Humans discovered that they did not have to rely on biological reproduction or human memory to perpetuate their names. If only they could accomplish worthwhile ventures, their achievements would forever be recorded in history, and persons coming after them would read about them. The story of society will become her-story or his-story, and history becomes her-story or his-story. Today, I do not know the children of Alexander the Great, Abraham Lincoln, Winston Churchill, Nnamdi Azikiwe, Booker T. Washington, and Sojourner Truth, but I know their achievements, and each one of them is more real to me than some of their descendants who may be my contemporaries. Memory engendered and sustained by writing has carried their names over the chasm of time to me.

Modern men and women also discerned that their ideas and wisdom can be passed on to generations after them and made to survive in society's pool of ideas if they recorded them themselves. Chinua Achebe, John P. Clark-Bekederemo, Jane Austen, Virginia Woolf, Plato, Aristotle, Karl Marx, and John Maynard Keynes are discussed more often in societies all over the world than some past local heroes who sired hundreds of children. Modern men and women have used various means, ranging from sports to unimaginable ways, to achieve a place in history. Mohammed Ali is there in the annals of history because of his boxing prowess and excellence.

We cannot exhaust the ways modern men and women create and sustain memories—the politics of memory. Many a woman drives to build first-class corporations that will outlive her. Modern man has toiled to invent things, burned the midnight oil, climbed treacherous mountains, traversed dangerous rivers, and stared down lions and bears to attain heights other men have not reached in order to earn the recognition that will put his name in history books. A modern woman with wealth has heavily contributed to public causes to earn a monument in her name in the public park. Many priests will tell you that a promise to engrave names on the walls of worship centers raises contributions to building funds faster than the world's most powerful sermon. All these examples suggest that humans, trapped in the ceaseless flow of time, helplessly caught in change and decay, resentful of another person's incredible capacity to forget their good deeds and feelings of insignificance in the vast universe, are looking for ways to achieve some permanence, some recognition, and to hold time, as it were, in the *Now*.

The question is: How do communities harness this powerful drive to shape the social ethics of lifemaking? The drive for legacy combines memory with ethical impulses. It is also a mode of narrative that shapes identity. Drive for legacy affects ethics because people in Kalabari communities are willing to have their lives shaped by the quest. The task ahead is to precisely show how this is done. We will begin by understanding the nature of their society. A small portion of the discussion in the next section may appear repetitious as I retrieve some salient ideas discussed earlier. I have to circle around ideas, reiterate facts and concepts, to progress to a better understanding of the Kalabari materials and to carry the reader along as I go into a better and deeper articulation of earlier materials in light of the new task (delineating the connection between social immortality, ethics, and lifemaking) before us. It was theologian and philosopher Robert Neville who once wrote:

> Good style is sometimes thought to consist in a clear treatment of one topic that leads to the treatment of the adjacent topic and so to build an edifice with block of analysis. This style makes it possible for a reader to turn to a specific chapter or section to ascertain the book's position on its topic. But better style has to acknowledge that, because of the plurality of approaches and angles of inquiry, no consistently written chapter can be more than a partial statement. Better style returns to the material again and again, treating it from one perspective and then the next, revising early statements in light of the latter, like a complex musical composition. Plato in the cumulative dialogues had a better style, more realistic to genuine thinking, than Aristotle in the little definitional essays.[6]

Society: Religion and Organization

The Kalabari live in the Eastern Niger Delta area of Southern Nigeria. They are noted as great entrepreneurs in the precolonial era and became mainly civil servants and professionals in colonial and post-independence Nigeria. Amaury Talbot, the British colonial administrator and anthropologist, remarked that "they are people of great interest and intelligence, hard-headed, keen-witted, and born traders."[7] These businesspeople and professionals have evolved a religious system that is very "theoretical" in orientation. For Kalabari, explanation, as noted by many scholars including Robin Horton, is based on the use of the idea of unobservable underlying reality of gods to make sense of the contingencies of everyday existence. The vast diversity of everyday experience is interpreted in terms of a scheme of three forces: ancestors, founding or village heroes, and water-spirits.[8] (Could there be a fourth category or only a variation of one the three?[9])

There are two main epistemological categories in the Kalabari world-view. *Oju* (body) represents material objects. *Teme* (spirit) is the other and represents the immaterial realm. The three categories of spirits or gods are defined with respect to different combinations of the attributes of spirits and bodies. Spirits are defined as incapable of direct observations but by reference to their effects. Unlike bodies, they can be in multiple places at the same time—they are anywhere and everywhere. There are ancestors (*duein*), village heroes (*oru*), and water-spirits (*owuamapu*). Ancestors and village heroes exist only in the spirit realm, but water-people are believed to have both bodies and spirits and live in definite localities.

The water-spirits (*owuamapu*) are the forces behind cultural innovations and social creativeness. They enable individuals to acquire abnormal skills, power, or wealth. They are the forces an individual could summon or collaborate with to pursue individualistic dreams or temporarily deviate from social norms or common standards so as to reach superhuman heights. They are the source of the creative impulse of society and hence vital to all persons interested in the drive for significance.

Ancestors (only those who had "good death" make it to this stage)[10] are part of the Kalabari life cycle because it is deemed that life does not end with physical death but continues in another form in the next world. "The idea of survival after death is essential to the theoretical model which Kalabari use to cope with the vicissitudes of everyday life. The ancestors underpin the strength of the lineages, and punish those who contravene lineage norms. They and their actions account for many of the fortunes and misfortunes both of the lineage and of their individual members."[11]

These three forces and God have varying relations with the observable world. God, the Supreme Being, known as *Teme-órú*, is at a different level and before the advent of Christianity was not an object of direct worship or daily concern. God and the tripartite forces are the source and sustainer of life. While God oversees the universe, the whole of creation, or the macrocosm, the powers beneath her (him, after Christianity arrived) look after the microcosm. God and the three forces constitute the realm of the spirit, a crucial arm of the cosmological order. The Kalabari community, like most African societies, is composed of five levels of interdependent relationships situated within a cosmological order consisting of the realms of spirits, nature, tribal or ethnic community, the family, and the individual.[12] A crucial goal of life is for the community to be in "harmony and equilibrium" with respect to all these related and overlapping dimensions.

For over four hundred years, from the fifteenth to the twentieth centuries, the Kalabari were among the pivotal merchant groups in transatlantic trade along the West Coast of Africa. Critical to their success in the transatlantic trade was the house (*wari*) system and competitiveness within the traditional society. The *wari* was the most characteristic political and social institution of the Eastern Niger Delta states in the eighteenth and nineteenth centuries. The *wari* was made up of a man and his household, extended family members, trading assistants, adoptees, and servants. Because of the need to maintain adequate labor supply for their burgeoning trade and because of the definition of wealth as the number of persons in the *wari*, leaders of the canoe houses absorbed a great number of non-Kalabari into their houses.

The society was also very competitive and fluid. For instance, a leader of a house only held his position (except for two women, only men have been elected chiefs[13]) as long as he was successful in his business endeavors. If he were to stumble or fall, leadership was taken from him and given to any member (native-born or nonnative-born) whose character, commercial ability, and wealth most suited the furtherance of the fortune of the house.[14]

The mobilizing and orientating impulse for the men-controlled prodigious merchant business and culture in the eighteenth and nineteenth centuries can be discerned in two symbols of hope for the future. First, the expectation of any trader, whether native-born or adoptee, was that he could rise to full citizenship and leadership with the accumulation of personal achievements, not by ascriptive distinctions. Second, there was an expectation that if his achievements were to further advance his ward, house, or community, his name would not be cut off among the living. He could see a future for himself when he was gone. In this interpretative framework for human activities and actions, the past no longer dominates the present.

In this competitive and entrepreneurial environment, the primary religious question that dominates thinking is not "Whence?" or "Where one is to reside in eternity?" but "What can I hope for?" It is only in the future, when one is living in the memory of future generations, that one has truly transcended the limits of human existence and political powers. It is this concern for the future that gives meaning to human acts and achievements, the necessary perseverance that births progress and lifemaking. Kalabari say, "I bobiri saki ibite ke I dede saki nengi," meaning "Let the evening of my life be better than the morning of my life." Basically, "All's well that ends well."

This hope for the future is at "its heart a hope for resurrection." Resurrection is not about bringing of dead persons to life in this world or in the one to come. But it is still a raising of the dead, a kind of raising by which the living encounter their past, their histories, and their past moments of solidarity that had kept the harmony in the community. It is only in remembrance, the bringing to mind of things past, that the hope for the future of those striving for legacy, excellence, can be realized. As Jürgen Moltmann put it, "Only the person who remembers can look this future in the face, the future called 'the raising of the dead.' And only the person who looks into this future is able really to remember those who have gone, and to live in the presence."[15] It all seems that the quest for legacy is a certain disposition to hope.

What is the ground of this hope? What reasons does one who hopes and strives for legacy give as the basis of his or her hope? Without a ground, hope becomes illusion, false hope, or wishful thinking.[16] The ground of hope does not lie in the subject who hopes but outside of him or her. The Kalabari person's confidence is derived from the self-sufficiency of the living relatives to realize his hope; the ground of hope is immanent to human relationality. This, however, could be completely misplaced, lacking in any basis, if there is no proportionality between the ground of hope and the object of hope (living in the memory of future relatives). For the ground of hope to be relevant or proportionate to the object of hope there has to be caring and active maintenance of harmony in one's social relationships insofar as one is alive. It is the knowledge of past instances of caring, the participatory experience of relationality in the community, and the *horizons* of constitution of the experience that give good reason to believe that the vision of remembrance will be realized. I turn now to the place of relations in ethics and lifemaking in Kalabari.

Grounding of Ethics

Kalabari say, "Daeregoabo efere finji-a" ("Whoever does not introduce him or herself through his or her ancestors should not begin his or her speech or act in the public realm"). This is one of the ways members of the community fight against forgetting the memory of their ancestors. In the society under study, to forget one's ancestors is to abandon the virtue of piety (*kpain ma*). Piety is understood as the deference and fitting response to, and virtuous acknowledgment of, dependence on the community's social structures, the sources of the community's existence and progress through life.[17] A refusal to introduce oneself through one's ancestors, that is, a refusal to "stand in" the memory of one's "living dead" in the public realm, is interpreted as stepping away from one's story, which defines the "who" of the person in Kalabari. To answer the question "I yeri tubo?" ("Who are you?") a person must place his story within the bigger narrative of his family (house, *wari*).

One thing is not lost on the person who introduces him- or herself through an ancestor or who answered the "who" question by telling a story. Legacy is a mode of narrative and narrating; it is both a story and the continuous narration of a story to keep it alive in the ongoing, unfolding narrative of one's people. The striving for legacy is part of the cultural shaping of biographies.[18] Persons order their legacies on the pattern of the structure that prevails in the relationships of their communities. Achievements are classified and reclassified into cultural constituted categories whose valuation and identity mirror what prevails in the social world of people. The narrative is not a mere story but a plot that is a coherent story told with causal sequences and motivations in order to form a literal picture of life. The narrative is a medium through which those who come after can experience the lives of their ancestors. As the ancestors' names are mentioned, it is believed that the "living dead" are called into communion with the living. Kalabari say the gods or "spirits stay and come in their names."[19] The name enjoys some intimate link with the ancestor it represents, and "as to the nature of this link between sign and referent, Kalabari do not speculate. It is something almost implicit in the meaning of 'name.' "[20]

This dependence of the "living dead" on the living to keep them "alive" is one of the paradoxical aspects of the traditional religion. While piety points to the recognition by the living that the source and substance of their well-being is partly anchored to the ancestors, memory is the dependence of the dead on the living. In fact, memory is recognition of the other, the dead who are vulnerable. Yes, in Kalabari both gods (spirits and ancestors) and humans are mutually vulnerable. It is believed that spirits and gods do not have intrinsic powers of their own such that the withdrawal of worship from or worshipful dependence on a god deprives it of power and authority to act on humans or control human activities. Kalabari insist that a god that is not worshipped loses its power.[21] So if a god becomes too furious or demanding, they will tell it from which tree it was carved ("Agu nsi owi baka kuma en k'o kara sin en dugo o piriba"[22]). This means that a community can unanimously annul the power of a god by refusing it worship.[23]

Thus, mutual dependence, this recognition of one another (gods and humans) as jointly vulnerable, engenders the ethical impulse of compassion. Compassion (*okuru kuru isibi ba*, literally "painful emotions that overcome one's head") is the movement toward the other as one looks into the face of the other and participates in his vulnerability and actively remembers the vulnerability of the other. It is also a movement that acknowledges that one may face similar possibilities and vulnerabilities in the future. The living family members do not hide their faces from the dead but hear their cry, and the ancestors also heed the voices of the living. A neglected ancestor is usually reported by local seers as crying and walking lonely in the spirit world and needs due recognition from the living in order to overcome isolation and occupy its proper place. Such neglect (poor eudaemonistic judgment) by the living can also be source of ruin to them.

Social ethics is anchored in relations rather than properties of the individual. Kalabari social ethics is based on *thick relations*—relations to the near and dear that are suffused with shared past or memory. Thick relations refer to persons with whom we have dense, enduring, and meaningful relations.[24] The required introduction in the public square, which *author-izes* a speech act, is couched in "I Mister Daketima, being the son of . . ." not "being rich or rational." The use of multiplace predicates ("being son of") rather than a one-place predicate gives a clue to Kalabari understanding of ethics as grounded in relations, not properties of autonomous individuals.[25] The instant that a living person introduces him- or herself in the public forum is a moment of invocation of family, lineage memory, and an affirmation of being one with the lineage and its shared memories. It is a pious display of the relationships that define a person qua person.

The use of multiplace predicates not only indicates anchoring of ethics and morality on personal relations but also points to a hesitancy on "making each person an autonomous human being. Autonomy is characterized by properties rather than relations."[26] For Kalabari the community and its shared experience are constitutive of the individual self-definition. The social milieu is not only what an individual has or possesses but also what the individual is; it is constituent of his or her identity and character. The community is the most important reality for the individual, and he or she cannot exist or realize his or her full humanity without participation in it. As John Mbiti puts it, "To be human is to belong to the whole community."[27] The drive for legacy importantly links the entire Kalabari moral system to community well-being. The link is part of the ethical self-formation and a ground of people's experience of themselves as virtuous citizens. The drive for legacy, which in a sense is a deliberate way of confronting and accepting mortality, is far more than a social fact. It shapes and molds social consciousness.

How the Drive for Legacy Shapes Ethical Behavior

In this section of the chapter, I will examine how the quest for legacy shapes social ethics in Kalabari society using two related steps: first, investigate the cultural forces behind the drive for legacy in Kalabari; second, present how the drive for legacy affects social behavior.

WHY KALABARI BOTHER WITH LEGACY?

The Kalabari person is concerned with legacy not because he or she wants to gain personal glory or desires to be "worshipped" as an ancestor. It is not egoism. The legacy quest is a fight against the threat of *nonbeing*; it is a form of courage to be in spite of nonbeing.[28] The man or woman who has died, as I have explained above, continues life in another world, that of the spirit realm. Physical death is not thought to bring an end to being.[29] It is believed in Kalabari that the spirit of the dead continues in some kind of existence, *beingness*, albeit not physical. The spirits of the dead finally reach nonbeing when they become the *nameless dead*.[30] Depending on their achievements while on physical earth and the support of living relatives who immortalize them in memory, ancestors, the *living dead*, can go on for a long time. But once the ancestors' names (collectively reenacted names) are "lost" among the living—that is, "the means by which they could be immortalized" becomes defunct—they are presumed to have reached the "stage of total dis-incorporation."[31] They have become *decommunalized* and succumbed to nonbeing or second death. I interpret the drive for legacy as a vigorous attempt to avoid decommunalization in the spirit realm and therefore avoid the suffering of a second death.

The second reason the quest for legacy is important is that there is no doctrine of immortality of the soul in Kalabari traditional religion—that is, no theory of being reconstituted as body and soul in some afterlife realm (heaven). So what really gives the assurance that the person at death is not everlastingly lost as a vapor? The drive for legacy is therefore a cry for social immortality, for the survival of a person's "essence," which is carried in his name. The threat of the blotting out of a deceased person's name among the living engenders a terrible fear of utter oblivion. So no one wants to die without leaving a trace.

Third, the concern with legacy is also a concern with life. For the Kalabari, life (of the individual and the community is seen as interdependent) is the highest good. Physical life is where the past and future meet in the cycle of collective "eternal life" (or shall we say existential eternal life?). The child is born, receives life, actualizes his or her destiny, and works out his or her fate. It is also in the life of here and now that the adult prepares for their place in the next, for the rank of the honorably departed. So life may be miserable, hard, and painful, but it is still life and without it there would be no community and no preparation for the next world. It is life in the land of the living that sustains life in the hereafter. Only by living in the memory of those alive do the ancestors avoid the decommunalization that effectively "evaporates" their beingness. A person must make the best use of their time by advancing and contributing to the overall quality of life in order to leave a mark for the future life of the community. A person must strive for significance in their community.

The drive for legacy is like driving a car into the future and making use of the rearview mirror from time to time. More appropriately, the drive for legacy is like steering a canoe with virtuoso piloting skills. An excellent Kalabari steersman can maneuver his vessel to go forward with his face looking forward, but he can put the same boat in reverse without turning his face or the boat around, doing his magic with deft handling of his paddle in the water (*tata kri ta juein doku*). The drive for legacy is like looking forward into the horizon of life's course yet steering one's canoe into a nice berth in the stream of a remembered past. The preferred berth is the stuff identities are made up of. If the remembered past helps to give a people their identity, then legacy is creating the content of memory and thus ultimately of identity. Kalabari is a society where people care a lot about their identity and public image. Kalabari people like to always project a certain aristocratic image or pursue a certain aristocratic ideal.[32] This ideal partly has to do with their involvement in external trade—both internal long-distance trade and transatlantic trade. Living as intermediaries between Europeans on the coast and Africans in the hinterland and being among the first groups of Africans on the West Coast to acquire European manufactured goods and technology, they developed a certain "attitude," a kind of a complexity and mystique as part of their trading, political, and military domineering strategy.

Also, as part of maintaining their image or leaving a legacy, Kalabari men and women work to have certain valuable clothes named in their honor while they are still alive. For instance, Kalabari will import Madras cotton cloth from India (something they have done for centuries, first via the Portuguese and later directly) and reinterpret and give them names of prominent personalities as a way of ingesting them into their culture. Sometimes, as part of creating a distinctively Kalabari image for these Madras, they lift and cut the threads or lift certain weft threads with needles and pull them out to create patterns and designs drawn from their environment.[33] Some of them directly negotiated with Indian manufacturers to design special patterns for them.

Finally, the drive for legacy is an effort by the individual, the hard-bitten businessperson, noted for their "almost ruthless respect for wealth and power," to be creative factors in the progress, improvement, and the well-being of their communities. Kalabari men and women in pursuit of projects to develop their communities say "Iyama ibi, ibuu kunu," meaning "Let my town prosper so that I will exude fragrance." A good person promotes the well-being of the community and in so doing etches his or her name into the community's memory.

Now that we have identified the forces behind the drive for legacy, let us investigate how that legacy shapes social ethics.

How Social Immortality Shapes Social Ethics

The living or dying woman expects her people to remember her because she has had thick relations with them. Thick personal relations are qualitative relations of caring, loyalty, and intensity. The kind of thick relations that survive death require a person to comport herself in a way that does not fracture lineage morality. Thick relations demand that she builds the kind of relations that will have an impact on the lives of her relatives. The fear of being forgotten is not just fear of falling into utter oblivion or decommunalization after death, but, according to Avishai Margalit, "it is what it says about relationships now. It is the fear of not amounting to much in our present relations with others."[34] This fear encourages good behavior and caring for persons in the community even at great personal cost. Life is judged by how it is remembered rather than the way it was experienced.

The achievements of the man or woman who does not become an ancestor will not be remembered. Therefore, in addition to garnering achievements and building and maintaining thick relations, a person needs to adhere to the standards of the whole community, which define who qualifies to be an ancestor. For instance, death by drowning automatically disqualifies a person from becoming an ancestor. The Kalabari inhabit a riverine environ, and acquiring the skill of swimming is paramount to survival in such an environment. So a person who does not know how to swim is seen as someone who has not mastered the vital aspects of their physical—and therefore cultural—environment. Failure to swim is taken as a bad case of inadequate socialization. Those who are not properly socialized are not expected to be good ancestors in the next world, which is only a replica of the earthly social world.

Family size is another area where the drive for legacy affects ethics. Since people carry the memory of the dead, especially in an oral society, one has to have many descendants who can carry one's name into the future. It is not just about having children but raising them to be respectable, virtuous persons in society. What good is a tale told by idiots? There is a Kalabari aphorism that says "the eye" had seven children and just looked at them until they became nonentities, lacking the necessary virtues, but "the mouth" had one child and talked it into a great virtuous person. Caring for one's children and directing them aright is integral to the drive for legacy.

A man or woman's name can also live through material achievements and skill development. There are men and women who were such good dancers that their names are mentioned decades after their death. The originators of certain proverbs and aphorisms are still credited to this day. For instance, it is still acknowledged that King Amakiri I, in the eighteenth century, purportedly formulated this proverb: "Ama bebe buru ngeribo buru pakiri," meaning "The whole yam belongs to the town and the individual has only a part."[35]

The fifth way the drive for legacy shapes social ethics is its impact on the concept of future. The quest for legacy is an expression of hope of continuity—a belief about future itself. It expresses the hope that in the future, when the living person is gone, the community will listen to the story of his or her life. This belief in the possibility of the community is the courage to say yes, to affirm life, to overcome threats to one's well-being and that of the community. As such, it is heroic. This is heroism ensconced in hope in such a way that it engenders deeds that can live in the memory of future generations.

The drive for legacy is not merely a wish to live in the memory of future generations, but it is also about working for future generations, enriching one's descendants in the same way that the present generation has been enriched by the labor of past men and women. There is a saying in Kalabari: "Furo te awome lolo te ke ina iyin-apu nengi-a wari ane faari wari," meaning "In a family where the children are not better than the parents, that is a family in decline." This is one of the ways they express the doctrine of progress, an essential article of faith in the traditional religion and in their entrepreneurial culture. They think of progress in terms of the gradual improvement in the fortunes of their descendants (*wari*).

The drive for legacy inspires men and women to do great works and noble actions. Young men and women are encouraged to model themselves on village heroes, emulating their virtues. We have earlier indicated that there are three main categories of gods (not including the Supreme Being) in Kalabari. The category called *amŏru*, village heroes or hero gods, consists of persons of extraordinary achievements and commitment to community well-being, founding communal institutions, who were deified after their "disappearance" without leaving any descendants (heroes do not die; they just vanish without trace of descendants but with indelible marks of achievement).[36] In the last couple of centuries, no human being has been deified, but the stories of persons who achieved that status (a level beyond that of ancestors) or reached the ideals they embodied are still trumpeted as models for young persons to emulate. The models are not pristine or unchangeable; they are usually emended, adapted, and adjusted to suit present purposes. The elders' stories, molded for the young ones to serve as their models, often involve playing a pack of tricks on the dead, as Voltaire would say. All use of legacy is consciously subjective "since every age is bound, in spite of itself, to make the dead perform whatever tricks it finds necessary for its own peace of mind."[37]

Legacy and Its Political Erasure

There is an opposite of legacy: the erasure of the person, symbolically expunging a chief and his war-canoe house from society, from memory.

This happens when a chief dies in war. The erasure means his chieftaincy stool will be dissolved as if it were never created; it is never to be raised again, and the members of his house will be absorbed into another house or houses, losing their independent corporate existence. The memory of their disgraced chief is cleansed from any glorious oral history and condemned to obscurity, oblivion, or ignominy.[38] His existence is never denied but is symbolically denuded. This process of becoming nothing is a mirror image of the successful entrepreneur becoming a chief discussed in chapter 4. The symbolic order that produced him as a glorious person has now turned him into a "naked life," a mere pre-political substrate, or a void. This is an outworking of a certain imaginative political logic of sovereignty. Kings and his chiefs in Kalabari have no mystical, unliving remainder of their physical bodies that continues on their thrones or seats as "kingly body politic" that can even fill the void or compensate for their finitude when they die. It is only the remembrance of their legacies that survives their finitude. A chief who dies in a disgraceful way loses even this bit of recognition. He truly enters a void.

Is this act of political erasure not tantamount to saying that the bullet (sword, cannonball) that killed a chief killed no one? A chief did not die because no chieftaincy in his name or a house he led existed. His disgraceful death proved that his stool had always been empty; when the lethal weapon fell on him it killed no chief. The past is retroactively changed to hide or fit the exigencies of the present. This, as I have already noted above, is part of the imaginative logic of sovereignty. Leaders that die in war are killed without transcendental remainder, no claim to some immortal, sacred, and inviolable flesh that hovers above the people. Their sovereignty was contracted to them by the people, and they were regarded as fellow citizens. (We saw in chapter 2 how Amakiri emerged as a king through a contract with the people.) The chiefs as war-canoe commanders were living martyrs who were always already dead before death was declared, and a dead chief's political glorification (ceremonial and liturgical lordship) was retroactively swept away as if he were never a chief. Nothing of a disgraced dead chief's body survives his finitude. Both of what Giorgio Agamben named as power and glory (economy and glory) of sovereignty are erased: the dissolution of the *wari* takes aim at power as government and effective management. The damnation of the memory of the chieftaincy stool targets the glory.[39] Because sovereignty (or, more precisely, chieftaincy) itself is never subtracted from lifemaking, which occupies an infinite network that generates, undergirds, and promotes chieftaincy, the chief (or the king who is also a chief) is always a temporary figure, organ, or conjugated political subjectivity in the stream ("body") of lifemaking. When a chief dies an unacceptable death, this temporary figure is seen in its true form as an "unbearable life," a life located neutrally between life and death, a political subject whose "name" cannot live or die.[40] The confinement of the legacy, the "name" of the chief killed in war, to the state of inexistence takes us to another key dimension of the Kalabari philosophical-theological-political imaginary.

The Kalabari chief is also conceived as a katechontic figure who restrains or delays lawlessness. Therefore when he dies there is the ceremonial *igira sara* where the youth in his *wari* engage in utter recklessness and lawless behaviors to signify the symbolic birth of anomie. While alive he stands not only between law and lawlessness and between historical and eschatological time but also between the internal space of peace and security and the external open space of destruction and death. Thus, this figure's disgraceful death in the external space of anomie and disaster, whose very death represents chaos in the internal space, is symbolically papered over by the act of smoothing, erasing his specific claims to glory (the liturgical, ceremonies, and acclamations) and governance (administration and execution) that took form in the community's immanent flows of life, in the "phase spaces" of lifemaking.[41] The erasure as a political trick pretends as if the traumatic event never happened by positing that the chieftaincy never existed.

There is something curious to be learned in this practice of political erasure. The erasure of the disgraced dead chief's place in the community is a form of biopolitics of immunization, as Roberto Esposito might put it. He might argue that in order to protect itself the Kalabari polity incorporates the external threat, which the extraterritorial death of a disgraced chief represents, as its own negation within its internal space of peace and security. We can, therefore, read the erasure, the lawlessness of *igira sara*, and the bad death of the chief as veritable lenses with which to examine the katechontic figuration of Kalabari chiefs and, by extension, the Kalabari lifemaking process. Esposito's compelling reading of the Pauline restrainer comes in handy to shed light on my last two statements. His reading is useful in interpreting the paradoxical, immunological operation of the katechontic character of the Kalabari chieftaincy institution, its capacity to incorporate chaos (as exemplified by *igira sara* or erasure) into its working.

> The *katechon* restrains evil by containing it, by keeping it, by holding it within itself. It confronts evil, but from within,

hosting it and welcoming it, to the point of binding its own necessity to the presence of evil. It limits evil, defers it, but does not eradicate it, because if it did, it would also eliminate itself. We could go so far as to say that the *katechon*—its constitutive juridical principle—opposes the absence of law by taking it up inside itself, and thereby, in some way, giving it form, rule, and norm. The *katechon* antinomically assigns a nomos to anomie, thus restraining its catastrophic unfolding.[42]

Concluding Remarks

In this chapter, I have explained the role the quest for legacy plays in maintaining the web of relationships that sustains Kalabari society. The drive for legacy appears to be a relationship-maintenance mechanism in the community as it dynamically connects future-oriented human actions to the lived present and the remembered past of the community. As the living attempt to transcend death and transience by creating social forms of immortality, they contribute to the well-being of the community. The drive for legacy is a bold way of dealing with the future, which both values and contributes to the present by seeking significance and meaning of today's actions in relation to how they will be considered once the actions move into the past.

The study of ethics in Kalabari (and, by extension, Africa) cannot be reasonably divorced from socially constructed notions of legacy. This is so, among other factors, because African traditional religion has not developed a concept of soul immortality or resurrection of person. It seems reasonable for them to posit the importance of the quest for legacy, for social forms of immortality rather than soul immortality, which depends on the citizens' faith (or lack of it) in some eternal personal existence in a heavenly realm. In a society whose main religion or philosophical outlook does not promise an immortal soul or resurrected person in communion with some appropriately named Being, or where such promise is weakened, as it happened in eighteenth-century Europe, more attention will be focused on social forms of immortality.[43] How men and women choose to immortalize themselves has tremendous impact on their ethics. In one sense, Max Weber, in the *Protestant Ethics*, links the motivation for capitalist development in Western Europe to concerns about the afterlife.

Can one claim that the concern with legacy and posterity is a foundation of morality and the good life in Kalabari? If we see the drive as contributing to the welfare of society, to the safeguarding and improvement of the community's well-being, then one may be able to say it is foundational to ethics in Kalabari. As the African philosopher Kwasi Wiredu argues, the basis of ethics and morality in Africa is human welfare and religion.[44]

Wiredu's point compels me to highlight an important observation, which might have escaped some of my readers. One of the discoveries of this book is that the Kalabari political system has no recourse to any form of transcendence. The Kalabari people worked out the political problem of citizens living together as individuals or groups without any (obvious) recourse to religious transcendence. This is not to say they are not a religious people; they are. This is not to say that the community as a whole does not recognize fundamental sources of authority beyond humanity. I am not denying the religious foundations of the Kalabari society. I am only saying that the political is not driven by the theological but by immanence of life. Life is immanent to itself; life is life to itself. The political is immanent to lifemaking, a process that permeates the whole community, and this process is affected by its immanent relation with the political. Immanence of the political here means at least three things. First, the primary orientation of the political is not imposed by an outside source; it is from the power of immanence operative within the functions of human history, within the biological, cultural, and social processes of human existence. Second, the political is truly immanent only when it is in immanent relation with all dimensions or goods of lifemaking in the society. The political affects every good of lifemaking (or lifemaking itself) and is affected by (goods of) lifemaking. By definition, the political and lifemaking are co-constitutive of each other; no one of them is transcendent or transcendental to the other. Finally, the Kalabari people consider themselves solely responsible for creating the society of lifemaking they want to inhabit.

The systems of norms and principles that govern their political sphere did not come from outside humanity itself. This should not be construed to mean that the laws, principles, and norms of the political (as a part of the overall culture) have no religious meanings. The proper interpretation is that the political is not under the heteronomous weight of transcendence; for better or worse, the relationship between the two is theonomous. This means political creativity or actions are linked to the divine depths of existence, not as an external imposition of the latter on the former. The political actualizes itself in accordance with the society's ultimate concern or lifemaking attentively pursued. The quest for such an accordance is driven by an understanding that the divine or the sacred is about actualization of human potentialities and for enabling each person to be the best that they can be. The divine stands for the essence (the perpetual actualization of potentialities) of humanity.

The non-reliance of the Kalabari political system on religious transcendence and exteriority is even discernible from the story of how King Amakiri I and Abbi, Amakiri IV, became rulers. Their success had to do with lifemaking rather than mobilization of logic of exteriority. There was nothing magical about the method of their choice as kings by the people. Amakiri, as we have learned, saved the city-state from economic ruin after a disastrous fire. No voice spoke from heaven, no priest danced or went into trance to (arbitrarily) impose him on the people. The people made a pragmatic deal with him. Kariboye Abbi, his grandson, who reigned from 1863 to 1900, also emerged as king under similar circumstances. In 1863 Kalabari palm produce merchants could not access the Orashi markets, which Nembe considered as its exclusive trading zone. "By the last years of Karibo's [Abbi's father's] reign, Kalabari traders were being attacked by the Nembe and their Engenni and Ogbia allies. Nembe seized the opportunity of Karibo's death in 1863 to instigate her Engenni allies to a full-scale blockade of Orashi River at Okarki; a blockade that completely paralysed Kalabari trade in the north-west."[45]

Abbi and Alambo, two powerful heads of trading houses, presented themselves to the community as capable of breaking the blockade through military force. The community made a pact with them: whoever was able to break the blockade would be the king, *amayanabo*. Alambo tried first and failed. Abbi embarked on the task and was successful. Subsequently he was installed *amayanabo*. Alambo was deposed from headship of the Odum House and was replaced by Chief Igbanibo.[46]

What role did transcendence play in the choice of Abbi as the new king? Abbi might have sought the aid of some supernatural force to boost his confidence in the fierce competition, but they were not the powers that chose or legitimized him as the new king. What mattered was that he succeeded at a task filled with uncertainty and risk, and his main rival failed. Later, Abbi attributed his victory on the battlefield to the benevolence of the Kalabari national deity *Owamekaso*. Her priest had prophesized that the new king of the community would emerge in the battlefield, and kingship would go to the one who would successfully eliminate the military blockade. There was no effort to impose her divine will on the community. Her prophecy only gave religious meaning to their decision. Religious meaning is not some ahistorical or true essence to which Kalabari community would lay claim or appropriate as a strange object from outside. When they discover or invent religious meaning, they discover themselves. They discover something that is deep in the process of life-making (the profound mystery of creativity and human sociality), though its potentialities infinitely exceed them, but they are never separated from it. The generation of religious meaning is a performance of being-with, an intervention within the creative possibilities of the symbolic order of lifemaking, the directedness and attraction of human cultural life toward the unity of the "ought" and with the "what is."

What do all these (the overall matrix of arguments in this chapter) tell us about lifemaking in the Kalabari context? In a certain sense, the value of a person's life in relation to others is ultimately seen in its contributions to her legacies for her own community. The significance and meaning of today's work is sought in relation to how it would be considered in the future as the actual performance moves into the past. Work (as creativity leaving behind legacy) is considered in the context of the *togetherness* of the three temporal modes of the human creativity: past, present, and future. In the same way, lifemaking, which is the context of the drive for legacy, is not limited to the present of the individual's or community's activities but also involves the togetherness of the three temporal modes. Through legacy, past work (actualities) enters the presence of lifemaking to fashion and refashion it. Present ongoing work can only actualize itself as a finished product by taking account of the potential that past work offers and the potential and possibilities for future work. Past work is involved in present work, and future work is also involved as anticipated. The concern with legacy is not about "timing" the value of one's work or legacy but about maintaining the web of relationships that undergirds a community's lifemaking. This is the connection between legacy (work as social creativeness or social ethics) and lifemaking. How can the nature of the link between social ethics and lifemaking be further explored? I will address this question in the next chapter.

In order to adequately prepare the reader for the discourse of chapter 6, I need to examine how bodiliness, the political, and sovereignty are connected with social ethics of lifemaking. The social ethics that flows from Kalabari political philosophy and politics is about bodiliness: keeping healthy connections between human bodies and between human bodies and nonhuman bodies (biotic and abiotic). Bodiliness is about access to the resources of life (human flourishing and ennobling livelihood) and the community's capabilities in the context of the person in community. Bodiliness is the fundamental notion of politics; thus, politics is guided by life. Life is the source and resource of politics. It is the matrix and prius of the political order. Life is the intention, the protention, the fullness, the justness, and the integrity of things political. Politics as life-esteem does not insist on the way of death, nor does it walk on the path of destruction, nor does it sit on the seat of decay. Its delight is human flourishing.

Politics is the activity that enables Kalabari communities to act on the basis, trajectory, and telos of bodiliness. This nexus of bodiliness and politics is the criterion for how the community or social relationships among human beings should be organized. Out of the sensuous spell of bodiliness and politics, subjects arise fragrantly—subjects "existing for life and not for death."[47] These men and women, when acting in concert, are capable of initiating something new amid ongoing social processes. As we learned earlier, these are the subjects who proclaim "Iyama ibi, ibuu kunu," meaning "Let my town prosper so that I will exude fragrance."

This book examines the relationship between politics and life. It demonstrates how life (human bodies and human flourishing) is the raw material, product, and telos of politics. It also points us to the inner meaning of sovereignty in Kalabari, the relation of the community to nothing other than itself. Sovereignty as self-relation, a relation without end, is about making provisions for the future possible so that life can flourish. For the Kalabari, sovereignty is materially grounded in social relations constituted through the protection, promotion, and prosecution of the good life. In this community, life is sovereign over law, and sovereignty cannot be contracted to an individual or a supreme authority. Sovereignty is the presence of life from which no one can flee, nor can anyone command or commandeer it. At the height of social interactions, it is there. If the people fall to the depths of coexistence, it is there. Even there, its power and pulsations guide the people and hold them fast. Even death is not deadly to life; the dead will speak like the living, and the unborn is as the living is to it. Though its connective energy may grow old in social interactions and its nodes decay or die in the soil of negating forces of being, at the scent of "water" it will flourish and bring forth connections as a young rhizome. In the abode of life are the roots of sovereignty. This is a hidden abode of mutual response: spheres of social relations answer to life consistently and responsibly, and life unfolds, refolds, and enfolds itself in social relations.

Sovereignty is the supreme symbol of the community to accept responsibility for the outcomes of all its actions and not only for those with good intentions behind them. What has decisive power over social relations in the community is the impetus to organize society to support life as a function of collective work and a refusal to organize human relationships as a production of sociological weapons of death. On the basis of the insights of the preceding two statements, we come to a Kalabari-specific understanding of sovereignty. We will not understand the Kalabari notion of sovereignty if we start from sovereignty and go to find in it the powers (elements) of life and death. The proper way is to start with real life and see how the images (powers, elements) of sovereignty make their appearance in it. Is this appearance that of a being-with attributes of a conscious subject or a physical-metaphysical hyperobject? Sovereignty is the *spirituality* (faith in natality as the immanent spirit of existence as such, fundamental impulse of being-with) institutionalized in community members by their quest for life, human flourishing, and their opposition to death.[48]

In political theoretic terms, sovereignty is the name for the community's political responsibility and obligation to enhance life, to promote human flourishing. Sovereignty is the *answerability* of the political to life. Answerability here means that the political seriously takes on its responsibility to be *itself*; that is, recognize itself as the site where a community's being and being-with are at stake; being and co-being are at risk and could be lost, severely damaged, or threatened. Coexistence is at stake through the interactions of the political with other spheres of society in their diverse orientations toward life. This acting through or with the other spheres is always shot through with the tension between completing interactions among the political and the other spheres and the unfinalizability of the dialogical act of the political-other (spheres) relations. Thus, the answerability of the political is not only about acting through or taking seriously the (potential) behaviors, rhythms, or actions of the other spheres (other axiological positions), but it also involves a normative recognition that these others can answer it (the political) back.

Sovereignty in this context is two-sided answerability of the political to all spheres of life. Let us not forget that the relationships of the political to the other spheres of life are images of social relations between human beings, expressionist portraits of the "dialogic process that builds on the practical problems associated with answerability."[49] Sovereignty is not a transcendental category but a category of practice that arises and abides in the social relations of acting subjects. Sovereignty (as transgredient architectonics) is not conceptualized as an ultimate ideal authority (power) or an already-made construction, but "as a site of polyphony, conflict, and domination whose unity is that which is always 'yet-to-be-attained.' "[50] Thus, the Kalabari king is a *symbol* (or a living image) of this form of sovereignty. He points to and participates in the power and authority of national sovereignty, but he is not a sovereign—definitely not a Hobbesian or Schmittian sovereign.

The preceding interpretation of Kalabari indigenous notion of sovereignty flows from my understanding of bodiliness, unfinishedness of life, and the unfinalizability of the dialogic and participatory process of intersubjective actions. These are acts of subjects who are "existing for life and not for death." Among them, some will arise fragrantly as the excellent selves. This is the theme of the next chapter.

Chapter 6

The Excellent Self

Existential End Goal of Lifemaking

Introduction

This book explores how to refound politics beyond death, against death, in contemporary Africa. Against the pernicious and persistent presence of necropolitics in African public life, it speaks to being and being-together, which are always at stake, and human existence being at stake is the nature of the political in Africa. It offers a creative analysis of the values, social practices, and institutions that can move African societies away from necropolitics to lifemaking. Lifemaking is a new thinking that stages or constructs political philosophy as a theorization of a community's commitment to the love of life and human flourishing. Drawing insights from an indigenous African political philosophy and using the tools of philosophy, postcolonial studies, political theory, cultural studies, social ethics, and religious studies, the book reveals how the questions implicit in existence could be met and answered by politics in the form of lifemaking. Lifemaking is an answer to existential needs.

Lifemaking is a passion for existence. A proper understanding of lifemaking involves a deep cultural or religious understanding of a people's conception of existence, how they explain human existence to themselves. The accent of this passion and conception of existence in Kalabari is the production of a certain subjectivity or citizen: the excellent self. Subjectivity is the event of apprehending that for which the person is apprehended by existence (or *So*, God). But whatever it is, it cannot be fully apprehended, so the person presses on, pushing outward the frontiers of human flour-ishing, reaching forward for the prize of the apprehension. Subjectivity is an event, and the person is engaged in its unfolding.

In this book we have attempted to penetrate the Kalabari philosophy of lifemaking in order to plumb the existential matrix of human flourish-ing, exposing their passionate attachment to life and living. Lifemaking is to accomplish the desire of human flourishing as a state of the world, existence as such. The Kalabari idea of actualizing their destiny or poten-tial is not founded on needs or on the order of possession but on the justice of the citizen's existence as a child of *Tamuno* (*Temeso*, God) with a particular destiny. It is necessary to make this fine distinction if one is to fully grasp the fervency with which Kalabari pursue what they think is their God-given destiny. With this orientation to lifemaking and the attendant view of justice, one can say, following Giorgio Agamben, that there is "a striking contraction of ethics and ontology, justice is presented not as a virtue but as a 'state of the world,' as the ethical category that corresponds not to having-to-be but to existence as such."[1] This is not about the right of possession but the right of existence itself, the right of actualization of destiny itself. And it is akin to how Walter Benjamin understands justice: "Justice does not appear to refer to the good will of the subject, but, instead, constitutes a state of the world. Justice desig-nates the ethical category of the existent, virtue the ethical category of the demanded. Virtue can be demanded; justice in the final analysis can only be as a state of the world or as a state of God."[2]

Lifemaking is the unfinalizable working out of human flourishing as a state of the world. This work of lifemaking never finishes. It is a desire to close the gap between justice as a state of the world—justice as the ethical category or fundamental impulse of being-with—and justice as the goodwill of leaders of a polity, the yet-to-be quality of justice that perpetually awaits actualization, or justice that is in "heaven." The desire to close the gap demands seeing justice as a quality of their current world and not for the world that is to come. This desire (*tari*, beginning[3]) is a mode of existing, a living-well that signifies a way of properly living a life of potentiality. Such desire is always haunted by a split between what is accomplished and the not-yet. Desire is an opening that every movement toward actualization of potentialities creates between actuality and the not-yet.

Here desire is not conceptualized as want for goods or fulfillment of needs but as the passion for existence because of the perceived goodness of destiny or *telos* of individual lives. The Kalabari citizen is a being moved by her destiny (*fiyeteboye* or *fiyeteboye* as amended by *bibibari*). This is different from desire as the seeking after goods because others in one's culture want them. Desire for the citizen is delighting in the actualization of one's potentials in the context of the wholesome integration of the essential and conditional components of one's life "and thus occupying one's ownmost place and identity" in one's existential field.[4] Basically, the person becomes the subject of the becoming of her own destiny, working out what she perceives as ideal possibilities of life allotted to her and what she has already actualized. Subjectivity is dialogic, polyphonic, and unfinalizable. There is a constant interaction between the self, the individual *telos* received from *So*, the *telos* of the house (*wari*) or group in which one was thrown into existence, and the dynamic balancing of essential and conditional features of one's life.

Desire as the gap between what is realized and the total range of possibilities in *So*, or *So*'s promise to an individual or community, is structural. It is structural in two senses. First, the gap cannot be made to totally disappear. The object of desire—the pursuit of human flourishing—cannot become a permanent possession. An existent in the Kalabari view cannot completely realize her possibilities; the justice of existence can never become a fixed (complete) possession. There is always a new projection of possibilities after every actualization because possibilities always exceed actualities. Human existence (*se-pakabo*) is being-concerned-with-this-gap. This being-concerned-with, being-after-something is what *tari* (desire) is about. In this space of *longing-for*, the temporal structure of desire consists in the retentive reaching back into the past and the anticipatory reaching out for the not-yet and the possible from the present, the gap. The *long-for* also comes from *Temeso* (God) as a force that energizes human "possibilizing" capacity or human creativity. Indeed, a person desires because *So* desires her or first desired or claimed her. The community (whose being is *amatemeso*) also desires or claims her.[5]

Second, the desire is structural with respect to the *rhythm* of existence as theorized by Giorgio Agamben. The temporal structure (already and not-yet) of desire or human existence also refers to the proper ("original") place of an individual or group existence, the inner rhythm that allows her (the group) to take the original measure of her (its) dwelling on earth.

Existence by itself is shapeless, without any structure, an inarticulate substratum of being that can be subjected to desired forms. When the experience of the struggle to cover the gap that is desire is added to it, existence acquires rhythm, structure. Structure here is not just a simple aggregation of the facts of life into an ensemble of meaning, creating a whole that has more meaning than the sum of the parts. Similarly, structure is not the "something else" that is added to an ensemble of life's facts and interpretations that makes the whole more than the sum of the parts and solidifies them into a unity. Thus, the thinking here about structure is not about a search for either "that which causes something to be what it is" or that ultimate, minimum irreducible element of the new life. It is about *form* that maintains existence in presence, puts it in its "proper station in presence."[6]

But what grants existence its proper place? Existence is an ongoing flow of activities, a pure flow in an infinite space-time continuum (or fabric, if you like). Social existence, in particular, appears as a perpetual movement of instants, the inexorable course of daily mortal life, running toward ruin, destruction, and death. This flow, when interrupted or interfered with, creates rhythm, introducing a split and stop in its relentless match. "Thus in a musical piece, although it is somehow in time, we perceive rhythm as something that escapes the incessant flight of instants and appears almost as the presence of an atemporal dimension of time."[7] In the same way, when the Kalabari person has put herself in the mundane transformational context, "panel-beating" the self into a relevantly shaped vehicle of her lowercase *so*, a particular type of moral subject, she perceives a stop in time, "as though she is suddenly thrown into a more original time. There is a stop, an interruption in the incessant flow of instants that, coming from the future, sinks into the past, and this interruption, this stop, is precisely what gives and reveals the particular status," the mode of presence proper to her existence.[8] The pursuit of her individual *so* appears to have broken the automatism, the inexorability of social existence, and lets her find her present space between past and future.

This split is enacted in the midst of a flow: in the flow of time, in the flow of social existence. While pursuit of her individual *so* reveals the proper place of existence, locates her in the presence proper to her as a work of *Temeso's* hand, the flight of life's instants goes on that do not reveal their meaning and place fully as they move on. The split is thus an inside that is "also a being-outside, an *ek-stasis* in the more original dimension."[9] The experience of the pursuit gives her the sense of her proper place (an ecstatic dwelling in it) but still retains her in the quotidian draw of existence.

So now we understand structure as rhythm, as what determines the proper ("original") place of existence. By opening to the Kalabari man his perceived authentic spatial and temporal dimension of existence, the pursuit also "opens for him the space of belonging to the world, only within which he can take the original measure of his dwelling on the earth and find again his present truth in the unstoppable flow of linear time [and inexorable course of daily movement to destruction and death]."[10] It is in this authentic space in the world or temporal dimension that the Kalabari person sallies forth to re-create the self and the world, is able to put his being and the past and future at stake in order to achieve the transformation of his subjectivity and access the full promises of *Temeso* in his life. This is why the experience of working out *fiyeteboye* (lowercase *so*)—that is, desire, *tari*—is called "beginning" and is architectonic in the archaic sense of production of origin.[11]

In sum, the efforts to close the gap that we have named desire can be considered as a form of production of temporality, new temporality to fashion relevant subjectivity for the *telos* from *Temeso* and as a route to legacy. The mindfulness of desire, this consciousness that breaks the automatism of ongoing social processes, that interrupts the normal patterns of sights and rhythms of sounds of social existence to create the space for human existence, a space of appearance, renews (re-creates) the person's sense of reality. The consciousness of one's destiny involves intentional acts of ruptures, which lift off the crust of tradition and habitude over the common world, to offer a new gap of existence.

I will use an event of the mid-nineteenth century to illustrate the ethos of rupture, emancipatory politics of interruption, that is built into Kalabari social practices, or to demonstrate how its politics is keyed to freedom, the capacity to begin, to initiate something new amid ongoing social-political processes. On September 27, 1857, Kalabari people announced to other Africans and Europeans in the Niger Delta that they had just killed one of their gods (Owu Akpana, the shark-god) and proceeded to celebrate the deicide and its ensuing freedom. This act, which was not metaphysical but historical, involved eating the divine flesh and drinking the blood of the god, incorporating the divine into the human, and thus recognizing sovereignty in the people. The killing illuminates, at the minimum, one ethico-political element: the materialization of some higher or untouchable power, spirit, or reality could be cast down to *nothing* by the people. The concert of actions of the people is the immanent

Spirit of the community and it obstructs the gods or the any agent from usurping popular sovereignty.

The people (the emancipatory political collective), at least for a moment in 1857, hovered "above the entire life of the state" and all forms of realization of the divine.[12] How can this tradition be retrieved to illuminate democratic politics or counter the politics of near-divine impunity by leaders on the African continent? What social-ontological power did the revolutionary act of deicide recognize, reveal, or portray? It is the capacity to initiate something new amid ongoing social-political processes, the possibility of radical new beginning. What is the implication of all this for democratic sovereignty in Africa?

The Executed God

Monday, 28th [September 1857]

[I] went up to [New] Calabar town this morning and while there heard that the chiefs had a meeting in their palaver house yesterday, in consequence of several of the natives having been killed lately by their big Jew Jew [juju, god], the Sharks, they came to the conclusion that it no be use for have wowo jew jew [useless god] all same shark no more and it is therefore no longer held as such, but the natives are catching them as fast as possible and now allow "white men" to do the same if they like which of course we shall do whenever we have a chance as the shark is the sailor's greatest enemy.[13]

William Oates, a trader from Liverpool who was in New Calabar (Elem Kalabari, the headquarters of the Kalabari people at the time), recorded this event in his diary. When growing up as child in the 1970s, I heard the elders in my town, Abonnema, talk about this event, and later I read about the same story recorded as oral history by British anthropologists such as P. Amaury Talbot, G. I. Jones, and Robin Horton. People in my town had always been suspicious about whether the event actually happened—my people could not have killed their god. Furthermore, no written record existed to support the tale.[14] But there were enough insights in the native worldview or philosophy that were repeated often as proverbs to suggest that my Kalabari ancestors were capable and even prone to killing their gods.[15] According to a popular Kalabari aphorism: "If a god becomes too furious or demanding, we will tell it from which wood it was carved" ("Agu nsi[16]owi baka kuma en ke o kara sin en dugo o piriba"). In other words, a community can unanimously annul a god's power by refusing it worship.[17]

The divine-human relationship is not above the belief in the human capacity to begin something new. As the event of 1857 in Elem Kalabari and other similar stories in Izon (Ijo) communities in the nineteenth century demonstrate, Izon people are willing to start afresh with their gods. If a god initiates a process that is not conducive to human flourishing, humans can disrupt the process to start something new. If a god becomes too violent, humans will cause it to cease to exist.

The power of community to interrupt powerful people or agents is also asserted or enacted in the ceremony of becoming chiefs. One of the questions a would-be chief must answer is, If you are with a beautiful woman, a new woman, and you are about to have sex or are already engaged in it, will you interrupt the coitus and come when the community calls?[18] If the aspirant is not capable of resisting libidinal impulses to promptly leave for community services when he hears a clarion call for action in the face of a new naked lover who is alone with him in the room, then he does not qualify for leadership, and he has exhibited a failure to understanding a basic requirement of citizenship. The man is questioned so the community can learn something about his willingness to consciously move from the private realm to the public, to interrupt his private interests for the sake of the public.

This chance to interrupt or gauge the preparedness of citizens for interruption is also evident in one of the primordial relations Kalabari-Ijo believe exists between God (the Supreme Being, Tamarau/Teme-órú/ Tamuno) and them. Here I am talking about the tension between *fiyeteboye* (prenatal decision, God-given destiny of a person before he or she was born) and *bibibari* (recanting or change of such destiny). If *fiyeteboye* is the "timeless," ontological structuring of the range of possibilities within a person's life, then *bibibari* is the radical temporality of subjectivity as an openness to the future in Kalabari thought. The individual has the opportunity or right to interrupt the primal voice, the preexistent speech in her life. Here the person is actually interrupting the voice speaking from the throne room of the Supreme Being. Yes, in the beginning was the word, but there is always a re-beginning of the beginnings. And owing to the disruptions caused by interruptions, the beginning does not stop itself from occurring more than once.

Perhaps it is now clear to the readers that lifemaking in Kalabari holds the potential for some dramatic upheavals, a radical discontinuity with authority or tradition, a fierce protection of freedom. In light of the traditional African spirit of communality, freedom is something enjoyed in public, not in private; free people participate in public actions for the common good with one's peers. Freedom is the power to act together, to initiate new possibilities in the community, to think and act in new ways. It is about appearing to others as a distinct, irreplaceable individual "who" in the public space (the shared world) and performing immortal deeds.[19]

This notion of freedom embeds the idea of the *capacity to do*; to do what a person needs to do irrespective of obstacles, burdens, or circumstances; a striving to achieve the improbable. Thus, one can bring something new into an already existing situation. One way this capacity to do is rendered in Kalabari is *I ye gbeye ye*, pure doability, to manifest the human character as acting to establish a new reality. *I ye gbeye ye* demands doing or acting to bring in the new, even the unexpected, to disrupt automatic political, historical, and religious processes by persuading other citizens to act collectively with him or her rather than be a slave to them. This freedom to act, to begin afresh, which is the key quality of intercourse among fellow citizens, is integral to lifemaking.

There is an aphorism that captures this commitment to freedom and the inclination to show the "who" of oneself in the public square. It was coined by Chief Frank Obu Briggs (1864–1958) of Abonnema, a man of immense courage and initiative who was well-regarded for his pithy philosophical sayings.[20] One that is still popular today is "O bere bere ibitein te ke o tiye mieba nengim." This philosophically dense statement is difficult to translate into English in one sentence. So I will offer multiple translations with the hope that the totality will capture the richness of the statement as a native Kalabari person understands it. Below are five translations of the Briggs statement.

1. Literally, it means that his trouble is better than [testing] "What can he do?"

2. It is better to avoid his trouble than to dare him.

3. To avoid his wrath is better than to throw down the gauntlet at him.

4. Let everyone cognize him for his limitless capability to give a fierce fight to any person that crosses him than say to themselves "What can he do?"

5. Avoiding his wrath is better than challenging him.

We can add three more that speak in an expansive way to the kernel of the idea in his pithy statement. These would bring his idea into the area of law and sovereignty.

1. To fear (respect) the law is better than to disregard it.

2. Respecting the wrath of the law is better than daring it.

3. Finally, by implication, it is better to respect the popular sovereignty than challenge it.

The reasons for this additional perspective of the law and sovereignty will become clear as I situate his thought in the cultural and historical context of his time.

The pithy statement speaks to Frank Briggs's willingness to protect and defend his dignity, personal sovereignty, or pursuit of justice. In any society where men and women are not respected for their fierce response to defend encroachment of their freedom, their liberty will be challenged or taken away. As explained in chapter 4, Kalabari chiefs are subjects to freedom, and Briggs was an exemplary chief.

Why did Briggs formulate the key principle of freedom in this seemingly belligerent expression? I would offer two reasons. First, Kalabari chiefs are also warriors. As we learned in chapter 4, would-be chiefs are asked, "Are you willing to pick a yam or a cannonball?" Yam represents the ability to feed his household, and cannonball represents taking risks on behalf of the community. In other words, is the man willing to put his physical self and financial resources toward defending the community in times of war and upholding its freedom? The man knows he must pick the cannonball to make it through the ceremony, going against his self-centered well-being. His upbringing has prepared him for how to respond to tests like this. Fathers tell their sons and nephews that if forced to choose between losing freedom and death, you choose death to keep your freedom of choice. Choosing freedom under the threat of death is unmanly and cowardly, offering no proof of freedom. Young men learn that when a proper Kalabari man faces such a condition (a kind of declaration of war), he should be able to quietly cut off his breath instead of "eating phlegm."

The second reason I give now sheds light on why I expanded the translation of Frank Briggs's philosophical expression into the areas of law and popular sovereignty. Briggs was a product of his era; he spent most of his adult life under British colonial rule, and the exercise of power or freedom was closely associated with the capacity to interrupt or disrupt. Kalabari people interpret political action—among other views—as the capacity to interrupt, to disrupt the power dynamics, or to lob in a voice or a thing that halts or diverts an ongoing system or process. Persons or institutions that have this kind of power to maximally interrupt others' lives become "gods." In the early twentieth century, for instance, the British colonial imposition as consulate authority in the life of the Kalabari people caused so many disruptions in their everyday lives and in how local institutions functioned that the consulate became a "god." In the 1970s, years after Nigeria's independence, old folks were still invoking this terrible god against an adversary: *Konsin bere i buu paka*, meaning "May you be persecuted by the consulate" or "Let the trouble of government befall you." Consulate as a god that interrupted local power dynamics was now called on to visit its form of interruption on an adversary, to deploy its wickedness and impunity to interrupt a person's ongoing life. Thus, people generally believed that it was better to avoid a fight with the government, the ruthless colonial authority, than to challenge it to a fight.

Frank Briggs was claiming this kind of power, fear of government, and adoration (if that is the right word) for near omnipotent domination for himself as a head of a collective, the large Oruwari group of houses in Abonnema. This claim, which he made through his pithy statement, has more than one meaning. Indeed, it is ambiguous. On one level it signals his desire for the kind of interruptive, disruptive powers the colonial government enjoyed. On another level, it signifies a kind of resistance. He puts himself up as an alternative god or a human being that can disrupt the arbitrary colonial god. It seems he was shooting an arrow across the bow of the colonial government, perhaps warning it to be careful not to further challenge the popular sovereignty of the people, whose "trouble" needed to be avoided.

In the logic of the colonial relationship with the Kalabari people in the early twentieth century, both sides knew not only that gods were interruptive forces but also that human beings could interrupt gods. British colonial governors knew well that under the influence of a local deity, the people they controlled could summon enough collective energy to disrupt their oppressive imperial rule. Thus, under the guise of Christian "civilization" that frowned on the worship of local gods, colonial rulers proceeded to discredit them. In some cases, colonial authorities destroyed the shrines of deities and even passed laws against people invoking the names of their gods against their opponents in a dispute. The colonial authorities brutally put down persons who dared to challenge their authority or persons who offered themselves as a site to concentrate resistance against undemocratic rule.

Now that we have dealt with the issues relating to the translation of Briggs's pithy statement, let me focus on the construction of the aphorism itself: "His trouble is better than [testing] 'What can he do?' "[21] There is a gap between "his trouble" and "what can he do." The trouble, which is to be avoided, is based on historical experience, what he has done in the past, how he has forcefully put down those who brought fights (*palava* in Nigerian pidgin English) to him. "What can he do" is futural. Thus, there is a gap between the past and future, which is the present (and its possibilities). Every would-be challenger has to make up his mind whether it is worth traversing the present based on the known historical fact. Briggs's aphorism is a warning to people not to tempt (or "attempt") him.[22]

The warning that Briggs issued bears two interpretative weights. First, history is behind it. He has a record of defeating those who challenged him in the past. This is the fact of history as implied in the aphorism. Second, this fact of history is not completed and buried in the past. Its performance in the past is not simply a fact but a past that is alive. He could give life to it anytime through his freedom to act, the power to initiate something new or to bring the (what is) past into existence. Given this perspective, Briggs is presenting himself or his capability as not only a *fact* of history but, more important, a *factor* of history. He is the factor of history that has the power of freedom to create facts of history. As a factor, Briggs does not just happen; he is happening and will happen (or the one who is to come to challengers of his authority).[23]

This factor-dimension of his being is both a gap and the bridge between the two components of his pithy statement, a drawbridge between "his trouble" and "what can he do." To his would-be challengers it is a gap, a distance they dare to cross at their own peril. He posits or poses himself as the cause of his challengers' anxiety, the destroyer of their joyful expectation of victory. For him, the distance between the two components of the statement is a bridge he embodies. He connects both of them (or both sides) and gives meaning and depth to each of them. Without him, without his biography, they are nothing, mere words carried away as chaffs by the wind.

The gap so analyzed speaks more to the celebration (fear) of past victories and its role in deterrence. Does this analysis of the gap ignore critical insights about Kalabari understanding of freedom? The liberating possibility that the Kalabari notion of freedom emphasizes is not in the past but in the future. What does it mean to have the pastness of "his trouble" (*o bere bere*) as the dominating factor in predicting the behavior of future challengers, even if we agree that no human is completely free of the past? How does the aphorism square with hope (*biokpo*)? Those who were likely to challenge him and all those who detested his philosophy could act only because they hoped for victory, while he and all those who subscribed to his philosophy hoped for victory because they had acted in the past or will act in the future. Note this distinction: act because you hope for victory or hope for victory because you have successfully acted in the past and can repeat it in the future. Both forms of hope are for those who want to create history, to actualize freedom to initiate something new amid ongoing politics. At the end, those who came along to challenge him and hoped for victory embarked on their task because they could act like him. Their hope was grounded in their ability to act regardless of the encumbrances of the past. And they won. The challengers were not exactly what Chief Briggs expected. It was the postcolonial Nigerian society that rendered obsolete the kind of powerful, strong man that he was. His era was washed away by the sands of time. While men like Briggs lasted, his pithy statement was an important language of politics in Kalabari history. It was a language of hope for the people in his own *wari*. His statement pointed to his capability to defend them. For those outside his realm of defense, it was a threat of deployment of overwhelming force to defeat his enemies or opponents in any struggle.

Chief Frank Brigg's pithy statement resonated with the Kalabari people and got passed down to generations after him. It captured something fundamental about Kalabari understanding of freedom as they writhed under the burden of British colonial rule. The Kalabari person is culturally formed to interrupt not only his speech-agreement with God but also his very being or own desire. This is enacted in a set of practices I have named elsewhere *counterfoil choice*.[24] The characteristic feature of counterfoil choice is that whenever A is offered, the Kalabari offer its negative (non-A) to deter the person from a specific decision or to gauge the person's willingness to interrupt their desire. During rites of passage or in situations in which citizens must rethink their actions or behavior, the community gives them a forced choice between A or non-A.

The politics of interruption in various forms that I have laid out points to the limitations of power, whether supernatural or natural, and to the fact that the citizens, worshippers, or subjects under authority must always have something to disrupt ongoing social processes, to overturn overbearing power. The people as a collective always have something through which they can control or successfully revolt against, a god or person in authority. This "something" is their action or their capacity to begin. The generative impulse of the political is that the actions of human beings work to eliminate the impossible by creating new possibilities. Simply put, coexistence (among humans and between human beings and gods) carries a high-voltage charge of disruptive possibility and is delicately balanced on a fragile consensus in which each actor has agreed not to overstep their bounds.

The Excellent Self

By way of reaching conclusion, let me now ask, What is the point of the cultural formation for freedom and the politics of interruption? It is to build up citizens who can promote freedom and human flourishing. Lifemaking is fashioned as an ethics and philosophy of *care of the soul*,[25] the pragmatic concern for and social practices to engender what I would call the *excellent self* (*krakra tombo*), a self faithfully committed to full-orbed freedom and flourishing as the event of "life and the good life."

The entry point into the Kalabari understanding of the excellent self is in their particular conception of God (*Tamuno/So*). *Tamuno* is the creative modality, and *So* is the dynamic directing agency, the dimension of divinity that orders the life outcome of all created beings. Let us recall that uppercase *So* is the universe of possibilities from which some are defined as available to persons and institutions and others remain either unfulfilled or simply the set of possibilities excluded to them at any given time. *So*, when applied to the individual, is called lowercase *so*. The lowercase *so* is the ideal that the individual receives from God and that the person works out within history, that is, achieves its actualization, by the way he or she unifies its efficient causes. The person transforms the pure possibilities given to him or her into possibilities realizable under the conditions of the world.

The idea of God's directing activity being present in each person suggests that every person or group incarnates some degree of God's purpose in the world. The excellent self is the one who has (almost) fully realized his or her particular divine aim with little or no distortion or is in search of the maximum potential in his or her historical circumstances. The particular divine aims have been decisively realized in the lives of few individuals in history, and they became *gods* or *community heroes* (*amaoru*). The heroes, human-gods, became the embodiments of divine creative purposes, the specific divine addresses (speeches, *bibi*) to the community at a specific time, and a sort of transparent medium through which the people could read (comprehend and prehend) So's aim for the community. The men and women who had so realized themselves became effective concrete lures for both individual and collective actions. They served also for personal and corporate self-understanding at a given historical juncture and what stood beyond them. Such men and women, in actualizing So's particular ideals for themselves, expressed So's general aim for their entire community, and it was received by all members of the community.

The interpretation of the work of *community heroes* and their reception is not timeless. When the historical situations that brought their works into collective consciousness and sustained them changed, their valuation also altered. And lifemaking continues as a politically transformative practice. This is complexly and intricately tied to a particular kind of political philosophy. This is a way of being and living (not a body of discourse or analytical arguments) by which nations deliberately set the conditions of possibility for all their citizens to creatively actualize their potentialities. When this philosophy reigns supreme, lifemaking will be the *katechon* (restrainer, *daasamaye*) of necropolitics in Africa.

Notes

Introduction

1. This sentence comes from Isaiah 5:14; "He was wounded for our transgressions" is from Isaiah 53:5; and "There was no beauty that we should desire him" comes from Isaiah 53:2.

2. For a discussion of the lotus-self, see Nimi Wariboko, *Ethics and Society in Nigeria: Identity, History, Political Theory* (Rochester, NY: University of Rochester Press, 2019), 4–5, 13–14, 19, 21, 23, 25–34, 99, 101, 160–62, 165, 171, 177.

3. Lifemaking is a translation of these Kalabari words: *dumotelema* (rightly order life); *dumokorinama* (work of life); *dumoteme* (make life); *dumoibima* (beautify life); *dumodori* (weave life); and *dumonama* (build life).

4. Pardon the allusion to Hannah Arendt, *The Origins of Totalitarianism* (New York: Schocken Books, 2004), 616.

5. Catherine Keller, "Theopoetics: A Becoming History," in *The Art of Anatheism*, eds. Richard Kearney and Matthew Clemente (London: Rowman & Littlefield, 2018), 29–41, at 38.

6. For a discussion of the transcripts of the sacred, see Nimi Wariboko, *Transcripts of the Sacred in Nigeria: Beautiful, Monstrous, Ridiculous* (Bloomington: Indiana University Press, 2023).

7. Wariboko, *Transcripts of the Sacred*.

8. Tejumola Olaniyan coined the term the *postcolonial incredible* in *Arrest the Music! Fela and His Rebel Art and Politics* (Bloomington: Indiana University Press, 2004). "The incredible is not simply a breach but an outlandish infraction of 'normality' and its limits" (2). He describes the reign of the incredible in these words:

> The "incredible" inscribes that which cannot be believed; that which is too improbable, astonishing, and extraordinary to be believed. The incredible is not simply a breach but an outlandish infraction of "normality" and its limits. If "belief," as faith, confidence, trust, and

conviction, underwrites the certainty and tangibility of institutions and practices of social exchange, the incredible dissolves all props of stability, normality, and intelligibility (and therefore of authority) and engenders social and symbolic crisis. . . . A presupposed interregnum that increasingly threatens to become the norm, a norm with a rapidly consolidating hierarchy of privileges feeding on and dependent on the crisis for reproduction. (2)

9. The rhythm of the preceding sentence is indebted to Paul Tillich, *Systematic Theology*, vol. 1: *Reason and Revelation, Being and God* (Chicago: University of Chicago Press, 1951), 157.

10. Achille Mbembe, *On the Postcolony* (Berkeley: University of California Press, 2001), 13.

11. Achille Mbembe, *Necropolitics* (Durham, NC: Duke University Press, 2019), 38.

12. Mbembe, 38–39.

13. This paragraph and the next were inspired by Gustav Mahler's song "Nun will die sonn," in Martha C. Nussbaum, *Upheavals of Thought: The Intelligence of Emotions* (Cambridge: Cambridge University Press, 2001), 293–94.

14. Mahler, "Nun will die sonn," in Nussbaum, *Upheavals of Thought*, 294.

15. X. Bichat, *Physiological Researches upon Life and Death*, trans. Tobias Watkins (Philadelphia: Smith & Maxwell, 1809), 43–44; quoted in Robert Esposito, *Third Person: Politics of Life and Philosophy of the Impersonal*, trans. Zakiya Hanafi (Cambridge: Polity Press, 2012), 21.

16. My way of conceptualizing political philosophy in this book is influenced by Richard Rorty, *Contingency, Irony and Solidarity* (Cambridge: Cambridge University Press, 1989), 1–43. It is germane to mention that in these pages he did not address the issue of political philosophy, but the general drift of his arguments for pragmatic/analytical philosophy informed my thinking about political philosophy.

17. Isaiah Berlin, *Four Essays in Liberty* (Oxford: Oxford University Press, 1969), 172.

18. The canoe house (*wari*) was the most characteristic political and social institution of the Eastern Niger Delta states in the eighteenth and nineteenth centuries. It was not a lineage or descent group; rather, it was, as Jones (55) puts it, "a compact and well organized trading and fighting corporation, capable of manning and maintaining a war canoe." Similarly, in 1913 the canoe house was defined by the British protectorate administration as "a number of persons grouped together for the purposes of trade and subject by native law and custom to the control, authority, and rule of a chief known as the head of the house" (Alagoa 15). A canoe house continued to function as long as it was dynamic, flourishing, and profitable. A prosperous, senior canoe house would spin off sub-canoe houses, which kept their connections with the parent-canoe house.

If a sub-canoe house became more prosperous than its parent, it absorbed the parent house and in turn became the senior house. An unsuccessful canoe house folded up, voluntarily merged with another, or was acquired by another house. In the nineteenth century, the leaders of the canoe house system were wealthy traders who commanded the support of their organizations. A chief (manager) only held his position as long as he was successful in his business endeavors. If he were to stumble or fall, leadership was taken from him and given to any member (slave or freeborn) whose character, commercial ability, and wealth most suited the furtherance of the fortune of the house. See G. I. Jones, *Trading States of the Oil Rivers: A Study of Political Development in Eastern Nigeria* (Oxford: Oxford University Press, 1963); E. J. Alagoa, *The Small Brave City-State: A History of Nembe (Brass) in the Niger Delta* (Madison: University of Wisconsin Press, 1964); and Nimi Wariboko, "The African Worldview and the Structure and Strategy of Traditional Business Enterprises: The Case of Kalabari of Southern Nigeria," *Nordic Journal of African Studies* 8, no. 2 (1999): 18–51.

19. Susana Narotzky and Niko Besnier, "Crisis, Value, and Hope: Rethinking the Economy," *Current Anthropology* 55, no. 9 (2014): 4–16, at 10; quoted in Sibel Kusimba, "Embodied Value: Wealth in People," *Economic Anthropology* 7, no. 2 (2020): 166–75.

20. Nimi Wariboko, "Three against Four: A Cultural Analysis of the Disappearance of Women in Kalabari," *Journal of Asian and African Studies* 37, no. 1 (2002): 66–95.

21. Nimi Wariboko, *The Split Time: Economic Philosophy for Human Flourishing in African Perspective* (Albany: State University of New York Press, 2022).

22. For a discussion of these issues in a different context, see Enrique Dussel, *Ethics of Liberation: In the Age of Globalization and Exclusion* (Durham, NC: Duke University Press, 2013), 55–107.

23. Mbembe, *Necropolitics*, 189.

24. Roberto Esposito, *Two: The Machine of Political Theology and the Place of Thought*, trans. Zakiya Hanafi (New York: Fordham University Press, 2014), 1.

25. I have slightly expanded Fanon's thought to meet my requirements here. See Frantz Fanon, *The Wretched of the Earth* (New York: Grove Press, 1968), 40.

26. Paul Tillich, *Systematic Theology*, vol. 2, *Existence and Christ* (Chicago: University of Chicago Press, 1956), 115–16.

27. Terry Cross, "Tillich's Picture of Jesus as the Christ: Toward a Theology of the Spirit's Saving Presence," in *Paul Tillich and Pentecostal Theology: Spiritual Presence and Spiritual Power*, eds. Nimi Wariboko and Amos Young (Bloomington: Indiana University Press, 2015), 71–83.

28. "The weak force of a call is something we can (*posse*) or have the power to ignore—at our peril, perhaps, but just so. The call comes packing only a vocative power—not power pure and simple, but the powerless power of a provocation or a summon, a soliciting, seductive power—but it does not have

an army to lend it support, and nothing stops us from turning a deaf ear to it. It lacks the sheer brawn to coerce or to translate what it calls for into fact. It must make do with the power of powerlessness, not the power of pure strength." John D. Caputo, *The Weakness of God: A Theology of the Event* (Bloomington: Indiana University Press, 2006), 13.

29. For a discussion of the transcripts of the sacred, see Nimi Wariboko, *Transcripts of the Sacred in Nigeria: Beautiful, Monstrous, Ridiculous* (Bloomington: Indiana University Press, 2023).

30. bell hooks, "Theory as Liberatory Practice," in *Feminist Theory: A Reader*, eds. Wendy K. Kolmar and Frances Bartkowski (Mountain View, CA: Mayfield Publishing, 2013), 28–33, at 28–29.

31. Slavoj Žižek, "Only a Suffering God Can Save Us," in *God in Pain: Inversions of Apocalypse*, by Slavoj Žižek and Boris Gunjević (New York: Seven Stories Press, 2012), 155–92, at 171.

32. Mihaly Csikszentmihalyi, *Flow: The Psychology of Optimal Experience* (New York: HarperCollins, 1990), 72–73.

Chapter 1

1. Maurizio Lazzarato, *The Making of the Indebted Man* (Los Angeles: Semiotext[e], 2007), 147.

2. Lazzarato, 70–71.

3. Lazzarato, 146.

4. Lazzarato, 60.

5. Laurenti Magesa, *African Religion: The Moral Traditions of Abundant Life* (Maryknoll, NY: Orbis Books, 1997), 279.

6. Magesa, 64, 65, 67, 120.

7. Lazzarato, *Making of the Indebted Man*, 60.

8. The prose style in this paragraph is influenced by Lazzarato, 34.

9. Martin Hägglund, *Dying for Time: Proust, Woolf, Nabokov* (Cambridge, MA: Harvard University Press, 2012), 7.

10. Hägglund, 8; italics in the original.

11. See "Explaining Hegel's 'Substance as Subject,'" *Reddit*, https://www.reddit.com/r/philosophy/comments/al1213/explaining_hegels_substance_as_subject/.

12. Slavoj Žižek, *Tarrying with the Negative: Kant, Hegel, and the Critique of Ideology* (Durham, NC: Duke University Press, 1993), 30.

13. Žižek, 26.

14. Catherine Malabou, *What Should We Do with Our Brains?*, trans. Sebastian Rand (New York: Fordham University Press, 2008), 5; italics in the original.

15. Is community or a deeper philosophical sense Being not plasticity? See Malabou, *What Should We Do with Our Brains?* See also Catherine Malabou,

Plasticity at the Dusk of Writing: Dialectics, Destruction, Deconstruction, trans. Carolyn Shread (New York: Columbia University Press, 2010).

16. Edmund Phelps, *Mass Flourishing: How Grassroots Innovation Created Jobs, Challenge, and Change* (Princeton, NJ: Princeton University Press, 2013), 14.

17. "The Eastern Ijaw people have drum language with which they communicate among themselves; and all clans, towns, chiefs, deities, noblemen, and even landmarks have their drum names. This is a medium used to identify themselves during inter-clannish wars; times of danger, during festivities, and during masquerade displays, where they give and receive instructions about what to do." Sonny Braide, *Owuame-Kengema Kalabari* (Bloomington, IN: Xlibris, 2017), 145. See also G. O. Tasie, *Kali Kulu Kulu Kalika: A Checklist of Kalabari Drum Names*, Suppl. *Journal of Niger Delta Studies* (Jos, Nigeria: Ehindero, 1999), vii–xiii, 5. Drum names sometimes capture the "signature" of a person or group. The whole or part of it can serve as an indicator of a philosophy of life and snippets of the grand narrative of a group or people.

18. Braide, *Owuame-Kengema Kalabari*, 150. See also Tasie, *Kali Kulu Kulu Kalika*, 27.

19. Tasie, *Kali Kulu Kulu Kalika*, 17–18. See also 24. Italics in the original.

20. My discovery or conception of these three forms of life in Kalabari was inspired by Miguel Vatter, *The Republic of the Living: Biopolitics and the Critique of Civil Society* (New York: Fordham University Press, 2014), 3, 7, 8.

21. Vatter, 142–43.

22. Hannah Arendt, *The Human Condition* (Chicago: Chicago University Press, 1958).

23. Vatter, *Republic of the Living*, 34.

24. Hannah Arendt, *The Promise of Politics* (New York: Schocken Books, 2005), 95.

25. Roberto Esposito, *Two: The Machine of Political Theology and the Place of Thought*, trans. Zakiya Hanafi (New York: Fordham University Press, 2015), 3.

26. Esposito, 20.

27. G. I. Jones, *Trading States of the Oil Rivers: A Study of Political Development in Eastern Nigeria* (London: Oxford University Press, 1963), 55.

28. E. J. Alagoa, *The Small Brave City-State: A History of Nembe (Brass) in the Niger Delta* (Madison: University of Wisconsin Press, 1964), 15.

29. Jones, *Trading States*, 56; E. J. Alagoa, "The Development of Institutions in the States of the Eastern Niger Delta," *Journal of African History* 7 (1971): 269–78; Robin Horton, "From Fishing Village to City-State: A Social History of New Calabar," in *Man in Africa*, eds. M. Douglas and P. M. Kaberry (London: Tavistock, 1969), 46–48; Nimi Wariboko, *The Mind of African Strategists: A Study of Kalabari Management Practice* (Madison, NJ: Fairleigh Dickinson University Press, 1997), 33–34.

30. Adolphus G. Karibi-Whyte, *Chieftaincy Institution among the Kalabari Ijaw* (Port Harcourt, Nigeria: Ulamba, 2017), 6–11.

31. Karibi-Whyte, 8.

32. I have adapted Norton's words and ideas for my purposes here. See Anne Norton, "Pentecost: Democratic Sovereignty in Carl Schmitt," *Constellations* 18, no. 3 (2011): 389–402, esp. 397.

33. Kay Williamson and A. O. Timitimi, "A Note on Ijo Number Symbolism," *African Notes* 5, no. 3 (January 1970): 9–16.

34. Susan O. Michelman and Tonye V. Erekosima, "Kalabari Dress in Nigeria: Visual Analysis and Gender Implications," in *Dress and Gender: Making and Meaning in Cultural Contexts*, eds. Ruth Barnes and Joanne B. Eicher (Oxford: Berg, 1992), 164–82, at 171.

35. Nimi Wariboko, *The Depth and Destiny of Work: An African Theological Interpretation* (Trenton, NJ: Africa World Press, 2008), 125.

36. Gibson Winter, *Community and Spiritual Transformation: Religion and Politics in a Communal Age* (New York: Crossroad Publishing, 1989), 45.

37. Winter, 41.

38. Beverly Wildung Harrison, *Making the Connections: Essays in Feminist Social Ethics*, ed. Carol S. Robb (Boston: Beacon Press, 1985), 19.

39. *Eros* is "the drive towards the other, towards an ultimate goal, striving of the person or subject for union with that which it is separated from though it belongs to it." *Eros* "strives for a union with that which is a bearer of values because of the value it embodies." See Paul Tillich, *Love, Power, and Justice: Ontological Analyses and Ethical Applications* (London: Oxford University Press, 1954), 25–30.

40. Wariboko, *Depth and Destiny of Work*, 37–39.

41. *Agu-nsi* is an Igbo word that has been adopted in Kalabari. The Kalabari word for carved or sculptured idol is *ẹkẹkẹ-tamụnọ*, and *ẹkẹkẹ* means stone, piece of stone, or rock.

42. Robin Horton, *Kalabari Sculpture* (Lagos: Department of Antiquities, Federal Republic of Nigeria, 1965), 8–9; see also Robin Horton, "The Kalabari Worldview: An Outline and Interpretation," *Africa* 32, no. 3 (July 1962): 204; Robin Horton, "A Hundred Years of Change in Kalabari Religion," in *Black Africa: Its People and Their Cultures Today*, ed. John Middleton (New York: Macmillan, 1971), 194–98.

43. Horton, "Kalabari Worldview," 204. I have heard of at least two cases of gods that have been disrobed of their powers. One is the Owu Akpana (shark) cult and the other is Ogboloma (called *Kun-ma* in Okrika, also a Niger Delta community) cult.

44. Horton relates the story of how a spirit who misbehaved was summoned before an assembly of its worshipers, found guilty, and fined. See Horton, "A Hundred Years of Change in Kalabari Religion," 194–98.

45. Nimi Wariboko, *Ethics and Society in Nigeria: Identity, History, Political Theory* (Rochester, NY: University of Rochester Press, 2019), 35–40.

46. Karibi-Whyte, *Chieftaincy Institution*, 178,

47. Horton, "Kalabari Worldview," 204.

48. Stathis Gourgourris, *Lessons in Secular Criticism* (New York: Fordham University Press, 2013), 130–37, inspired these lines. His comments are on Claude Lefort's contribution to political theory.

49. Nimi Wariboko, *The Principle of Excellence: A Framework for Social Ethics* (Lanham, MD: Lexington Books, 2009).

50. Paul Tillich, *Morality and Beyond* (Louisville, KY: Westminster John Knox Press, 1963), 20.

51. Arendt, *Human Condition*, 9, 177–78, 247.

52. This paragraph and the two before it come from Nimi Wariboko, *The Split Time: Economic Philosophy for Human Flourishing in African Perspective* (Albany: State University of New York Press, 2022), 43–44.

53. See Friedrich Hayek, *Law, Legislation and Liberty*, vol. 1, *Rules and Order* (Chicago: University of Chicago Press, 1973); See also his *The Road to Serfdom* (Chicago: University of Chicago Press, 1944); *The Constitution of Liberty* (Chicago: University of Chicago Press, 1960); *Law, Legislation and Liberty*, vol. 2, *The Mirage of Social Justice* (Chicago: University of Chicago Press, 1976); and *Law, Legislation and Liberty*, vol. 3, *The Political Order of a Free People* (Chicago: University of Chicago Press, 1979).

54. Hayek, *Law, Legislation and Liberty*, 1:108.

Chapter 2

1. Tonye Erekosima, W. H. Kio Lawson, and Obeleye MacJaja, eds., *Hundred Years of Buguma History in Kalabari Culture* (Lagos, Nigeria: Sibon Books Limited, 1991), 15.

2. *Kirikiri mine* is a rare religious funeral rite that traditionally *must* be given to only two categories of people in Kalabari: *akaso-alabo* (chief priest of the national goddess, *Owamekaso*) and *akwa-alabo* (the drum chief of Ekine society). Another version of the oral tradition has it that in addition to these two figures every freeborn chief was entitled to it. It was a normal part of the rites of the funeral of freeborn Kalabari chiefs.

After Amakiri's successful request, he was added to this exclusive list as the third person. The body on which this significant and rare burial rite is performed is called *mine duein* ("embamable corpse requiring extra rites"). The corpse, instead of being put on a bed (*ede*), is laid on a mat on the floor for the rite. The body is dressed with three cloths: *injiri* (imported madras cotton), *ikakibite*, and a white cloth. Other adornments or accessories are *igo piko* (fish eagle feather), red cap, *toru* (kaolin), *buruma* (indigo), and *ila* (native coral bead). Corpses that undergo this rite are buried in a different posture—upright position in the grave for the *akaso-alabo* and *akwa-alabo*, seated position for *amanyanabo*. The normal burial position in Kalabari is flat, face-up.

For further details on Kalabari funeral practices, see Joanne B. Eicher and Tonye Victor Erekosima, "Celebration and Display" in *Global Trade and Cultural Authentication: The Kalabari of the Niger Delta*, ed. Joanne B. Eicher (Bloomington: Indiana University Press, 2022), 221–38; Joanne B. Eicher and Tonye Victor Erekosima, "Fitting Farewells," in *Global Trade and Cultural Authentication*, 239–49.

3. Nimi Wariboko, *The Mind of African Strategists: A Study of Kalabari Management Practice* (Madison, NJ: Fairleigh Dickinson University Press, 1997), 56–63.

4. Erekosima, Kio Lawson, and MacJaja, *Hundred Years*, 17–18.

5. Gwilym Iwan Jones, *The Trading States of the Oil Rivers: A Study of Political Development in Eastern Nigeria* (Oxford: Oxford University Press, 1963), 206–7.

6. Erekosima, Kio Lawson, and MacJaja, *Hundred Years*, 20.

7. For the common as a basis of communication, collaboration, and cooperation, see Michael Hardt and Antonio Negri, *Multitude: War and Democracy in the Age of Empire* (New York: Penguin Books, 2004), 128.

8. Erekosima, Kio Lawson, and MacJaja, *Hundred Years*, 19.

9. Erekosima, Kio Lawson, and MacJaja, 19.

10. See Roberto Esposito, *Third Person: Politics of Life and Philosophy of the Impersonal* (Cambridge: Polity Press, 2012); Roberto Esposito, *Immunitas: The Protection and Negation of Life*, trans. Zakiya Hanafi (Cambridge: Polity Press, 2011); Roberto Esposito, *Communitas: The Origin and Destiny of Community*, trans. T. Campbell (Stanford, CA: Stanford University Press, 2010); and Roberto Esposito, *Bios: Biopolitics and Philosophy* (Minneapolis: University of Minnesota Press, 2008).

11. Miguel Vatter, *The Republic of the Living: Biopolitics and the Critique of Civil Society* (New York: Fordham University Press, 2014), 18.

12. This expectation or obligation of generosity does not, however, mean that in the traditional Kalabari society an individual's assets, endowments, or rewards belong to the whole community as common assets.

13. Robin Horton, "From Fishing Village to City-State: A Social History of New Calabar," in *Man in Africa*, eds. M. Douglas and P. M. Kaberry (London: Tavistock, 1969), 41–42, 45, 50; E. J. Alagoa, "The Niger Delta States and Their Neighbours to c. 1800," in *History of West Africa*, eds. J. A. Ajayi and M. Crowder (London: Longman, 1969), 381.

14. The language from which tonal patterns are extracted is often the ancient form of the Kalabari language. This makes it difficult even for those who are fluent in the modern version to grapple with drum language.

15. Robin Horton, "Igbo: An Ordeal for Aristocrats," *Nigeria Magazine* (September 1966): 168–83.

16. Horton, 179–81.

17. Horton, 181.

18. Erekosima, Kio Lawson, and MacJaja, *Hundred Years*, 89–90. (Note the chapters do have the contributors' names.)

19. Nimi Wariboko, "Three against Four: A Cultural Analysis of the Disappearance of Women in Kalabari," *Journal of Asian and African Studies* 37, no. 1 (2002): 66–95.

20. Robin Horton, "Social Psychologies: African and Western," in *Oedipus and Job in West Africa*, eds. M. Fortes and Robin Horton (Cambridge: Cambridge University Press, 1983), 41–82, at 54.

21. See discussions of existence *sopaka* and *pakabo* in chapter 4.

22. Paul Tillich, *The Socialist Decision* (1933), trans. Franklin Sherman (New York: Harper & Row, 1977), 2.

23. Nimi Wariboko, *The Depth and Destiny of Work: An African Theological Interpretation* (Trenton, NJ: Africa World Press, 2008), 95–115.

24. There cannot be any entity that is a collection of all there is. French philosopher Alain Badiou in *Being and Event*, using the mathematical theories of Georg Cantor (1845–1918), has shown that such an entity is an impossibility; no set can belong to itself. The number of parts or subset of elements in a set is larger than the elements themselves—there is an irremediable excess of subsets over elements such that there cannot exist a set of all sets. See Alain Badiou, *Being and Event*, trans. Oliver Feltham (London: Continuum, 2005).

25. Richard Kearney, *The God Who May Be: A Hermeneutics of Religion* (Bloomington: Indiana University Press, 2001), 95.

26. This idea was inspired by Jean-Luc Nancy, *The Sense of the World*, trans. Jeffrey S. Librett (Minneapolis: University of Minnesota Press, 1997), x.

27. Nancy, 152.

28. Nancy, 136.

29. Roberto Esposito's comment on Martin Heidegger's distinction between part and piece goes like this: "Heidegger talks about the 'piece' (Stück) rather the 'part,' since 'the part shares itself with parts in a whole. It takes part in the whole, belongs to it. The piece on the contrary is separated and indeed, as the piece, is even isolated from the other pieces.'" See Esposito, *Two*, 20.

30. For a deep discussion of the agonistic communitarianism in Kalabari, see Nimi Wariboko, *The Split Time: Economic Philosophy for Hunan Flourishing in African Perspective* (Albany: State University of New York Press, 2022), 109–39.

31. Nancy, *Sense of the World*, 152.

32. Nancy, 111.

33. Wariboko, *Split Time,* 109–39.

34. Paulina Ochoa Espejo, *The Time of Popular Sovereignty: Process and the Democratic State* (University Park: Pennsylvania State University Press, 2011), 59; italics in the original.

35. Espejo, *Time of Popular Sovereignty*, 143.

36. Espejo, 161.

37. Espejo, 161–62; parentheses in the original.

38. Nimi Wariboko, "A Theory of the Canoe House Corporation," *African Economic History* 26 (1998): 141–72.

39. Jan Assmann, *Cultural Memory and Early Civilization: Writing, Remembrance and Political Imagination* (Cambridge: Cambridge University Press, 2011), 178–81, 190–93.

40. Adolphus G. Karibi-Whyte, *Chieftaincy Institution among the Kalabari Ijaw* (Port Harcourt, Nigeria: Ulamba Publishers, 2017), 8–9.

41. Michael Hardt and Antonio Negri, *Empire* (Cambridge, MA: Harvard University Press, 2000), 166.

42. Hardt and Negri, 182.

43. Nimi Wariboko, "Kalabari: A Study in Synthetic Ideal-Type," *Nordic Journal of African Studies* 8, no. 1 (1999): 80–92.

44. Nigel Barley, *Forehead of the Dead: An Anthropological View of Kalabari Ancestral Screens* (Washington, DC: Smithsonian Institute, 1988), 6.

45. For more on the problems of indigeneity in Africa, see Mahmood Mamdani, *When Victims Become Killers: Colonialism, Nativism, and the Genocide in Rwanda* (Princeton, NJ: Princeton University Press, 2001); Mahmood Mamdani, "Making Sense of Political Violence in Postcolonial Africa," *Socialist Register* (2003): 132–51.

46. See Constitution of the Federal Republic of Nigeria 25(1) & (2); 26 (1) &(2), 27 (Abuja, Nigeria: Federal Government of Nigeria Printing Press, 1999).

47. I am deploying the term "apparatus" in its Agambenian sense. See Giorgio Agamben, *What Is an Apparatus? and Other Essays*, trans. David Kishik and Stefan Pedatella (Stanford, CA: Stanford University Press, 2009). It is not in the Foucauldian sense of "a set of strategies of the relations of forces supporting, and supported by, certain types of knowledge." Michel Foucault, *Power/Knowledge: Selected Interviews and Other Writings, 1972–1977*, ed. Colon Gordon (New York: Pantheon, 1980), 196, quoted in Agamben, *What Is an Apparatus?*, 2.

48. Agamben, *What Is an Apparatus?*, 14.

49. Slavoj Žižek, "Only a Suffering God Can Save Us," in *God in Pain: Inversions of Apocalypse*, by Slavoj Žižek and Boris Gunjević (New York: Seven Stories Press, 2012), 155–92, at 171.

50. Slavoj Žižek, "Christianity against the Sacred," in Žižek and Gunjević, *God in Pain*, 58.

Chapter 3

1. Tsenay Serequeberhan, *The Hermeneutics of African Philosophy: Horizon and Discourse* (New York: Routledge, 1994), 28.

2. See Nimi Wariboko, *The Pentecostal Principle: Ethical Methodology in New Spirit* (Grand Rapids, MI: William B. Eerdmans, 2012).

3. Nimi Wariboko, *Ethics and Time: Ethos of Temporal Orientation in Politics and Religion in the Niger Delta* (Lanham, MD: Lexington, 2010), 60–61n13.

4. In every society there are three sets of possibilities: one that is open to all individuals, another that is available to only a few and the rest of society is excluded, and the universe of possibilities that are yet to be fulfilled or not yet available to all persons and institutions. The latter is actually the *horizon of unfulfilled possibilities*. And there is the law (as acts of legislature, *nomos* and *ethos*, symbolic structures that regulate practices and representations, or specific regimes of interpretations of the [oral or written] scripture/faith, and so on). The law acts to bring the range of possibilities to manageable proportion and distributes them into the three sets. There are included and excluded possibilities in every existing state of affairs. It is the law that defines the boundaries of these three sets, what is possible and what is impossible. The law is the power that regulates possibilities and access to them. It is the law that tells members of a community what works within a given framework of relations.

5. From here on, I am going to adapt Richard Fenn, "Sociology and Religion: Searching for the Sacred," in *The Oxford Handbook of Religion and Science*, eds. Philip Clayton and Zachary Simpson (Oxford: Oxford University Press, 2006), 253–70.

6. Fenn, "Sociology and Religion," 258.

7. Fenn, 259.

8. Fenn, 257–58.

9. If a person does not like the course of her life on earth she goes to a diviner to change her *so* or *fiyeteboye*. The process of changing destiny is called *bibibari* (altering or nullifying the spoken word, recanting). The person visits a diviner to let *Teme-órú* (the supreme goddess) know that the person would like to change how he or she wants to live his or her life-course on earth. Once the change of destiny is made, the new *so* (which becomes a new point of fixity) determines the whole course of the person.

10. For discussions of *amatemeso*, see Wariboko, *Ethics and Time*.

11. See Judith Butler, *Bodies That Matter: On the Discursive Limits of "Sex"* (New York: Routledge, 2011), 9. I have borrowed Butler's words to use in a very different context.

12. Here I reference French philosopher Jean-Luc Nancy's insight on apportioning as it relates to *nomos*: "*Nomos* is the distribution, apportionment, and allocation of its [a community's, world's] parts: a piece of territory, a portion of food, the delimitation of rights and needs in each, and at every time, as it is fitting. . . . This is not an accomplished distribution." See Jean-Luc Nancy, *Being Singular Plural*, trans. Robert D. Richardson and Anne E. O'Byrne (Stanford, CA: Stanford University Press, 2000), 185.

13. Nimi Wariboko, *Ethics and Society in Nigeria: Identity, History, Political Theory* (Rochester, NY: University of Rochester Press, 2019), 35–50.

14. Miguel Vatter, *The Republic of the Living: Biopolitics and the Critique of Civil Society* (New York: Fordham University Press, 2014), 257.

15. Jean-Luc Nancy, *The Inoperative Community*, trans. Peter Connor, Lisa Garbus, Michael Holland, and Simona Sawhney (Minneapolis: University of Minnesota Press, 1991), 25.

16. See Nancy, *The Inoperative Community*.

17. Jean-Luc Nancy, *Birth to Presence*, trans. Brian Holmes et al. (Stanford, CA: Stanford University Press, 1993), 155; emphasis in the original.

18. Nancy, *Being Singular Plural*, 185.

19. Nimi Wariboko, *The Split Economy: Saint Paul Goes to Wall Street* (Albany: State of University of New York Press, 2020).

20. Malidoma Patrice Somé, *Ritual: Power, Healing, and Community* (New York: Penguin Group, 1993), 12; see also 24, 59.

21. I am alluding to Paul Tillich here.

22. Nimi Wariboko, "Kalabari: A Study in Synthetic Ideal-Type," *Nordic Journal of African Studies* 8, no. 1 (1999): 80–92.

23. Note that *so* refers both to the "second person" of the duality and the destiny of human beings. Destiny is *so* because it is a "program" put in place for the individual by the second person of the duality (*So*). The context of usage in this chapter makes it clear which of the two senses is referred to at any point.

24. Mark Lewis Taylor, *Remembering Esperanza: A Cultural-Political Theology for North American Praxis* (Minneapolis, MN: Fortress Press, 2005), 205–6.

25. Nimi Wariboko, *The Split Time: Economic Philosophy for Human Flourishing in African Perspective* (Albany: State University of New York Press, 2022); Wariboko, *The Split Economy*.

26. Robin Horton, *Kalabari Sculpture* (Lagos: Department of Antiquities, Federal Republic of Nigeria, 1965); Robin Horton, "The Kalabari Ekine Society: A Borderline of Religion and Art," *Africa* 33, no. 2 (1963): 94–114; Nigel Barley, *Forehead of the Dead: An Anthropological View of Kalabari Ancestral Screens* (Washington, DC: Smithsonian Institute, 1988).

27. Richard Kearney, *Strangers, Gods and Monsters: Interpreting Otherness* (London: Routledge, 2003), 4–7 inspired this thought.

28. Nimi Wariboko, *The Depth and Destiny of Work: An African Theological Interpretation* (Trenton, NJ: Africa World Press, 2008), 35–63.

29. All this means that this stuff is not reworked by the relations in which it finds itself or is manifested.

30. Paul Tillich, *Theology of Culture* (London: Oxford University Press, 1959), 25; italics in the original.

31. This definition was inspired by Roger H. Mitchell and Julie T. Arram, *Discovering Kenarchy* (Eugene, OR: Wipf and Stock, 2014), 90.

32. Slavoj Žižek, *Interrogating the Real* (London: Continuum, 2005), 38.

33. Žižek, 37.

34. Žižek, 125.

35. Vatter, *Republic of the Living*, 34.

36. Giorgio Agamben, *The Kingdom and the Glory: For a Theological Genealogy of Economy and Government*, trans. Lorenzo Chisea with Matteo Mandarini (Stanford, CA: Stanford University Press, 2011).

37. Roger Haydon Mitchell, "What Are the Politics of Love," in *Cultivating New Post-Secular Space*, ed. Roger Haydon Mitchell (London: Routledge, 2019), 26–43, at 28.

38. Paul Tillich, *The Courage to Be* (New Haven, CT: Yale University Press, 2014), 138.

39. Tillich, 138.

40. Pardon the Hegelian turn of phrase here.

41. Wariboko, *The Split Time*, 13, 55–63.

42. Nimi Wariboko, "Three against Four: A Cultural Analysis of the Disappearance of Women in Kalabari," *Journal of Asian and African Studies* 37, no. 1 (2002): 66–95.

43. Slavoj Žižek, *Violence: Six Sideways Reflections* (New York: Picador, 2008).

44. Kay Williamson and A. O. Timitimi, "A Note on Ijo Number Symbolism," *African Notes* 5, no. 3 (January 1970): 9–16.

45. Pardon my allusion to Alasdair McIntyre.

46. For an admirable discussion of politics-as-statecraft and politics-as-soulcraft, see Bradley B. Burroughs, *Christianity, Politics, and the Predicament of Evil: A Constructive Theological Ethic of Soulcraft and Statecraft* (Lanham, MD: Lexington Books, 2019).

Chapter 4

1. Margaret Canovan, *The Political Thought of Hannah Arendt* (New York: Harcourt Bruce Jovanovich, 1974), 48.

2. John Wall, *Moral Creativity: Paul Ricoeur and the Poetics of Possibility* (Oxford: Oxford University Press, 2005), 17.

3. Patricia Bowen-Moore, *Hannah Arendt's Philosophy of Natality* (New York: St. Martin's Press, 1989), 7.

4. Hannah Arendt, *Between Past and Future: Eight Exercises in Political Thought* (New York: Penguin Books, 1954), 148.

5. Hannah Arendt, *On Revolution* (New York: Penguin Books, 2004), 59.

6. Hannah Arendt, *The Human Condition* (Chicago: University of Chicago Press, 1958), 176.

7. Hannah Arendt, *The Origins of Totalitarianism* (New York: Schocken Books, 2004), 616.

8. Arendt, *Human Condition*, 179.

9. Arendt, 247.

10. Arendt, *Between Past and Future*, 105.

11. Arendt, 99.

12. Arendt, 118.

13. It is important to mention that chiefs did not behave toward their subjects ex nihilo. There was a tradition of lawfulness that both chiefs and their subjects and slaves recognized. The Kalabari tradition of lawfulness was sustained neither by commitment to foundation on a beginning alone, like the Romans, nor by adherence to an otherworldly, transcending concept of justice alone, as the Greeks. Theirs was a combination of immanentism and transcending measurements. The legitimacy of law or authority is traced back to human actions. The tradition of the elders or the village heroes is the stabilizing force in human affairs, the positive law that provides the legal restrictions on action. Religion (the village heroes are part of the pantheon of gods) was also retained as a motivating principle and as the source of ultimate standards.

Amatemeso (literally the "destiny of town" or "creator-god of town"), which is also invoked as a power behind law, a motivating principle, captures something of the Romans' commitment to foundation and augmentation and throwness to human actions. Since the *amatemeso* is in some crucial sense not a being but the collective will (the spirit or mind of the town, *Volksgeist*) or, better, the signification of the coming together of the people to found a community and its derived national character, it is open to refounding, to amendment, and to augmentation. This process is similar to and linked to the augmentation of houses. As houses grow and segment and merge, they each get their own *waritemeso*, which supposedly adds up to form or is sublated into the *amatemeso*.

14. Bowen-Moore, *Hannah Arendt's Philosophy of Natality*, 2; italics in the original.

15. Arendt, *Origins of Totalitarianism*, 611.

16. "Arendt's understanding of natality is viewed from the standpoint of what she called *amor mundi*, in which the potentiality of human beginnings is directed toward the world and for the sake of the world rather than toward oneself in isolation from the world and for the sake of oneself independent of others. Thus, natality is disclosed as an entirely world-oriented (that is, worldly) phenomenon whose capacity for beginning anew is ideally for the sake of the durability and futurity of the world we hold in common." See Bowen-Moore, *Hannah Arendt's Philosophy of Natality*, 2.

17. Nimi Wariboko, *The Mind of African Strategists: A Study of Kalabari Management Practice* (Madison, WI: Fairleigh Dickson University Press, 1997), 58–59, 70–80.

18. Robin Horton, "From Fishing Village to City-State: A Social History of New Calabar," in *Man in Africa*, eds. M. Douglas and P. M. Kaberry (London: Tavistock, 1969), 38–59, at 48.

19. Bowen-Moore, *Hannah Arendt's Philosophy of Natality*, 42.

20. See Nimi Wariboko, "A Theory of the Canoe House Corporation," *African Economic History* 26 (1998): 141–72; and also his *Mind of African Strategists*.

21. Depending on the era, the number of required men to man a war-canoe ranged from twenty to thirty.

22. Arendt, *Origins of Totalitarianism*, 586.

23. Arendt, *Human Condition*, 176–77.

24. Nimi Wariboko, *The Depth and Destiny of Work: An African Theological Interpretation* (Trenton, NJ: Africa World Press, 2008), chap. 5.

25. Bowen-Moore, *Hannah Arendt's Philosophy of Natality*, 52.

26. The house system is open to expansive movements, anchored to a boundless and inclusive framework. The notion of sovereignty implicit in the house system is akin to that of the United States as recently described by Michael Hardt and Antonio Negri, *Empire* (Cambridge, MA: Harvard University Press, 2000), 164–72.

27. Horton, "From Fishing Village to City-State," 41–42, 45, 50; E. J. Alagoa, "The Niger Delta States and Their Neighbours to c. 1800," in *History of West Africa*, eds. J. A. Ajayi and M. Crowder (London: Longman, 1969), 381.

28. Canovan, *Political Thought of Hannah Arendt*, 59–60.

29. Arendt, *Between Past and Future*, 161.

30. Arendt, 161.

31. See D/0/18, National Museums of Liverpool (Maritime Archives and Library). See his diary note of September 28, 1857.

32. Shiraz Dossa, *The Public Realm and the Public Self: The Political Theory of Hannah Arendt* (Waterloo, ON: Wilfrid Laurier University Press, 1989), 82; italic in the original.

33. Arendt, *Human Condition*, 242.

34. Nimi Wariboko, "Three against Four: A Cultural Analysis of the Disappearance of Women in Kalabari," *Journal of Asian and African Studies* 37, no. 1 (2001): 66–95.

35. Tonye V. Erekosima, W. H. Kio Lawson, and Obeleye MacJaja, *Hundred Years of Buguma History in Kalabari Culture* (Lagos, Nigeria: Sibon Books Limited, 1991), 117. See also Robin Horton, "The Kalabari Ekine Society: A Borderland of Religion and Art," *Africa* 33, no. 22 (1963): 94–114, at 99.

36. Alain Badiou's word from another context. See his *Saint Paul: The Foundation of Universalism*, trans. Ray Brassier (Stanford, CA: Stanford University Press, 2003), 59.

37. Arendt, *Human Condition*, 200.

38. Søren Kierkegaard, *Philosophical Fragments*, trans. Howard V. Hong and Edna H. Hong (Princeton, NJ: Princeton University Press, 1985), chap. 4.

39. Horton, "Kalabari Ekine Society," 101–2.

40. Horton, 108.

41. Horton, 107.

42. Robin Horton, "Igbo: An Aristocratic Ordeal for Aristocrats," *Nigerian Magazine* (September 1966): 168–83.

43. Arendt, *Between Past and Future*, 151.

Chapter 5

1. This is a lineage-based trading *corporation* (*wari* in local parlance), the major vehicle for trading and political activities in the eighteenth and nineteenth centuries. It is now the major form of political and kinship organization of Kalabari society.

2. This drive is always and everywhere culturally and socially constructed. I am not here talking about a biological drive but a culturally conditioned quest for self-actualization and affirmation. Henri J. M. Nouwen sees it as humanity's attempt to "project himself [*sic*] beyond the limitations of human existence." *The Wounded Healer: Ministry in Contemporary Society* (New York: Doubleday, 1972), 14. Robert Jay Lifton posits it as the compelling, universal urge "to maintain an inner sense of continuity over time and space with the elements of life . . . man's way of experiencing his connection with all human history." *Boundaries* (New York: Random House, 1970), 22.

3. Philippe Aries, *Western Attitudes toward Death from the Middle Ages to the Present* (Baltimore, MD: John Hopkins University Press, 1974), 63–64.

4. Robert J. Lifton identified five modes of expression of immortality: (1) the biological mode, living on through one's children; (2) the theological mode, the idea of transcending death through spiritual attainment; (3) the mode of creativity, this immortality achieved through "works"; (4) eternal nature, "the sense of immortality achieved through being survived by nature itself," as believed among the Japanese; and (5) experiential transcendence, ecstatic mystic experience that gives a feeling of "continuous presence." "The Sense of Immortality: On Death and the Continuity of Life," in *New Meanings of Death*, ed. Herman Feifel (New York: McGraw-Hill, 1977), 278–79. What Lifton assigns to the Japanese is also found among the Chinese, as Michael C. Brannigan explains in another context elucidating the philosophy of Chuang Tzu: "There is no essential difference between ourselves and all that surrounds us. We are one with the universe, and the universe, as revealed through the seasonal cycle, is permanent. Living in harmony with Nature ensures one's immortality in oneness with Nature." *The Pulse of Wisdom: The Philosophies of India, China, and Japan* (Belmont, CA: Wadsworth Publishing, 1995), 331. John Bodin, on the other hand, identified only three forms of social immortality: (1) continuity of the breed or the tribe; (2) immortality of the personal soul in some heavenly realm; and (3) socialized immortality through social creativeness, works. "In this third stage, the conception of immortality is

socialized. Man finds his meaning and salvation in the social community with its continuity of life and ideals. The kingdom of heaven has now become a kingdom to be progressively realized in this world. Loyalty to the community and sacrifice for its progress now become dominant motives. The immortality of the individual and of the social group of which he is a part are now recognized to be reciprocal. Man must find his life and joy in the creative service to the community." "Social Immortality," *International Journal of Ethics* 25 (191): 195–212, at 196.

5. Understanding how men and women choose to strive for legacy in any particular era is a study of the prevailing philosophies of the time. Carl Becker argues that the notion of personal immortality was replaced in the eighteenth and nineteenth centuries with concern over posterity and social forms of immortality as eighteenth-century philosophies overtook the theological concern with afterlife with the notion that works and commitment of people to the progress of their societies will enable them to live in the memory of future generations. *The Heavenly City of the Eighteenth-Century Philosophers* (New Haven, CT: Yale University Press, 1932 [2003]), 119–68). Viviana A. Zelizer argues that notions of immortality in the nineteenth and early twentieth centuries in America yielded to the predominant capitalist ethos. "For instance, life insurance assumed the role of a secular ritual and introduced new notions of immortality that emphasized remembrance through money. A 'good death' was no longer defined only on moral grounds; the inclusion of a life policy made financial foresight another prerequisite." "Human Values and the Market: The Case of Life Insurance and Death in 19th-Century America," *American Journal of Sociology* 84 (1978): 591–610.

6. Robert Cummings Neville, *Eternity and Time's Flow* (Albany: State University of New York Press, 1993), xv.

7. Amaury Talbot, *Tribes of the Niger Delta: Their Religions and Customs* (London: Frank Cass & Co., 1932), 9.

8. Robin Horton, "The Kalabari Worldview: An Outline and Interpretation," *Africa* 33, no. 1 (July 1962): 197–219; "The Kalabari Ekine Society: A Borderline of Religion and Art," *Africa* 33 (1963): 94–114.

9. There is a category of spirit, *Kumbu-ama-kala-ama-apu*, that may be called sacred dwarves, dwarf spirits, or tiny men. They are known to carry axes (*kumbu* in Kalabari). Sometimes they are men known to carry sticks in the form of a hoe or axe. Their name is very descriptive of them. *Ama* means village/city/territory, sphere/realm, otherworld. *Kala* means small, tiny, or dwarfish. *Ama-apu* means residents. Their name indicates two of their features. They are people of the land/realm/*ama* of axe. Second, *kala-ama-apu* means people of small of dwarfish realm. Literally, the name means dwarfs who carry axes or dwarfs of the axe realm. The long name doubles on their dwarfishness and their weapon of attack. Tiny-men-with-axes.

They are land-based gods or spirits, dwelling in the forest. They are good, bad, or both. A person who works with or worships them can appease them or offer them what they need and then send them to do whatever the person desires, and that could be bad or good. Yes, they befriend little children and take them into the forest and teach them herbal medicines and the language of herbs. Once a person learns the herbal language he or she can communicate with plants/plant life. The plants will tell such a person their individual usefulness, what they can be used for in terms of healing, affliction, prosperity, and so on.

I got this information in an interview I conducted in Port Harcourt, Nigeria, on Saturday, December 14, 2019, with two Kalabari brothers, a doctor (in his fifties) and a lawyer (late forties). The lawyer claims to have had a personal encounter with them when, he believed, his enemies sent them to attack him in the night. According to him, this happened in the mid-1990s. He was a young practicing lawyer then. The doctor said he heard about them from the elders. I also heard about dwarf spirit-men while growing up in Abonnema. But I forgot about such stories until my interviewees brought them up on that fateful December day during a conversation about illness and spiritual attack.

On December 13 or 14, 2021, I started reading Malidoma Patrice Somé's book *Of Water and the Spirit: Ritual Magic, and Initiation in the Life of an African Shaman* (New York: Penguin Books, 1994) and came across a description of tiny men, little spirits he met in the forest as a child. They are named Kontomblé in the language of the Dagara of Burkina Faso, West Africa. See Somé, *Of Water and the Spirit*, 17–19.

10. Not every person can become an ancestor. There are several conditions a person has to meet before qualifying to be ancestor. They include dying after age fifty; being buried in the hometown; not passing away in abnormal circumstances such as suicide, childbirth, pregnancy, drowning, eating, and death accompanied by sores or infectious diseases, general swelling of the body, and elephantiasis. The person should not be known as a wizard or witch and should be of integrity, of honesty, and supportive of house and community. These rules are not mere conditions that qualify a person for his or her place in the world beyond the grave. They go past that. If a person does not meet these rules before death, the person brings disgrace to the living relatives. Robin Horton writes that "people who die in any of these ways [abnormal circumstance] are considered to have brought abomination to the community. They are wrapped in mats and are buried as quickly as possible, without any coffin, in a special tract of mangrove reserved for the 'bad dead.' After burial, special priests purify the village. People who have died in this way are not normally called upon when lineage members invoke their ancestors. Indeed, the funeral rite performed for them has the effect of severing all ties between themselves and the living." "Ikpataka Dogi: A Kalabari Funeral Rites," *African Notes* 5, no. 3 (1970): 57–72.

11. Horton, "Ikpataka Dogi," 68.

12. See Peter Paris, *The Spirituality of the African Peoples: The Search for Common Moral Discourse* (Minneapolis, MN: Fortress Press, 1995), 25.

13. He or she is usually elected to the post by house members. Only two women in Kalabari history have become house leaders and thus chieftaincy titles established in their names. They are Orupumbu of Buguma and Oruguta of Abonnema. They were not actually installed as chiefs.

14. Robin Horton, "From Fishing Village to City-State: A Social History of New Calabar," in *Man in Africa*, eds. M. Douglas and P. M. Kaberry (London: Longman, 1969), 38–39.

15. Jürgen Moltmann, "Progress and Abyss: Remembrances of the Future of the Modern World," in *The Future of Hope: Christian Tradition amid Modernity and Postmodernity*, eds. Miroslav Volf and William Katerberg (Grand Rapids, MI: William B. Eerdmans, 2004), 18.

16. James K. A. Smith, "Determined Hope: A Phenomenology of Christian Expectation," in Volf and Katerberg, *Future of Hope*, 200–27.

17. Here I have relied on Jeffrey Stout's insightful definition of piety to capture the enigmatic "spirit" of the Kalabari notion of piety. See his *Democracy and Tradition* (Princeton, NJ: Princeton University Press, 2004), 25–37.

18. For the notion of cultural biography, see Igor Kopytoff, "The Cultural Biography of Things: Commoditization as Process," in *The Social Life of Things: Commodities in Cultural Perspective*, ed. Arjun Appadurai (Cambridge: Cambridge University Press, 1988), 64–90.

19. This is rendered in Kalabari as "Orume ere-bu ane eke-boari ane ipiki ke simeari."

20. Robin Horton, *Kalabari Sculpture* (Lagos, Department of Antiquities, Federal Republic of Nigeria, 1965), 10.

21. This way of thinking is not at all surprising once one grasps the importance of relations as constitutive of both society and personhood in Kalabari (African) communities. Worship is not just reverence, obeisance, praise and exaltation, or appropriate response to deity but the dynamic maintenance of deep, thick relations, a social bond with a deity. All forms of power, be it political or spiritual, are always predicated on the strength of social bonds among persons and the fracture or rapture of the bond or the displacement of harmony in the bond means erosion of power and authority.

22. *Agu-nsi* is an Igbo word that has been adopted in Kalabari. The Kalabari word for carved or sculptured idol is *ẹkẹkẹ-tamụnọ*, and *ẹkẹkẹ* means stone, piece of stone, or rock.

23. Horton, *Kalabari Sculpture*, 8–9. See also Horton, "The Kalabari Worldview," 204. Horton relates the story of how a spirit who misbehaved was summoned before an assembly of its worshipers, found guilty, and fined. Robin Horton, "A Hundred Years of Change in Kalabari Religion," in *Black Africa: Its People and Their Cultures Today*, ed. John Middleton (New York: Macmillan, 1971, 194–98.

24. For a description of thick relations, see Avishai Margalit, *The Ethics of Memory* (Cambridge, MA: Harvard University Press, 2002), 7–8, 37–38.

25. Margalit, 90.

26. Margalit, 90.

27. John Mbiti, *African Religions and Philosophy* (New York: Doubleday, 1970), 3.

28. Paul Tillich, *The Courage to Be* (New Haven, CT: Yale University Press, 2000).

29. Since everything arises from being in Kalabari philosophy, there is nothing like absolute nonbeing, and there was no time when there was no being or power of being. Death (*so*, depart from physical appearance) is not a precipitous drop into nothingness, into an abyss, but only a return into "no-more" or "not-yet" being, which is still animated in some sense by power of being. The spirit, the power of being, is an active relational principle, a substance that is shared by all men and connects all things to Being itself. Thus, a person exists by being in communion with others, sharing of this power. One may surmise that nonbeing in African philosophical thought is being that is *decommunalized*.

30. John Mbiti calls this "collective immortality." See Ifeanyi Menkiti, "On the Normative Conception of a Person," in *A Companion to African Philosophy*, ed. Kwasi Wiredu (Malden, MA: Blackwell Publishing, 2004), 328, for a critique of Mbiti's problematic and misleading terminology.

31. See Menkiti, "On the Normative Conception of a Person," 328.

32. For more details on this, see chap. 4.

33. See Tonye V. Erekosima and J. B. Eicher, "Kalabari Cut-Thread Cloth: An Example of Cultural Authentication," *African Arts* 14, no. 2 (1981): 48–51; Tonye V. Erekosima, "An Analysis of Learning Resources for Political Integration Applicable to Nigerian Secondary School Social Studies: The Case of Kalabari Men's Traditional Dress" (PhD diss., Catholic University of America, 1989); J. B. Eicher and T. V. Erekosima, "Kalabari Funerals: Celebration and Display," *African Arts* 19, no. 3 (1987): 38–45; M. C. Daly, "Kalabari Female Appearance and the Tradition of Iria" (PhD diss., University of Minnesota, 1984).

34. Margalit, *The Ethics of Memory*, 94.

35. It can also be translated as thus: "The community is the whole yam and the individual is only a part of the yam (community)." The part can exist only because the whole (the *we*) exists in which it is a part and it is such only through the whole.

36. Horton, "A Hundred Years of Change in Kalabari Religion," 193.

37. Quoted in Becker, *The Heavenly City*, 44.

38. G. I. Jones, *The Trading States of the Oil Rivers: A Study of Political Development in Eastern Nigeria* (Oxford: Oxford University Press, 1963), 213–14.

39. Giorgio Agamben, *The Kingdom and the Glory: For a Theological Genealogy of Economy and Government*, trans. Lorenzo Chiesa with Matteo Mandarini (Stanford, CA: Stanford University Press, 2011).

40. Arthur Bradley, *Unbearable Life: A Genealogy of Political Erasure* (New York: Columbia University Press, 2019).

41. According to J. Wentzel van Huyssteen: "Phase space is an image for the fact that every event that does happen is surrounded by a ghostly halo of nearby events that did not happen but could have. Phase spaces are large, since they comprehend a wide range of all possibilities." J. Wentzel van Huyssteen, *Alone in the World? Human Consciousness in Science and Theology* (Grand Rapids, MI: William B. Eerdmans, 2006), 56, citing Ian Stewart, *Life's Other Secret: The New Mathematics of the Living World* (New York: Wiley, 1998).

42. Roberto Esposito, *Immunitas: The Protection and Negation of Life*, trans. Zakiya Hanafi (Cambridge: Polity Press, 2011), 63.

43. Becker, *The Heavenly City*; Zelizer, "Human Values and the Market," 591–610; and Bodin, "Social Immortality," 195–212.

44. Kwasi Wiredu, *Philosophy and African Culture* (Cambridge: Cambridge University Press, 1980), 6. See also John Ayotunde Isola Bewaji, "Ethics and Morality in Yoruba Culture," in Wiredu, *A Companion to African Philosophy*, 396–403.

45. Tonye Erekosima, W. H. Kio Lawson, and Obeleye MacJaja, eds., *Hundred Years of Buguma History in Kalabari Culture* (Lagos, Nigeria: Sibon Books Limited, 1991), 23.

46. Erekosima, Kio Lawson, and MacJaja, eds., 24.

47. Frank J. Hinkelamert, *The Ideological Weapons: A Theological Critique of Capitalism* (Maryknoll, NY: Orbis Book, 1986), 264.

48. The insights of this paragraph are indebted to Hinkelamert, *The Ideological Weapons*, 18–72.

49. Greg M. Nielsen, *The Norms of Answerability: Social Theory Between Bakhtin and Habermas* (Albany: State University of New York Press, 2002), 121.

50. Nielsen, 122.

Chapter 6

1. Giorgio Agamben, *The Use of Bodies*, trans. Adam Kotsko (Stanford, CA: Stanford University Press, 2015), 81.

2. Walter Benjamin, "Notes Toward a Work on the Category of Justice," trans. Peter Fenves in his *The Messianic Reduction: Walter Benjamin and the Shape of Time* (Stanford, CA: Stanford University Press, 2011), 257, quoted in Agamben, *Use of Bodies*, 81.

3. *Tari* is the Kalabari-Ijo word for desire. *Tari* (which also means beginning, original, the first or primordial, to long for, being-after-something, or being concerned with) in its complex depths of meaning and nuance can carry most of the connotations of *gboloma* (togetherness, *eros*) and *belema* (love, like) and

go beyond them. *Tari* as desire is a potentiality, not a thing or substance, but the contextual ground for things or substance. *Tari* is singular and indeterminate. When desire (*tari*) meets its object, it become *gboloma*, an actuality, producing a determinate thing. See Nimi Wariboko, *The Depth and Destiny of Work: An African Theological Interpretation* (Trenton, NJ: Africa World Press, 2008), 87, 105, 119; Nimi Wariboko, *The Principle of Excellence: A Framework for Social Ethics* (Lanham, MD: Lexington Books, 2009), 87–88.

  4. Robert Cummings Neville, *Existence: Philosophical Theology*, vol. 2 (Albany: State University of New York Press, 2014), 79.

  5. The terminology in this paragraph is indebted to Ben Vedder, "Heidegger on Desire," *Continental Philosophy Review* 31 (1998): 353–68.

  6. Giorgio Agamben, *The Man without Content*, trans. Georgia Albert (Stanford, CA: Stanford University Press, 1999), 98; 94–103 of this book inspire this section on temporal structure of desire.

  7. Agamben, 99.

  8. Agamben, 99.

  9. Agamben, 99.

  10. Agamben, 101.

  11. Agamben, 101.

  12. Carl Schmitt, *Political Theology: Four Chapters on the Concept of Sovereignty*, trans. George Schwab (Cambridge, MA: MIT Press, 1985), 49.

  13. For a discussion of the killing of the shark-god, see Liverpool merchant William Oates, diary notes, September 28, 1857, D/0/18, International Slavery Museum (National Museums of Liverpool, Maritime Archives and Library), Liverpool, England. See also G. I. Jones, *The Trading States of the Oil Rivers: Study of Political Development in Eastern Nigeria* (Oxford: Oxford University Press, 1963), 217.

  14. Until I discovered Oates's diary in July 2009 at the International Slavery Museum, Liverpool, UK.

  15. The people of Bonny, another Izon group, also killed two gods that they considered wicked. "Kunbuyana and Tolofari . . . were wicked and capsized many Bonny canoes, going and coming from market, unless a small offering of palm-oil was thrown into the river. They so molested Bonny that my [B. M. Pepple] ancestor, King Dappa Pepple, went off and cut off their heads, which he brought back to Bonny. This happened long years ago." P. Amaury Talbot, *Tribes of the Niger Delta: Their Religions and Customs* (London: Frank Cass, 1967), 52. I have heard of another case in Okrika, another Izon community, where the god Kun-ma (which is called Ogboloma in Kalabari) was also "disrobed."

  16. *Agu-nsi* is an Igbo word that has been adopted in Kalabari. The Kalabari word for carved or sculptured idol is *ẹkẹkẹ-tamụnọ*; *ẹkẹkẹ* means stone, piece of stone, or rock.

17. Robin Horton, *Kalabari Sculpture* (Lagos: Department of Antiquities, Federal Republic of Nigeria, 1965), 8–9. See also Robin Horton, "The Kalabari Worldview: An Outline and Interpretation," *Africa* 32, no. 3 (July 1962): 197–219, esp. 204. Horton relates the story of how a spirit who misbehaved was summoned before an assembly of its worshipers, found guilty, and fined. See Robin Horton, "A Hundred Years of Change in Kalabari Religion" in *Black Africa: Its People and Their Cultures Today*, ed. John Middleton (New York: Macmillan, 1971), 194–98.

18. See a reinstatement of this question in the form of a public announcement in J. P. Clark, *Ozidi* (Ibadan, Nigeria: Oxford University Press, 1966), 18.

19. See Wariboko, *Depth and Destiny of Work* for the role legacy and social immortality play in the ethical formation of subjects in an Izon community.

20. His drum name in Kalabari accents his boldness, which comes from his wealth. *Isiowu-ye-obu: Kali-kulu-kulu-kalika. Igwangi bara pakabo toru kuro*, meaning in Kalabari, "The rich is bold." See Sonny Braide, *Owuame-Kengema Kalabari* (Bloomington, IN: Xlibris, 2017), 157.

21. The analyses that follow were inspired by Rubem A. Alves, *A Theology of Human Life* (Washington, DC: Corpus Books, 1969), 130–31, 136.

22. In the 1970s I heard two men quarreling in Onu-bio (the main square of the canoe house that Chief Frank Briggs once ruled). One of them, Ifeanyi from Jack Compound, not well educated in the English language, busted out in anger against his opponent, stating, "Don't attempt me" instead of "Don't tempt me."

23. This distinction between fact and factor was inspired by Alves, *A Theology of Human Hope*, 130–32.

24. Nimi Wariboko, *Pattern of Institutions in the Niger Delta: Economic and Ethological Interpretations of History and Culture* (Port Harcourt, Nigeria: Onyoma Research Publications, 2007), 301–37.

25. What I call the *care of the soul* for the generation of the early twenty-first century. The care of the soul (not to be confused with a pastoral technique of preparing the self for an elsewhere) is a matter of defining, sustaining, and harnessing the most adequate form and multiplicity of the becoming of de-finalized freedom for a people, a civilization, or an era. The care of the soul, as the micropolitics of freedom, precedes any order or being, always searching for the crack or line of fight to explode any socioeconomic order that resists human flourishing. Care of the soul in this sense is the praxis of taking on one's own existence always as potentiality. See Nimi Wariboko, *Economics in Spirit and Truth: A Moral Philosophy of Finance* (New York: Palgrave Macmillan, 2014), xi–xvii, 159–71.

Bibliography

Books and Journals

Agamben, Giorgio. *The Kingdom and the Glory: For a Theological Genealogy of Economy and Government*. Translated by Lorenzo Chisea with Matteo Mandarini. Stanford, CA: Stanford University Press, 2011.

———. *The Use of Bodies*. Translated by Adam Kotsko. Stanford, CA: Stanford University Press, 2015.

———. *What Is an Apparatus? and Other Essays*. Translated by David Kishik and Stefan Pedatella. Stanford, CA: Stanford University Press, 2009.

Alagoa, E. J. "The Development of Institutions in the states of the Eastern Niger Delta." *Journal of African History* 7 (1971): 269–78.

———. "The Niger Delta States and Their Neighbours to c. 1800." In *History of West Africa*, edited by J. A. Ajayi and M. Crowder, 372–411. London: Longman, 1969.

———. *The Small Brave City-State: A History of Nembe (Brass) in the Niger Delta*. Madison: University of Wisconsin Press, 1964.

Alves, Rubem A. *A Theology of Human Life*. Washington, DC: Corpus Books, 1969.

Arendt, Hannah. *Between Past and Future: Eight Exercises in Political Thought*. New York: Penguin Books, 1954.

———. *The Human Condition*. Chicago: Chicago University Press, 1958.

———. *On Revolution*. New York: Penguin Books, 2004.

———. *The Origins of Totalitarianism*. New York: Schocken Books, 2004.

———. *The Promise of Politics*. New York: Schocken Books, 2005.

Aries, Philippe. *Western Attitudes toward Death from the Middle Ages to the Present*. Baltimore, MD: John Hopkins University Press, 1974.

Assmann, Jan. *Cultural Memory and Early Civilization: Writing, Remembrance and Political Imagination*. Cambridge: Cambridge University Press, 2011.

Avishai Margalit. *The Ethics of Memory*. Cambridge, MA: Harvard University Press, 2002.

Badiou, Alain. *Being and Event*. Translated by Oliver Feltham. London: Continuum, 2005.

———. *Saint Paul: The Foundation of Universalism*. Translated by Ray Brassier. Stanford, CA: Stanford University Press, 2003.

Barley, Nigel. *Forehead of the Dead: An Anthropological View of Kalabari Ancestral Screens*. Washington, DC: Smithsonian Institute, 1988.

Becker, Carl. *The Heavenly City of the Eighteenth-Century Philosophers*. New Haven, CT: Yale University Press, 1932. Reprinted in 2003.

Benjamin, Walter. "Notes Toward a Work on the Category of Justice." Translated by Peter Fenves. In *The Messianic Reduction: Walter Benjamin and the Shape of Time*, by Peter Fenves, 257–58. Stanford, CA: Stanford University Press, 2011.

Berlin, Isaiah. *Four Essays in Liberty*. Oxford: Oxford University Press, 1969.

Bewaji, John Ayotunde Isola. "Ethics and Morality in Yoruba Culture." In *A Companion to African Philosophy*, edited by Kwasi Wiredu, 396–403. Malden, MA: Blackwell Publishing, 2004.

Bichat, X. *Physiological Researches upon Life and Death*. Translated by Tobias Watkins, 43–44. Philadelphia: Smith & Maxwell, 1809; quoted in Robert Esposito, *Third Person: Politics of Life and Philosophy of the Impersonal*, trans. Zakiya Hanafi (Cambridge: Polity Press, 2012).

Bodin, John. "Social Immortality." *International Journal of Ethics* XXV (1915): 195–212.

Bowen-Moore, Patricia. *Hannah Arendt's Philosophy of Natality*. New York: St. Martin's Press, 1989.

Bradley, Arthur. *Unbearable Life: A Genealogy of Political Erasure*. New York: Columbia University Press, 2019.

Braide, Sonny. *Owuame-Kengema Kalabari*. Bloomington, IN: Xlibris, 2017.

Brannigan, Michael C. *The Pulse of Wisdom: The Philosophies of India, China, and Japan*. Belmont, CA: Wadsworth Publishing, 1995.

Burroughs, Bradley B. *Christianity, Politics, and the Predicament of Evil: A Constructive Theological Ethic of Soulcraft and Statecraft*. Lanham, MD: Lexington Books, 2019.

Butler, Judith. *Bodies that Matter: On the Discursive Limits of "Sex."* New York: Routledge, 2011.

Canovan, Margaret. *The Political Thought of Hannah Arendt*. New York: Harcourt Bruce Jovanovich, 1974.

Caputo, John D. *The Weakness of God: A Theology of the Event*. Bloomington: Indiana University Press, 2006.

Clark, John Pepper. *Ozidi*. Ibadan, Nigeria: Oxford University Press, 1966.

Constitution of the Federal Republic of Nigeria 25(1) & (2); 26 (1) & (2), 27. Abuja, Nigeria: Federal Government of Nigeria Printing Press, 1999.

Csikszentmihalyi, Mihaly. *Flow: The Psychology of Optimal Experience*. New York: HarperCollins, 1990.

Daly, M. C. "Kalabari Female Appearance and the Tradition of Iria." PhD diss., University of Minnesota, 1984.

Dossa, Shiraz. *The Public Realm and the Public Self: The Political Theory of Hannah Arendt*. Waterloo, ON: Wilfrid Laurier University Press, 1989.

Dussel, Enrique. *Ethics of Liberation: In the Age of Globalization and Exclusion*. Durham, NC: Duke University Press, 2013.

Eicher, Joanne B., and Tonye Victor Erekosima. "Celebration and Display." In *Global Trade and Cultural Authentication: The Kalabari of the Niger Delta*, ed. Joanne B. Eicher, 221–38. Bloomington: Indiana University Press, 2022.

———. "Fitting Farewells." In *Global Trade and Cultural Authentication*, 239–49.

———. "Kalabari Funerals: Celebration and Display." *African Arts* 19, no. 3 (1987): 38–45.

Erekosima, Tonye V. "An Analysis of Learning Resources for Political Integration Applicable to Nigerian Secondary School Social Studies: The Case of Kalabari Men's Traditional Dress." PhD diss., Catholic University of America, 1989.

Erekosima, Tonye V., and J. B. Eicher. "Kalabari Cut-Thread Cloth: An Example of Cultural Authentication." *African Arts* 14, no. 2 (1981): 48–51.

Erekosima, Tonye V., W. H. Kio Lawson, and Obeleye MacJaja. *Hundred Years of Buguma History in Kalabari Culture*. Lagos, Nigeria: Sibon Books Limited, 1991.

Espejo, Paulina Ochoa. *The Time of Popular Sovereignty: Process and the Democratic State*. University Park: Pennsylvania State University Press, 2011.

Esposito, Roberto. *Bios: Biopolitics and Philosophy*. Minneapolis: University of Minnesota Press, 2008.

———. *Communitas: The Origin and Destiny of Community*. Translated by T. Campbell. Stanford, CA: Stanford University Press, 2010.

———. *Immunitas: The Protection and Negation of Life*. Translated by Zakiya Hanafi. Cambridge: Polity Press, 2011.

———. *Third Person: Politics of Life and Philosophy of the Impersonal*. Translated by Zakiya Hanafi. Cambridge: Polity Press, 2012.

———. *Two: The Machine of Political Theology and the Place of Thought*. Translated by Zakiya Hanafi. New York: Fordham University Press, 2015.

Fanon, Frantz. *The Wretched of the Earth*. New York: Grove Press, 1968.

Fenn, Richard. "Sociology and Religion: Searching for the Sacred." In *The Oxford Handbook of Religion and Science*, edited by Philip Clayton and Zachary Simpson, 253–70. Oxford: Oxford University Press, 2006.

Fenves, Peter. *The Messianic Reduction: Walter Benjamin and the Shape of Time*. Stanford, CA: Stanford University Press, 2011.

Foucault, Michel. *Power/Knowledge: Selected Interviews and Other Writings, 1972–1977*. Edited by Colon Gordon. New York: Pantheon, 1980.

Giorgio Agamben. *The Man without Content*. Translated by Georgia Albert. Stanford, CA: Stanford University Press, 1999.

Gourgourris, Stathis. *Lessons in Secular Criticism*. New York: Fordham University Press, 2013.

Hägglund, Martin. *Dying for Time: Proust, Woolf, Nabokov*. Cambridge, MA: Harvard University Press, 2012.

Hardt, Michael, and Antonio Negri. *Empire*. Cambridge, MA: Harvard University Press, 2000.

———. *Multitude: War and Democracy in the Age of Empire*. New York: Penguin Books, 2004.

Harrison, Beverly Wildung. *Making the Connections: Essays in Feminist Social Ethics*. Edited by Carol S. Robb. Boston: Beacon Press, 1985.

Hayek, Friedrich. *The Constitution of Liberty*. Chicago: University of Chicago Press, 1960.

———. *Law, Legislation and Liberty*. Vol. 1, *Rules and Order*. Chicago: University of Chicago Press, 1973.

———. *Law, Legislation and Liberty*. Vol. 2, *The Mirage of Social Justice*. Chicago: University of Chicago Press, 1976.

———. *Law, Legislation and Liberty*. Vol. 3, *The Political Order of a Free People*. Chicago: University of Chicago Press, 1979.

———. *The Road to Serfdom*. Chicago: University of Chicago Press, 1944.

Hinkelamert, Frank J. *The Ideological Weapons: A Theological Critique of Capitalism*. Maryknoll, NY: Orbis Book, 1986.

hooks, bell. "Theory as Liberatory Practice." In *Feminist Theory: A Reader*, edited by Wendy K. Kolmar and Frances Bartkowski, 28–33. Mountain View, CA: Mayfield Publishing, 2013.

Horton, Robin. "From Fishing Village to City-State: A Social History of New Calabar." In *Man in Africa*, edited by M. Douglas and P. M. Kaberry. London: Tavistock, 1969.

———. "A Hundred Years of Change in Kalabari Religion." In *Black Africa: Its People and Their Cultures Today*, edited by John Middleton, 192–211. New York: Macmillan, 1971.

———. "Igbo: An Ordeal for Aristocrats." *Nigeria Magazine* (September 1966): 168–83.

———. "Ikpataka Dogi: A Kalabari Funeral Rites." *African Notes* 5, no. 3 (1970): 57–72.

———. "The Kalabari Ekine Society: A Borderline of Religion and Art." *Africa* 33, no. 2 (1963): 94–114.

———. *Kalabari Sculpture*. Lagos: Department of Antiquities, Federal Republic of Nigeria, 1965.

———. "The Kalabari Worldview: An Outline and Interpretation." *Africa* 32, no. 3 (July 1962): 197–219.

———. "Social Psychologies: African and Western." In *Oedipus and Job in West Africa*, edited by M. Fortes and Robin Horton, 41–82. Cambridge: Cambridge University Press, 1983.

Jones, G. I. *The Trading States of the Oil Rivers: A Study of Political Development in Eastern Nigeria*. Oxford: Oxford University Press, 1963.

Karibi-Whyte, Adolphus G. *Chieftaincy Institution among the Kalabari Ijaw*. Port Harcourt, Nigeria: Ulamba Publishers, 2017.

Kearney, Richard. *The God Who May Be: A Hermeneutics of Religion*. Bloomington: Indiana University Press, 2001.

———. *Strangers, Gods and Monsters: Interpreting Otherness*. London: Routledge, 2003.

Keller, Catherine. "Theopoetics: A Becoming History." In *The Art of Anatheism*, edited by Richard Kearney and Matthew Clemente, 29–41. London: Rowman & Littlefield, 2018.

Kierkegaard, Søren. *Philosophical Fragments*. Translated by Howard V. Hong and Edna H. Hong. Princeton, NJ: Princeton University Press, 1985.

Kopytoff, Igor. "The Cultural Biography of Things: Commoditization as Process." In *The Social Life of Things: Commodities in Cultural Perspective*, edited by Arjun Appadurai, 64–90. Cambridge: Cambridge University Press, 1988.

Lazzarato, Maurizio. *The Making of the Indebted Man*. Los Angeles: Semiotext(e), 2007.

Lifton, Robert Jay. *Boundaries*. New York: Random House, 1970.

———. "The Sense of Immortality: On Death and the Continuity of Life." In *New Meanings of Death*, edited by Herman Feifel, 274–90. New York: McGraw-Hill, 1977.

Magesa, Laurenti. *African Religion: The Moral Traditions of Abundant Life* Maryknoll, NY: Orbis Books, 1997.

Malabou, Catherine. *Plasticity at the Dusk of Writing: Dialectics, Destruction, Deconstruction*. Translated by Carolyn Shread with a foreword by Clayton Crockett. New York: Columbia University Press, 2010.

———. *What Should We Do with Our Brains?* Translated by Sebastian Rand. New York: Fordham University Press, 2008.

Mamdani, Mahmood. "Making Sense of Political Violence in Postcolonial Africa." *Socialist Register* (2003): 132–51.

———. *When Victims Become Killers: Colonialism, Nativism, and the Genocide in Rwanda*. Princeton, NJ: Princeton University Press, 2001.

Mbembe, Achille. *Necropolitics*. Durham, NC: Duke University Press, 2019.

———. *On the Postcolony*. Berkeley: University of California Press, 2001.

Mbiti, John. *African Religions and Philosophy*. New York: Doubleday, 1970.

Menkiti, Ifeanyi "On the Normative Conception of a Person." In *A Companion to African Philosophy*, 324–31.

Michelman, Susan O., and Tonye V. Erekosima. "Kalabari Dress in Nigeria: Visual Analysis and Gender Implications." In *Dress and Gender: Making and Meaning in Cultural Contexts*, edited by Ruth Barnes and Joanne B. Eicher, 164–82. Oxford: Berg, 1992.

Mitchell, Roger Haydon. "What Are the Politics of Love?" In *Cultivating New Post-Secular Space*, edited by Roger Haydon Mitchell, 26–43. London: Routledge, 2019.

Mitchell, Roger H., and Julie T. Arram. *Discovering Kenarchy*. Eugene, OR: Wipf and Stock, 2014.

Moltmann, Jürgen. "Progress and Abyss: Remembrances of the Future of the Modern World." In *The Future of Hope: Christian Tradition Amid Modernity and Postmodernity*, edited by Miroslav Volf and William Katerberg, 3–26. Grand Rapids, MI: William B. Eerdmans, 2004.

Nancy, Jean-Luc. *Being Singular Plural*. Translated by Robert D. Richardson and Anne E. O'Byrne. Stanford, CA: Stanford University Press, 2000.

———. *Birth to Presence*. Translated by Brian Holmes. Stanford, CA: Stanford University Press, 1993.

———. *The Inoperative Community*. Translated by Peter Connor, Lisa Garbus, Michael Holland, and Simona Sawhney with a foreword by Christopher Fynsk. Minneapolis: University of Minnesota Press, 1991.

———. *The Sense of the World*. Translated by Jeffrey S. Librett. Minneapolis: University of Minnesota Press, 1997.

Narotzky, Susana, and Besnier, Niko. "Crisis, Value, and Hope: Rethinking the Economy." *Current Anthropology* 55 (9): 4–16; quote 10. Quoted in Sibel Kusimba, "Embodied Value: Wealth in People," *Economic Anthropology* 7, no. 2 (2020): 166–75.

Neville, Robert Cummings. *Eternity and Time's Flow*. Albany: State University of New York Press, 1993.

———. *Existence: Philosophical Theology*, vol. 2. Albany: State University of New York Press, 2014.

Nielsen, Greg M. *The Norms of Answerability: Social Theory Between Bakhtin and Habermas*. Albany: State University of New York Press, 2002.

Norton, Anne. "Pentecost: Democratic Sovereignty in Carl Schmitt." *Constellations* 18, no. 3 (2011): 389–402.

Nouwen, Henri J. M. *The Wounded Healer: Ministry in Contemporary Society*. New York: Doubleday, 1972.

Nussbaum, Martha C. *Upheavals of Thought: The Intelligence of Emotions*. Cambridge: Cambridge University Press, 2001. Source for Gustav Mahler's song "Nun will die sonn."

Oates, William. Diary notes, September 28, 1857, D/0/18, International Slavery Museum, National Museums of Liverpool, Maritime Archives and Library, Liverpool, England.

Olaniyan, Tejumola. *Arrest the Music!: Fela and His Rebel Art and Politics*. Bloomington: Indiana University Press, 2004.

Paris, Peter. *The Spirituality of the African Peoples: The Search for Common Moral Discourse*. Minneapolis, MN: Fortress Press, 1995.

Phelps, Edmund. *Mass Flourishing: How Grassroots Innovation Created Jobs, Challenge, and Change*. Princeton, NJ: Princeton University Press, 2013.

Rorty, Richard. *Contingency, Irony and Solidarity*. Cambridge: Cambridge University Press, 1989.

Schmitt, Carl. *Political Theology: Four Chapters on the Concept of Sovereignty*. Translated by George Schwab. Cambridge, MA: MIT Press, 1985.

Serequeberhan, Tsenay. *The Hermeneutics of African Philosophy: Horizon and Discourse*. New York: Routledge, 1994.

Smith, James K. A. "Determined Hope: A Phenomenology of Christian Expectation." In *The Future of Hope*, 200–27.

Somé, Malidoma Patrice. *Ritual: Power, Healing, and Community*. New York: Penguin Group, 1993.

Stout, Jeffrey. *Democracy and Tradition*. Princeton, NJ: Princeton University Press, 2004.

Talbot, Amaury. *Tribes of the Niger Delta: Their Religions and Customs*. London: Frank Cass & Co., 1932. Reprinted in 1967.

Tasie, G. O. *Kali Kulu Kulu Kalika: A CheckList of Kalabari Drum Names*. Suppl. *Journal of Niger Delta Studies*. Jos, Nigeria: Ehindero, 1999.

Taylor, Mark Lewis. *Remembering Esperanza: A Cultural-Political Theology for North American Praxis*, 205–6. Minneapolis, MN: Fortress Press, 2005.

Terry Cross. "Tillich's Picture of Jesus as the Christ: Toward a Theology of the Spirit's Saving Presence." In *Paul Tillich and Pentecostal Theology: Spiritual Presence and Spiritual Power*, by Nimi Wariboko and Amos Yong, 71–83. Bloomington: Indiana University Press, 2015.

Tillich, Paul. *The Courage to Be*. New Haven, CT: Yale University Press, 2014.

———. *Love, Power, and Justice: Ontological Analyses and Ethical Applications*. London: Oxford University Press, 1954.

———. *Morality and Beyond*. Louisville, KY: Westminster John Knox Press, 1963.

———. *The Socialist Decision*. Translated by Franklin Sherman. New York: Harper & Row, 1933. Reprinted in 1977.

———. *Systematic Theology*. Vol. 1, *Reason and Revelation, Being and God*. Chicago: University of Chicago Press, 1951.

———. *Systematic Theology*. Vol. 2, *Existence and Christ*. Chicago: University of Chicago Press, 1956.

———. *Theology of Culture*. London: Oxford University Press, 1959.

van Huyssteen, J. Wentzel. *Alone in the World? Human Consciousness in Science and Theology*. Grand Rapids, MI: William B. Eerdmans, 2006.

Vatter, Miguel. *The Republic of the Living: Biopolitics and the Critique of Civil Society*. New York: Fordham University Press, 2014.

Vedder, Ben. "Heidegger on Desire." *Continental Philosophy Review* 31 (1998): 353–68.

Wall, John. *Moral Creativity: Paul Ricoeur and the Poetics of Possibility*. Oxford: Oxford University Press, 2005.

Wariboko, Nimi. "The African Worldview and the Structure and Strategy of Traditional Business Enterprises: The Case of Kalabari of Southern Nigeria." *Nordic Journal of African Studies* 8, no. 2 (1999): 18–51.

————. *The Depth and Destiny of Work: An African Theological Interpretation.* Trenton, NJ: Africa World Press, 2008.

————. *Ethics and Society in Nigeria: Identity, History, Political Theory.* Rochester, NY: University of Rochester Press, 2019.

————. *Ethics and Time: Ethos of Temporal Orientation in Politics and Religion in the Niger Delta.* Lanham, MD: Lexington Books, 2010.

————. "Kalabari: A Study in Synthetic Ideal-Type." *Nordic Journal of African Studies* 8, no. 1 (1999): 80–92.

————. *The Mind of African Strategists: A Study of Kalabari Management Practice.* Madison, NJ: Fairleigh Dickinson University Press, 1997.

————. *Pattern of Institutions in the Niger Delta: Economic and Ethological Interpretations of History and Culture.* Port Harcourt, Nigeria: Onyoma Research Publications, 2007.

————. *The Pentecostal Principle: Ethical Methodology in New Spirit.* Grand Rapids, MI: William B. Eerdmans, 2012.

————. *The Principle of Excellence: A Framework for Social Ethics.* Lanham, MD: Lexington Books, 2009.

————. *The Split Time: Economic Philosophy for Human Flourishing in African Perspective.* Albany: State University of New York Press, 2022.

————. *The Split Economy: Saint Paul Goes to Wall Street.* Albany: State University of New York Press, 2020.

————. "A Theory of the Canoe House Corporation." *African Economic History* 26 (1998): 141–72.

————. "Three against Four: A Cultural Analysis of the Disappearance of Women in Kalabari." *Journal of Asian and African Studies* 37, no. 1 (2002): 66–95.

————. *Transcripts of the Sacred in Nigeria: Beautiful, Monstrous, Ridiculous.* Bloomington: Indiana University Press, 2023.

Williamson, Kay, and A. O. Timitimi. "A Note on Ijo Number Symbolism." *African Notes* 5, no. 3 (1970): 9–16.

Winter, Gibson. *Community and Spiritual Transformation: Religion and Politics in a Communal Age.* New York: Crossroad Publishing, 1989.

Wiredu, Kwasi. *Philosophy and African Culture.* Cambridge: Cambridge University Press, 1980.

Zelizer, Viviana A. "Human Values and the Market: The Case of Life Insurance and Death in 19th-Century America." *American Journal of Sociology* 84 (1978): 591–610.

Žižek, Slavoj. *Interrogating the Real.* London: Continuum, 2005.

————. "Only a Suffering God Can Save Us." In *God in Pain: Inversions of Apocalypse,* by Slavoj Žižek and Boris Gunjević, 155–92. New York: Seven Stories Press, 2012.

———. *Tarrying with the Negative: Kant, Hegel, and the Critique of Ideology.* Durham, NC: Duke University Press, 1993.

———. *Violence: Six Sideways Reflections.* New York: Picador, 2008.

Web Links

Althuraya. "Explaining Hegel's 'Substance as Subject.'" *Reddit.* https://www.reddit.com/r/philosophy/comments/al1213/explaining_hegels_substance_as_subject/.

Index